16.70

THE GROUP TREATMENT OF HUMAN PROBLEMS:

A Social Learning Approach

Edited by
Gloria G. Harris, Ph.D.
Department of Psychology
American University
Washington, D.C.

GRUNE & STRATTON

A Subsidiary of Harcourt Brace Jovanovich, Publishers
New York San Francisco London

Library of Congress Cataloging in Publication Data
Main entry under title:

The Group treatment of human problems.

  Bibliography: p.
  Includes index.
    1. Group psychotherapy.   2.   Behavior therapy.
3.   Social learning.   I.   Harris, Gloria G.
RC488.G74   616.8'915   77-22371
ISBN 0-8089-1023-X

Grune & Stratton, Inc.
111 Fifth Avenue
New York, New York 10003

Distributed in the United Kingdom by
Academic Press, Inc. (London) Ltd.
24/28 Oval Road, London NW1

Library of Congress Catalog Number 77-22371
International Standard Book Number 0-8089-1023-X

Printed in the United States of America

78 011994

CONTENTS

PREFACE

Both group treatment and behavioral approaches to change have become increas
ingly popular during the past decade. In *The Group Treatment of Human Problems: A Social Learning Approach* these two major streams in contemporar)
psychotherapy are integrated for the first time, and the usefulness of behaviora
group treatment for a wide range of problems is presented. This book is addressed to practicing mental health professionals who wish to increase thei
clinical repertoircs as well as to researchers who seek to validate the effectiveness of particular interventions. The diverse affiliations of the book's contributors are indicative of the contents' potential areas of application. Represented are those who work in correctional institutions, university counseling
centers, community mental health centers, outpatient clinics, hospitals, and university research facilities.

The social learning approach reported in this book places emphasis on the
important role of the social environment in shaping and maintaining behavior,
describes the actual clinical practices of cognitive–behavioral therapists, and
reflects a firm commitment to report research data when they exist. The traditional distinction between therapy and training has not been drawn in order to
point out that a social learning approach subsumes both modes of intervention.
Remedial treatment of self-defeating and antisocial behaviors and the acquisition
of prosocial, life enhancing, skills are viewed as constituting a continuum rather
than forming a disease–health dichotomy.

Organization of the book's contents has been planned so as to emphasize the
diversity of areas of application. Part I examines the usefulness of behavioral
groups for the treatment of self-defeating behaviors. Focus in this section is on
behaviors that are clearly maladaptive for an individual. The first four chapters
discuss specific self-defeating behaviors; the last two explore the treatment of
nonhomogeneous groups, composed of either children or adults.

The chapters in Part II discuss the effectiveness of behavioral group approaches for the treatment of antisocial behaviors, those that adversely affect the
rights and the welfare of others. Part III reports the application of behavioral
group techniques to the treatment of alcoholism and drug addiction, and Part IV
examines the innovative treatment of two psychophysiologic disorders, sexual
dysfunction and dysmenorrhea. A training rather than a treatment model is
employed in Part V where the acquisition of a number of effective prosocial
skills is described. The concluding chapter attempts to explore the full implica-

tions of the group setting for behavior therapy with particular emphasis on the actual and potential influences of group processes on the conduct and outcome of therapy.

Interest in the emerging field of behavioral group treatment grew out of my interdisciplinary training and experience as a systems-oriented psychiatric social worker who 10 years later acquired a clinical psychology doctorate from a behaviorally oriented psychology department, at the University of Washington. Other significant influences on my career included my dissertation committee chairman, Irwin Sarason, who in 1968 was among the first to report the successful use of a skill training model to assist groups of institutionalized juvenile offenders in the acquisition of socially appropriate skills, and my coauthorship of *Assertive Training for Women* (Thomas, Springfield, Illinois, 1975), a behavioral group approach to eliminate women's self-defeating behavior patterns.

It is my hope that the information in this book will enable mental health professionals to conduct behavioral groups with large numbers of troubled people. Clear implications exist for the application of behavioral groups in the areas of prevention and community psychology. Since prevention is always an important goal of the clinician, the development of behavioral group approaches might free practitioners enough to begin dealing with this alleged luxury as a reality.

GLORIA G. HARRIS, PH.D.

Gloria G. Harris

Introduction

Recognition of the effectiveness of social learning approaches in the treatment of a wide range of human problems has grown rapidly in recent years. In this approach the important role that environmental as well as cognitive influences play in shaping and maintaining behavior patterns is emphasized; both adaptive and maladaptive behavioral and emotional responses are viewed as learned. Techniques described include desensitization, assertive training, observational learning (modeling), and cognitive restructuring. Rather than the traditional focus on personality and motivational factors, the chapters in this volume have behavioral and attitudinal change as their common target. Included among the considerable advantages of a social learning approach are the fact that it lends itself to evaluation at any point, it is economical to the client, and the length of treatment is considerably shorter than that of other psychotherapeutic interventions.

Small groups which employ a social learning approach to behavior change have many other advantages. First, group members are able to provide an additional source of positive social reinforcement and concern for the improved performance of group members. The therapist is no longer the sole determiner of group behavior. Second, the group further provides a laboratory in which to experiment with new behaviors. Group members provide a ready consensus for what constitutes appropriate behavior in a given situation. Furthermore, group members can experiment with new forms of communication with others in situations which closely simulate the real world. There is a broader base for social modeling in groups, and group members may facilitate the acquisition, and in many cases, the maintenance of prosocial or adaptive behaviors. Third, in a behavioral group, each participant is afforded a possibility of performing leadership or teaching roles for other group members. As a client learns treatment procedures, he may demonstrate them to other participants. If the client comes into the group with skills which are valued by other members, he can teach these to the group; he may be invited to assist them in achieving the same skills (Rose, 1973). Fourth, behavioral groups enable the clinician to quantify the extent to which group members are reaching their treatment goals.

Along with improvement frequently comes strong opposition from the client's family and friends who may object to any change, however small, in his/her behavior. Most behavioral clinicians have long recognized and attempted to seek solutions to this difficulty in achieving transfer of training from the group to the outside world. One further advantage of behavioral groups, thus, is that the importance of the group members may come to replace or to augment that of the therapist and, occasionally, that of family and friends. Since social reinforcement represents the most important source of motivation for human behavior (Ferster, 1968), group members who continue to meet regularly after the group has formally terminated may provide a continued source of support and encouragement.

EFFECTIVENESS OF BEHAVIORAL GROUP TREATMENT

The first experimental evidence of the effectiveness of behavioral group treatment was published by Lazarus (1961) who successfully employed group desensitization with patients who were mainly either height phobic, claustrophobic, or sexually impotent males. Paul and Shannon (1966) next extended Lazarus' study by applying group desensitization to college students who suffered from chronic interpersonal anxiety. According to Lazarus (1968), Paul and Shannon's study demonstrated that systematic desensitization can be successfully combined with more traditional methods of clarification and discussion and employed in groups without any loss of therapeutic effectiveness.

Paul and Shannon's results indicated that group desensitization was superior to both individual insight-oriented and attention-placebo programs; there were no significant differences between the effects of group desensitization and individual desensitization approaches. In fact the results were inclined to point toward combined group desensitization as having had a more positive generalized effect. Since the publication of these first reports, a sizable number of studies have been carried out in which the effectiveness of group desensitization has been demonstrated (Rimm & Masters, 1974).

Evidence for the effectiveness of group assertive training has been increasing. Gittelman (1965) first reported a case study in which behavior rehearsal was employed in a group situation to decrease the aggressive behavior of three acting-out, aggressive children. Another early published report assessing the efficacy of group assertive training was that of Lomont, Gilner, Spector, and Skinner (1969) who compared group insight therapy and group assertive training in the treatment of hospitalized psychiatric patients. The results indicated that the assertive group showed a significantly greater total decrease on the clinical scales of the Minnesota Multiphasic Personality Inventory (MMPI) than the insight group. Unfortunately, response measures did not include direct behavioral assessment. Empirical findings, including results of case histories and experimental investigations, provide relatively convincing evidence that group assertive training is a valid and efficient treatment method (Rimm & Masters, 1974).

Observational learning (modeling) procedures have been found to be most effective in promoting behavioral change in group settings. Modeling procedures are based on the premise that an individual may rapidly acquire (learn) a variety of complex responses simply by observing another person's (the model's) behavior. Sarason (1968) employed a group acquisition of skills modeling approach to assist groups of institutionalized juvenile delinquents in acquiring socially appropriate skills. His results indicate that this combined group approach was highly successful.

Ritter (1968) also successfully utilized a group observational learning procedure for the elimination of snake phobias in young children. In her procedure, peer models were employed to demonstrate fearless and bold interaction with snakes. Ritter's success in the use of group procedures for the elimination of fears led her to suggest the possibility of developing treatment centers on the model of "schools" that could devote concerted effort to the behavioral treatment of human problems. In such "schools," assistants could be trained to administer all assessment techniques, both behavioral and paper and pencil, as well as many of the behavioral treatment procedures. Professionally trained individuals, then, could devote their time to the construction of new therapeutic programs and to the evaluation of current therapeutic procedures. Such an institution might, as Ritter (1969) suggested, include the use of both in vivo and filmed treatments as well as films to teach "living skills."

A SOCIAL LEARNING APPROACH

Following the formulation by Bandura (1971), the social learning theory approach employed in this volume acknowledges the influence of both environmental and cognitive–mediating determinants of behavior:

> In the social learning view, man is neither driven by inner forces nor buffeted helplessly by environmental influences. Rather, psychological functioning is best understood in terms of a continuous reciprocal interaction between behavior and its controlling conditions.

According to social learning theory, the acquisition of behaviors, whether deviant or prosocial, is attributed to three distinct regulatory systems. The first behavioral control system is external. It is established as a result of the contiguous association between autonomic responses, such as changes in cardiovascular, gastrointestinal reactions, and emotional responses, and either direct or vicarious affective experiences. The second regulatory mechanism involves response feedback processes, mainly in the form of reinforcing consequences. The third, and in many respects, the most influential, regulatory mechanism operates through central mediational processes.

> At this higher level stimulus inputs are coded and organized: tentative hypotheses about the principles governing the occurrence of rewards and punishments are developed and tested . . . and, once established, implicit rules and strategies serve to guide appropriate performances in specified situations. (Bandura, 1969, pp. 62–63)

According to social learning theory, behavioral and emotional responses can be learned by direct experiences or vicariously by observation. Furthermore, symbolic mental representations may be acquired and may assist in the interpretation of events and in the conduct of actions. Social learning theory is fundamentally optimistic in its approach. Explaining human acts in terms of a learning model helps to establish a positive expectation that self-defeating attitudes can be overcome, behavior can change, more rewarding interpersonal relationships can be attained, and greater personal autonomy and independence from extrinsic influences can be reached.

Clinical behavior therapy began in the late 1950s with the appearance of Wolpe's now classic book, *Psychotherapy by Reciprocal Inhibition,* and the principal techniques reported in this collection stem from Wolpe's pioneering studies. Recently, however, the field has undergone many significant developments, and all behaviorally oriented clinicians are no longer in agreement with respect to the issue of which techniques or approaches belong to behavior therapy and which do not.

Despite the disagreement on specific issues, there is considerable agreement on more fundamental assumptions. For example, behavioral approaches are generally viewed as most effectively employed with clients who exhibit relatively specific maladaptive behavior patterns. These patterns are viewed by social learning theorists as learned (with the clear implication that they can be unlearned) or, in some cases, as a failure to have acquired adaptive, socially appropriate behaviors in the first place. Behavioral approaches make no attempt to investigate either the causes or motivations of a particular behavior. Childhood memories are not delved into nor are current dreams explored. Instead, the major emphasis is on the identification of the self-defeating aspects of the client's behavior in a "here and now" context, and systematic attempts to modify these aspects are made.

Behavioral approaches always involve setting explicit, clearly defined treatment goals. These goals generally place primary emphasis on the achievement of behavioral changes and the acquisition of skills that are positively valued by both society and the client. Whether maladaptive behaviors are unlearned or prosocial skills are acquired, the treatment methods should be as explicit and negotiable as the goals, and the outcome should be objectively monitorable. It is this emphasis on specifying goals, methods, and outcomes that places behavioral approaches to change in a unique position of accountability.

CONCLUSION

Although traditional approaches to personal change have maintained that fears and inhibitions are symptomatic of deep-rooted disorders and need long-term treatment for amelioration, empirical evidence indicates that behavior change may be facilitated, and that many self-defeating attitudes and behaviors may be effectively modified on a relatively short-term basis. Behavioral groups offer a challenging approach to the alleviation of behavioral maladaption and the potential for meeting the crucial needs of large groups of people.

The behavioral approaches reported in this book do not simplistically reduce the therapist–client interaction to dyadic contingencies of reinforcement. Rather, in direct contrast to this two-person model, contributors have utilized the findings of small group research in the service of behavioral change. This important recognition that groups represent a complex social system with unique properties for change is discussed in depth in the concluding chapter.

Many of the advantages of the approaches to treatment which are presented in this book still remain to be proven by research studies. No treatment procedure can be said to have demonstrated its effectiveness until the stability of improvements has been analyzed over time. A range of clinical and community applications of behavioral groups is represented in this volume, and many of them are still in the preempirical stage. Systematic research studies, however, are now proceeding, and it is hoped that the reader will be stimulated to extend the state of knowledge in this new field by further investigations on both the clinical and empirical levels.

REFERENCES

Bandura, A. *Principles of behavior modification*. New York: Holt, 1969.

Bandura, A. *Social learning theory*. Morristown, New Jersey: General Learning Press, 1971.

Ferster, C. B. *Behavior principles*. New York: Appleton, 1968.

Gittleman, M. Behavior rehearsal as a technique in child treatment. *Journal of Child Psychology and Psychiatry*, 1965, *6*, 251–255.

Lazarus, A. A. Group therapy of phobic disorders by systematic desensitization. *Journal of Abnormal and Social Psychology*, 1961, *63*, 504–510.

Lazarus, A. A. Behavior therapy in groups. In G. M. Gazda (Ed.), *Basic approaches to group psychotherapy and group counseling*. Springfield, Illinois: Thomas, 1968.

Lomont, J. F., Gilner, F. H., Spector, N. J., & Skinner: Assertion training and group insight therapies. *Psychological Reports*, 1969, *25*, 463–470.

Paul, G. L. & Shannon, D. T. Treatment of anxiety through systematic desensitization in therapy groups. *Journal of Abnormal Psychology*, 1966, *71*, 124–135.

Rimm, D. C., & Masters, J. C. *Behavior therapy: Techniques and empirical findings*. New York: Academic Press, 1974.

Ritter, B. The group treatment of children's snake phobias, using vicarious and contact desensitization procedures. *Behavior Research and Therapy*, 1968, *6*, 1–6.

Ritter, B. Eliminating excessive fears of the environment through contact desensitization. In J. D. Krumboltz & C. E. Thoreson (Eds.), *Behavioral counseling: Cases and techniques*. New York: Holt, 1969.

Rose, S. *Treating children in groups*. San Francisco: Jossey-Bass Publ., 1973.

Sarason, I. G. Verbal learning, modeling, and juvenile delinquency. *American Psychologist*, 1968, *23*, 254–266.

Wolpe, J. *Psychotherapy by reciprocal inhibition*. Stanford: Stanford University Press, 1958.

CONTRIBUTORS

James F. Alexander, Ph.D.
Department of Psychology, University of Utah, Salt Lake City, Utah.

Cole Barton
Department of Psychology, University of Utah, Salt Lake City, Utah.

Joel D. Block, Ph.D.
Private practice, Plainview, New York. Fellow, Institute for Advanced Study of Rational Emotive Psychotherapy, New York, New York.

Jonathan M. Chamberlain, Ph.D.
Department of Educational Psychology, Brigham Young University, Provo, Utah.

Frances E. Cheek, Ph.D.
Behavior Modification Training Programs, New Jersey Neuropsychiatric Institute, Princeton, New Jersey.

Margaret A. Chesney, Ph.D.
Stanford Research Institute, Menlo Park, California.

Myles Genest, B.I.S.
Department of Psychology, University of Waterloo, Waterloo, Ontario, Canada.

Martin Gittelman, Ph.D.
Department of Psychiatry, New Jersey Medical School, Newark, New Jersey.

James Gormally, Ph.D.
Department of Psychology, University of Maryland, College Park, Maryland.

Clara E. Hill, Ph.D.
Department of Psychology, University of Maryland, College Park, Maryland.

Carole Kirkpatrick, Ph.D.
Counseling Center, University of Oregon, Eugene, Oregon.

Joseph LoPiccolo, Ph.D.
Department of Psychiatry and Behavioral Sciences, SUNY at Stony Brook, Stony Brook, New York.

Barry W. McCarthy, Ph.D.
Department of Psychology, American University, Washington, D.C. Clinical Psychologist, Washington Psychological Center, Washington, D.C.

Kevin McGovern, Ph.D.
Columbia Psychiatric Clinic, Portland, Oregon.

Donald Meichenbaum, Ph.D.
Department of Psychology, University of Waterloo, Waterloo, Ontario, Canada.

Peter E. Nathan, Ph.D.
Alcohol Behavior Research Laboratory, Rutgers University, New Brunswick, New Jersey.

Henry R. Novotny, Ph.D.
Private practice, Marina del Rey, California.

Robert D. O'Connor, Ph.D.
Center for Studies of Social Behavior, Oklahoma City, Oklahoma.

Gerald W. Piaget, Ph.D.
Behavior Therapy Associates, Los Altos, California.

David C. Rimm, Ph.D.
Department of Psychology, Old Dominion University, Norfolk, Virginia.

T. Antoinette Ryan, Ph.D.
College of Criminal Justice, University of South Carolina, Columbia, South Carolina.

David L. Sansbury, Ph.D.
Counseling Psychology Program, School of Education, American University, Washington, D.C.

John J. Steffen, Ph.D.
Department of Psychology, University of Cincinnati, Cincinnati, Ohio.

Richard M. Suinn, Ph.D.
Department of Psychology, Colorado State University, Fort Collins, Colorado.

PART I

Treatment of Self-Defeating Behaviors

Donald Meichenbaum
and Myles Genest

Chapter 1
Treatment of Anxiety

This chapter illustrates the application of a *cognitive–behavior modification* approach to group therapy for anxiety. Cognitive–behavior modification has developed from an attempt to integrate the clinical concerns of cognitive or semantic therapists, such as Aaron Beck, Albert Ellis, and George Kelly, with the technology of behavior therapy. (See Meichenbaum, 1977, for a description of the theoretical and empirical basis for cognitive–behavior modification.) Cognitive–behavior modification procedures have also been applied to treatment of pain (Langer, Janis, & Wolfer, 1975; Levendusky & Pankratz, 1975; Turk, 1976), anger control problems (Novaco, 1975), social anxiety (Christensen, 1974), and hyperactive, impulsive children (e.g., Bornstein & Ouevillon, 1976, Camp, Blom, Herbert, & Van Doorwick, Note 1; Meichenbaum & Goodman, 1971).

Central to the cognitive–behavior modification treatment approach is the view that behavior change is accomplished through a sequence of mediations. The initial mediating mechanism of therapy is the client's "reconceptualization" of his problem. When a client enters therapy he is usually seeking some understanding of what is happening to him, trying to make sense of his behaviors. He wants to receive assurances that he is not going to "lose his mind," and that something can be done to help him change. A sense of helplessness, hopelessness, and demoralization often characterizes the client (e.g., see Frank, 1974; Strupp, 1970). It has been suggested that common to all therapy procedures, including the social learning approaches described in this book, is a translation process that helps to alter the client's internal dialogue (Meichenbaum, 1977). The client's symptoms and complaints are "translated" from his pretherapy meaning system to a conceptualization that is conducive to therapy. The questions the therapist asks, the homework assignments he gives, the tests he administers, the rationale he offers, all contribute to this translation process.

The specific content and viewpoint of the "translated" statement of the client's problem are dependent on the client's expectations, the specific goals of therapy, and the therapist's orientation. *Which* viewpoint the therapist espouses (whether Freudian, Jungian, behavioral, Rogerian, etc.) is of less importance than that the client and therapist arrive at a common conceptualization and that this conceptualization leads to specific suggestions for therapeutic intervention. Most patients have had sufficient experiences to substantiate the claims of most therapeutic approaches. The client's pretherapy view of his problem is quite likely to be that recovery is unlikely, or at least improbable, without the help of an external agent. The translation process should cause the client to see himself as an active participant, if not the primary agent, in accomplishing change.

The reconceptualization of the client's problem facilitates his heightened awareness of his own maladaptive behaviors, thoughts, and feelings. This awareness, this self-observation, is a prerequisite to behavior change.

What is usually considered the main concern of therapy, especially behavior therapies, is the acquisition of behaviors that are incompatible with the maladaptive ones. The client's self-observation enables him to initiate these skills that he learns in therapy when they are indicated by his own thoughts, feelings, behaviors, and/or the reactions of others.

The cognitive–behavioral approach to therapy explicitly capitalizes on this sequence of mediations, which is implicit in all behavior change. First, the treatment is specifically concerned with the evolution of a conceptualization of the client's problem that renders the problem solvable. The first focus of therapy is on changing what the client "says to himself" about his maladaptive behavior so that he and the therapist agree on a route that will lead to the desired change. Second, a cognitive–behavioral approach emphasizes the client's observation of his own behavior, so that he may recognize the contingencies involved in his problem. And finally, the self-observation must come to initiate appropriately the coping skills learned in therapy. Indeed, a great deal goes on in therapy prior to the initiation of any particular therapy technique. Aspects of therapy that have been viewed as nonspecific factors or "beyond behavior therapy," actively contribute to the change process. Recognition of this will make us more sensitive therapists. A group therapy setting provides a useful avenue for the development of a conceptualization and the accompanying increased self-observation, as well as a productive outlet for rehearsal of adaptive behaviors. Let us now illustrate how these processes come into play in the group treatment of clients with anxiety.

A GROUP THERAPY ILLUSTRATION

The initial session of cognitive–behavior group therapy begins with the therapist exploring the extent and duration of the clients' presenting problems.

The therapist conducts a situational analysis, asking questions concerning the generality of the problem, precipitating and consequent events, and so on (see Peterson, 1968, pp. 121–122, for an illustrative clinical interview). In addition, the cognitive–behavior therapist has clients report on the set of thoughts and images they experience in anxiety-producing situations. To encourage this report one of the clients may be asked to close his eyes and "run a movie through his head" of a recent incident involving his problem, reporting the sequence of thoughts, images, and behaviors. Such an imagery procedure has proved a useful adjunct to the standard interview. A second adjunctive technique that can be used is a behavioral assessment. For example, if the clients have speech anxiety or test anxiety or are low-assertive, a behavioral assessment can be arranged either in the office or laboratory, or in situ. The rationale offered to the clients for such an assessment is that each participant, as well as the therapist, will gain a better understanding of the presenting problem. In the subsequent therapy sessions the clients can then explore the feelings and thoughts they experience in their common behavioral assessment situation. The therapist may have the group consider what were the particular aspects of the environment that triggered specific self-statements and images. What were the self-statements that clients emitted at different points in the assessment? For example, on an exam day, a high-test-anxiety client reported engaging in a behavioral ritual of planning exactly what seat to sit in, remaining isolated from the other students prior to the exam in order not to hear what they were talking about, and so forth. A violation of the ritual, such as an overheard conversation, would trigger anxious thoughts in the client. During the initial phase of therapy, the therapist can wonder aloud about the purpose of behavior like the exam ritual. A plausible answer that the group will come to produce is that the ritual controls negative self-statements.

Note that in addition to serving the function of actual assessment, the behavioral assessment procedures may foster group identity and group cohension, and also provide the group with a common experience that they can verbally share in therapy. The group can discuss their thinking processes in the specific assessment situations, and then explore the range of situations in which they have the same or comparable thoughts. Group members are asked to engage in a homework assignment of listening to themselves with a "third ear," noting any negative self-statements (or any anxiety-engendering images) they emit. The purpose of the homework assignment is to have the clients become aware of how their thought processes contribute to how they feel and behave. Therapists differ in how demanding and structured their homework assignments are. Some therapists encourage monitoring, recording, and graphing specific behaviors, thoughts, urges, moods, and so on.

In the group therapy sessions the therapist can use clients' accounts to illustrate the self-defeating and self-fulfilling aspects of their "internal dialogues." Indeed, a client's behavior in the group itself may be used as a basis to explore self-statements. For example, if a client does not participate in the group, the therapist may begin to explore the thoughts that might keep a person from participating.

Through the group's examination of the relationship between their thinking styles and their behaviors and feelings, individual clients can begin to discover that their fears and anxieties are *not* a property of external events. Rather they will find that their own thoughts and behaviors contribute to anxiety. These are thoughts and behaviors that first of all, other members of the group also experience, and secondly, that they will be able to learn to control.

What has been described thus far is the initial phase of therapy, during which the therapist tries to assess the nature of the clients' presenting problems. He attempts to discern the degree to which clients' maladaptive behaviors are a result of a "can't" versus a "won't" problem. A "can't" problem reflects an inadequate response repertoire, suggesting the need for behavioral rehearsal and coping skills training. A "won't" problem indicates an internal dialogue of conflict, of negative self-statements, which interfere with adaptive behaviors. The "won't" problem suggests that the adaptive responses are already within the client's repertoire, that is, the client knows what to do and can do it under nonthreatening circumstances, but in anxiety-producing situations he engages in an internal dialogue that interferes with or prevents the appropriate behaviors. Thus, as the clients are examining the role of their internal dialogues and their behavioral repertoires, our therapist is busy "talking to himself" about the clients' problems.

How the therapist conducts the remaining phases of therapy will be influenced by what he is "saying to himself" at this point about the clients' cognitions. If the therapist views his clients' cognitions as reflections of "irrational" belief systems, á la Albert Ellis (1962), then he will go on to challenge their premises and beliefs. If the therapist views the clients' cognitions as reflections of faulty thinking styles, á la Aaron Beck (1976), then the therapist will have the client keep an account of his behavior in order to juxtapose the "behavioral data" with what the client is saying to himself (i.e., authenticate his cognitions). If the therapist views the clients' cognitions as a reflection of poor problem-solving skills, á la D'Zurilla and Goldfried (1971), then he will teach them how to generate hypotheses (i.e., behavioral alternatives), employ feedback, and so forth. In other words, the therapist has a variety of different ways to view his clients' cognitions and each of these views gives rise to different treatment procedures.

Two points are worth noting before describing the remainder of the therapy process. The first is that clients, before treatment, are *not* consciously and deliberately going about "talking to themselves." Rather, as Goldfried, Decentece, and Weinberg (1974) have indicated, because of the habitual nature of expectations or beliefs it is likely that most thinking processes become automatic and seemingly involuntary, like overlearned acts. The client's negative self-statements become a habitual style of thinking, in many ways similar to the automatization that accompanies the mastery of a motor skill such as driving a car or skiing. However, the cognitive–behavior therapist can make the client aware of such thought processes and increase the likelihood that the client will in the future notice maladaptive self-statements and images. The therapist attempts to "deautomatize," to have the client recognize the incipient or prodromal signs of his anxiety in order to short-circuit its occurrence at low intensity levels. Notice that in this approach generalization is built into the treatment regimen. The client's maladaptive behaviors (thoughts, feelings, physiological reactions, reactions of others) become the signals, the cues for the client to employ the coping procedures that will be taught in therapy. The client's recognition of his negative self-statements can take on a déjàvu flavor (i.e., "those are thoughts we discussed in the group"). Insofar as the therapist can anticipate and incorporate the clients' negative self-statements into the therapy procedure, treatment generalization will be ensured.

The second general note concerns the reluctance of some writers (e.g., Berenson & Carkhuff, 1967) to see cognitive assessment and change as of central importance in psychotherapy. This reluctance may be based on misconceptions, as noted by Murray and Jacobson (1971). For many psychotherapists cognitive change may imply an emphasis on purely intellectual insight. However, cognitive assessment and therapy as described in this chapter refer to cognitive changes that are closely tied to emotional, motivational, and behavioral processes. For the cognitive–behavior therapist, the client's cognitions are viewed as one part of a complex repertoire.

In summary, the basic premise of the treatment is that the client's anxiety is maintained by the self-statements and images in which he engages concerning evaluative and interpersonal situations. From this premise, three therapeutic objectives follow:

1. Clients explicitly examine the thoughts they have in the assessment situations.
2. Clients explore the *range* of situations in which they use the same or comparable self-statements and images.
3. The therapist provides the opportunity for the clients to realize the self-defeating and self-fulfilling aspects of such thoughts and to replace these with incompatible self-instructions, and incompatible behaviors.

In other words, the purpose of the initial phase of therapy—(a) the assessment procedures, (b) the group discussion, (c) situational analysis, (d) homework assignment—is to secure information about the clients' problems, to lay the groundwork for the therapist and clients to evolve a common conceptualization of the presenting problems, and to decide upon the means of therapy intervention. Once the clients come to accept the possibility that what they say to themselves influences their behavior, specific treatment can be introduced.

The treatment is introduced by means of the therapist presenting the rationale for the therapy procedures. In all therapy procedures, the therapist conveys to the client, either explicitly or implicitly, the rationale for the treatment steps that will be followed. Such rationales should be seen as active ingredients that significantly contribute to the change process.

RATIONALE

It may be useful to illustrate how the therapy rationale is conveyed by including excerpts from a cognitive–behavior modification treatment study. The excerpt is from a study involving the cognitive–behavior modification of test anxiety (Meichenbaum, 1972). The therapist said to the group:

As I listen to you discuss your test anxiety I am struck by some of the similarities in how each of you is feeling and what you are thinking. On the one hand there are reports of quite a bit of tenseness and anxiety in exam situations and in evaluative situations. This seems to take many forms, such as stomachs and necks becoming tense, pounding hearts, sweaty palms, heavy breathing, and so on (the therapist should use the specific reactions offered by group members). At the same time—and correct me if I am wrong—several of you describe how difficult it was for you to focus attention on only the task before you. Somehow, your attention wandered away from what you had to do (such as studying, or taking the exam) to something irrelevant. [Once again the therapist should use reactions offered by group members.] Your thinking or self-statements seem to get in the way of what you had to do. Your thoughts about catastrophies, and how awful the consequences will be because of your not doing well got in the way. [Pause.] Have I heard you correctly?

Then, the therapist had the group return to their description of their evaluation anxiety, specifically, to the test assessment situation in which each member participated. The kinds of thoughts and feelings that the clients experienced in the test situation could be summarized by the following categories:

1. Worrying about one's performance, including how well others are doing as compared with himself.
2. Ruminating too long and fruitlessly over alternative answers or responses.
3. Being preoccupied with bodily reactions associated with anxiety.
4. Ruminating about possible consequences of doing poorly on the test: disapproval, punishment, loss of status or esteem, damage to academic record or job chances.
5. Thoughts or feelings of inadequacy. These may include active self-criticism or self-condemnation, calling yourself "stupid," considering yourself worthless.

Following the discussion of the client's thinking processes, the therapist shared with the clients in lay terms the theory that led to the development of the treatment procedure. In this case, the two factors of emotionality and worry which characterize the high-test-anxiety individual's behavior (Morris & Liebert, 1970) and the problems with focusing attention (Sarason, 1973; Wine, 1971) constituted the basis of the therapy rationale.

The therapy rationale continued:

In the therapy sessions we are going to work on ways to control how you feel, on ways of controlling your anxiety and tenseness. We will do this by learning how to relax.

In addition to learning relaxation skills, you will learn how to control your thinking processes and attention. The control of your thinking, or what you say to yourselves, comes about by first becoming aware of when you are producing negative self-statements, catastrophizing, being task irrelevant, and so on. [Once again, the therapist should give examples of the client's thinking style.] The recognition that you are in fact doing this will be a step forward in changing. This recognition will also act as a reminder, a cue, a bell-ringer for you to produce different thoughts and self-instructions, to challenge and dispute your self-statements. In this way you will come to produce task-relevant self-instructions and new, adaptive behaviors. I'm wondering about your reactions to what I have described. Do you have any questions? [The therapist should determine how the rationale matches the clients' expectations for and conceptualization of change.]

In therapy contexts in which a specified target behavior is not well articulated or where there may be multiple problems, the conceptualization of therapy may evolve more slowly than in this example and change over the course of therapy.

Thus, the clients are presented with a conceptualization of their anxiety as consisting of two components: first, a heightened emotionality or tenseness, and second, a cognitive component, thinking process, or worry, which caused the clients to shift their attention to themselves and away from the task. In order to control the anxiety clients were given muscular relaxation exercises á la Paul (1966) and Meichenbaum (Note 2). The relaxation exercises emphasized slow, deep breathing and mental relaxation. For example, the therapist said:

Now that we have relaxed the muscles of both hands and both arms, I want you to tense and hold the muscles of the chest and back. You can do this by filling the chest cavity slowly, with short deep breaths. Let's begin by taking short deep breaths, holding each one. [At this point, the therapist models the breathing exercise while the client is also breathing in.] Fill the chest and hold. Now part your lips slightly and slowly exhale. Slowly. Good. Note as you slowly exhale, the sense of relaxation and warmth you are able to bring forth. Good. [Pause, letting the client get back to his normal, even breathing pattern.] Now once again, let's make the muscles of the chest and back tense by filling your chest by means of slow deep breaths. Now hold the breath, feel the tenseness across the top of the chest and throughout the upper portion of your body. Now bring forth a sense of relaxation by slowly exhaling, part the lips and let the air out slowly, slowly. Good. Note the distinction that you have been able to bring forth between tenseness and relaxation.

[While the patient is sitting quietly, the therapist continues.] One can bring forth a feeling of relaxation by the use of breathing. By means of using slow deep breaths and by exhaling slowly one can control any feelings of tenseness and anxiety. The breathing technique is especially effective because of the effect breathing has on heart rate and on the rest of the body. Breathing right slows the bodily processes, lowers arousal. Once again, let's try the breathing exercise. This time try it on your own, breathing in slowly and holding each breath and then parting the lips and letting the air out slowly. Try it. [This cycle is repeated once again.]

[The therapist can also suggest to the client] You can deepen the relaxation and relax away feelings of tension by thinking silently to yourself the words "relax" and "calm" as you slowly let out your breath. Think or picture these words to yourself as you slowly let out the breath. [The therapist can also use a pleasant relaxing image.] As you are exhaling, imagine that you are blowing softly and evenly on a spoon of hot soup. These exercises are especially helpful between sessions when you practice.

The pattern of inhalation modeled by the therapist occurs approximately one per second, usually filling the chest by four or five breaths, then holding the chest for 5 seconds or so, and finally slowly exhaling for another 5 seconds. The breathing sequence takes about 20 to 30 seconds. Obviously these parameters can be adapted to the characteristics of the clients and therapist. One warning is that the therapist should not have the client hold his breath to the point of breathlessness, but rather leave sufficient time for slow exhalation. Indicate to the clients both during the relaxation exercise and after training when everyone is sitting up, the distinction between a sudden sharp inhalation and exhalation which causes the heart rate to increase as compared to the slow inhalation--exhalation cycle which causes a quieting of the bodily processes, including heart rate.

The emphasis on breathing as opposed to muscular relaxation during the exercises derives from (a) our own clinical experience with the technique, (b) research literature (as cited in Meichenbaum, 1972) on the relationship between breathing, heart rate, and anxiety (e.g., research studies on sinus arrhythmia and the role of respiration in operant conditioning of heart rate), (c) the literature by Lader and Mathews (1968) on the questionable relationship between muscular relaxation and measures of autonomic arousal, (d) the conclusions by Rachman (1967), after reviewing the desensitization literature, that the major contribution of relaxation to the desensitization process is more a matter of *mental* relaxation than physical relaxation, and (e) finally, the general influence of other (Eastern) exercise procedures which have indicated the important role of breathing. Obviously, there is a need for research on the role of such breathing techniques in the behavior change process. We have tried to spell out the details of how we employed the procedure, in order to encourage such research.

The relaxation instructions to the clients emphasized how they had been able to bring forth the sense of relaxation or tenseness. This is consistent with the notion of viewing the treatment as a process in learning self-control.

In order to help clients control the cognitive activity that contributes to their anxiety, a number of self-instructional training procedures can be employed. The therapist has a variety of different therapy techniques available to influence the clients' thought processes. In the limited space remaining we can merely outline these alternative therapy procedures. The interested reader should see Meichenbaum (1975, 1977).

RECONCEPTUALIZATION OF THE PROBLEM

As part of the conceptualization process the therapist indicates that the clients' anxiety attacks, from their descriptions, seem to progress through various stages, including preparing for a stressor, such as an exam, confronting and handling the stressor, coping with the feeling of being overwhelmed, and self-reflection, which might occur at each of these phases. The therapist, using the clients' behavior, offers examples of each of these phases. The point of this reconceptualization process is to have the clients view their anxiety as consisting of two components (arousal and cognitive activity) which go through four stages. Prior to therapy the anxious client tends to view the experience of anxiety as an "all or none" phenomenon, always a harbinger of deterioration. By means of a reconceptualization the client develops a more differentiated view, one that sensitizes him to low intensity instances of the anxiety attacks, which now become "warning" signals. This reconceptualization contributes to the translation process we described earlier.

In addition, the therapist can explore with the group other areas in their lives in which they are able to cope with stress and anxiety. The therapist can elicit from the group members descriptions of coping techniques that are available in their repertoires, and discuss what prevents them from applying these coping skills to dealing with the presenting problem. The discussion of these skills serves the dual function of having clients begin to change their self-concepts and providing the basis for later discussions of coping techniques.

As the therapist examines with the group members the kinds of thoughts and feelings they experience at each of the various phases, the group can begin to explore in a collaborative fashion with the therapist, the coping self-statements that can be employed at each phase. Table 1 provides a list of the self-statements that were employed in the treatment of test anxiety. It is important to note that the therapist does *not* present these coping strategems in a Coué-like fashion, but rather, sensitively uses suggestions from the group members concerning which different thoughts they could employ to control their anxiety. The members actively contribute to the list. The self-statements encourage clients to (a) assess the reality of the situation; (b) control negative, self-defeating, anxiety-engendering ideation; (c) acknowledge, use, and possibly relabel the anxiety they are experiencing; (d) "psych" themselves up to perform the task; (e) cope with any intense anxiety they might experience; and (f) reinforce themselves for having coped.

There are a number of different ways the therapist can employ the coping

Table 1
Examples of Coping Self-Statements

Confronting and handling the stressor of taking an exam

What is it I have to do? No negative self-statements.
Just think rationally.
Don't worry; worry won't help anything.
Focus on the task; exactly what does the question really ask?
It doesn't say this . . . or this . . . it just asks. . . .
Just think about what I can do about it. That's better than getting anxious.
Don't look for tricks, just what does it say? What's the basic question, what's the main
    point?
I don't want to get lost in detail; stand back and look at the big picture.
I can't get the feel of how to say this . . . let me just start writing about that, maybe that'll
    get me into it.
That's a stupid question. O.K. It's stupid, or I don't get the point. I'll come back to it.
Wonder how many I can miss for a B. . . . I'll figure that up later; just pay attention and
    finish this up.

Coping with the feeling of being overwhelmed

Don't get anxious; just take off a moment and take a couple of slow, deep breaths . . .
    calm . . . and relax . . . good.
Don't try to eliminate the anxiety totally; just keep it manageable.
Keep the focus on the present; what is it I have to do?
Lots more to do before I finish. Just take one question at a time.
This is the anxiety that I thought I might feel. It's a reminder for me to cope.
Slow down a little; don't rush and get all in a panic . . . there's time for most of it.
They finished early. I wonder . . . hell, there's no way I can know what's going on; forget
    them.
I'm not going to be able to do it. I'm going to lose control. No, take a deep breath, part
    lips, relax.
Label my anxiety from 0 to 10 and watch it change.
Now, I'm under control—back to the exam.

Reinforcing self-statements

It's working. I can control how I feel.
Wait until I tell my group about this.
I am in control. I made more out of my fear that it was worth.
My damn ideas; that's the problem. When I control them I control my fear.
It's getting better each time I use the procedures. I did it.

Examples are taken from Meichenbaum (1972, 1974) and Richardson (1973).

self-statements in the therapy regimen. The therapist can use cognitive modeling procedures in which the client observes models coping with anxiety-producing situations. The evidence indicates that a coping model (one who manifests anxiety at the outset, and then copes with his falterings and eventually becomes a mastery model) is most effective in facilitating change (e.g., Meichenbaum, 1971; Sarason, 1973).

One can also employ imagery procedures, as in desensitization, in order to have clients cognitively rehearse the coping responses of relaxation and self-instructions. Once again, a coping imagery procedure seems to enhance the change process (Kazdin, 1973; Meichenbaum, 1972). Coping imagery in desensitization would result in the therapist not stopping the image when the client signals he is anxious, as would be done in traditional desensitization. Rather, the therapist would have the client continue imagining the scene while seeing himself use the coping techniques to reduce his anxiety. The modification to the imagery component of the desensitization procedure is based on the premise that when desensitized clients imagine hierarchy scenes, they are in fact providing themselves with a model for their own behavior. The greater the similarity between the imagined scenes and the real-life situation, the greater the likelihood of treatment generalization.

Other behavior therapy techniques, such as behavioral rehearsal, role-playing, thought stoppage, covert assertion, can be employed to teach the clients to use coping self-instructions, as well as to teach incompatible behaviors.

During the course of therapy the clients examine both their thinking processes and their behavioral repertoires. Implicit in this discussion is the notion that clients can come to control their thoughts and feelings, that they are not mere "victims" of such thoughts or helpless in controlling what they say to themselves or how they feel. Moreover, the group discussion provides an opportunity for the clients to learn how they inadvertently contribute to their own problems. In short, the translation process continues with the client altering what he says to himself about his symptoms. One useful tool in conveying the sense of control and in altering the clients' internal dialogue is the set of procedures offered by Ellis (1962) in his rational–emotive therapy (RET). A description of the RET procedures that challenge the premises underlying clients' negative self-statements is beyond the scope of this chapter. However, it is important to highlight that such procedures may often be a useful therapy.

Since RET has been so closely identified with Albert Ellis' "forceful" therapy style, it is important to remind the reader of the need to distinguish between the particular therapy technique and the therapist's style, personality, and demeanor. To make the point more succinct, conjure up the image of Carl Rogers, as compared to Albert Ellis, conducting RET therapy.

A second note concerning the RET approach is that it may not be the presence of "irrational" beliefs per se that distinguishes clients from "normals" or nonclients. Rather, it may be the set of management techniques employed to cope with stress. The nonclient may often have the same feelings and thoughts as clients, but what differentiates the nonclient is what he says to himself when experiencing anxiety. The "normal" is more capable of compartmentalizing events and can use a number of coping techniques such as humor, rationality, "creative repression," and/or support from significant others. In contrast, part of clients' problems is what they are saying to themselves. Thus, the clients' perceptions, attributions, expectations, images, and self-statements represent an important component of the treatment enterprise.

CONCLUSION

Our previous work (Meichenbaum, 1972; Meichenbaum, Gilmore, & Fedoravicius, 1971) has indicated that the cognitive–behavior modification described in this chapter was as effective as individual therapy. The group treatment proved easier and more valuable in fostering behavior change. The advantage in terms of therapist hours is obvious. Moreover, in group treatment clients can benefit from a group discussion of their faulty thinking styles and self-statements and by the group discussion of the incompatible thoughts and behaviors (e.g., study habits, assertive responses) they must employ to reduce anxiety and change their behavior. Other factors such as group cohesion and group pressure can be readily employed in a group treatment process.

REFERENCE NOTES

1. Camp, B., Blom, B., Herbert, F., & Von Boorwick, W. "Think aloud": A program for developing self-control in young aggressive boys. Unpublished manuscript, University of Colorado School of Medicine, 1976.
2. Meichenbaum, D. Therapist manual for cognitive behavior modification. Unpublished manuscript, University of Waterloo, 1974.

REFERENCES

Beck, A. *Cognitive therapy and the emotional disorders*. New York: International Universities Press, 1976.
Berenson, B., & Carkhuff, R. *Sources of gain in counseling and psychotherapy*. New York: Holt, 1967.
Bornstein, P., & Quevillon, R. The effects of a self-instructional package on overactive preschool boys. *Journal of Applied Behavior Analysis*, 1976, *9*, 179–188.
Christensen, C. *Development and field testing of an interpersonal coping skills program*. Toronto: Ontario Institute for Studies in Education, 1974.

D'Zurilla, T., & Goldfried, M. Problem-solving and behavior modification. *Journal of Abnormal Psychology*, 1971, *78*, 107–126.

Ellis, A. *Reason and emotion in psychotherapy*. New York: Lyle Stuart Press, 1962.

Frank, J. *Persuasion and healing*. New York: Schocken, 1974.

Goldfried, M., Decenteceo, E., & Weinberg, L. Systematic rational restructuring as a self-control technique. *Behavior Therapy*, 1974, *5*, 247–254.

Kazdin, A. Covert modeling and the reduction of avoidance behavior. *Journal of Abnormal Psychology*, 1973, *81*, 87–95.

Lader, M., & Mathews, A. A physiological model of phobic anxiety and desensitization. *Behaviour Research and Therapy*, 1968, *6*, 411–421.

Langer, E., Janis, I., & Wolfer, J. Reduction of psychological stress in surgical patients. *Journal of Experimental Social Psychology*, 1975, *11*, 155–165.

Levendusky, P., & Pankratz, L. Self-control techniques as an alternative to pain medication. *Journal of Abnormal Psychology*, 1975, *84*, 165–169.

Meichenbaum, D. Examination of model characteristics in reducing avoidance behavior. *Journal of Personality and Social Psychology*, 1971, *17*, 298–307.

Meichenbaum, D. Cognitive modification of test anxious college students. *Journal of Consulting and Clinical Psychology*, 1972, *39*, 370–390.

Meichenbaum, D. Self-instructional methods. IN F. Kanfer and A. Goldstein (Eds.), *Helping people change*. New York: Pergamon Press, 1975.

Meichenbaum, D. *Cognitive-behavior modification: An integrative approach*. New York: Plenum Press, 1977.

Meichenbaum, D., Gilmore, B., & Fedoravicius, A. Group insight vs. group desensitization in treating speech anxiety. *Journal of Abnormal Psychology*, 1971, *77*, 115–126.

Meichenbaum, D., & Goodman, J. Training impulsive children to talk to themselves. *Journal of Abnormal Psychology*, 1971, *77*, 115–126.

Morris, L., & Liebert, R. Relationship of cognitive and emotional components of test anxiety to physiological arousal and academic performance. *Journal of Consulting and Clinical Psychology*, 1970, *35*, 332–337.

Murray, E., & Jacobson, L. The nature of learning in traditional and behavioral psychotherapy. In A. Bergin and S. Garfield (Eds.), *Handbook of psychotherapy and behavior change*. New York: Wiley, 1971.

Novaco, R. *Anger control: The development and evaluation of an experimental treatment*. Lexington, Massachusetts: Heath, 1975.

Paul, G. *Insight vs. desensitization in psychotherapy: An experiment in anxiety reduction*. Stanford: Stanford University Press, 1966.

Peterson, D. *The clinical study of social behavior*. Englewood Cliffs, New Jersey: Prentice Hall, 1968.

Rachman, S. Systematic desensitization. *Psychological Bulletin*, 1967, *67*, 93–103.

Sarason, I. Test anxiety and cognitive modeling. *Journal of Personality and Social Psychology*, 1973, *28*, 58–61.

Strupp, H. Specific vs. nonspecific factors in psychology and the problem of control. *Archives of General Psychiatry*, 1970, *23*, 393–401.

Turk, D. *Application of expanded skills training to the treatment of experimentally induced pain*. Doctoral dissertation, University of Waterloo, 1976.

Wine, J. Test anxiety and directions of attention. *Psychological Bulletin*, 1971, *76*, 72–104.

Richard M. Suinn

Chapter 2
Treatment of Phobias

Among the neurotic conditions, the tensional states of anxiety and phobia represent a significant part of human concerns. Many clients may feel incapacitated by the effects of such states, yet feel reluctant to seek the means for better control. This chapter will discuss briefly both tensional states, with a greater emphasis on the phobic conditions. Descriptions will then follow concerning anxiety management methods that appear effective: systematic desensitization for phobias, and Anxiety Management Training for anxiety conditions.

Anxiety conditions and phobic conditions share much in common. Spielberger (1966) indicates they involve complex patterns of responses characterized by subjective feelings of apprehension and tension, accompanied by or associated with physiological activation or arousal. These response patterns may include cognitive sets ("I believe I am anxious"); autonomic responses such as changes in heart rate, GRS, blood pressure, respiration, or gastric motility; or somatic–behavioral responses, such as in tremors, avoidance behaviors, speech disruption, motor inhibition, or disruption of performances. The evidence currently is that these response patterns need not necessarily all be present simultaneously in tension states. In fact, a lack of congruence can sometimes be observed. For example, a client may verbally state being "anxious" or "fearful" yet show only reduced physiological evidence. Similarly, a person may demonstrate heightened autonomic arousal, yet demonstrate approach behaviors toward the feared object. Also, a client may display avoidance behaviors or disruptions in performance without reporting any perceived sense of distress. Diagnostically, these differences may be important for differential treatment recommendations. For example, the first client may be in need of help to change the verbal operants or learned negative self-reports as a means of gaining control. The second client may be able to profit from an emotional reconditioning or

17

counterconditioning program. The third client may benefit from a behavioral rehearsal program emphasizing the appropriate approach or adaptive response patterns (Suinn, 1972).

The stimulus dimensions of tension states are important. Where the anxiety response patterns are triggered by a large number of diverse stimuli, or where the stimuli are diffuse such that the client is yet unable to identify the stimuli cognitively, then the tensional state may be called "anxiety," "general anxiety," or "trait anxiety." Where the cue conditions fall within a common class of stimuli (e.g., high places), it is convenient to label this as "phobias." Thus, a working distinction between anxiety and phobias relates to the specificity of the stimulus prompting the tensional responses. Based on such a distinction, the selection of a treatment regime can be determined. Thus, desensitization is appropriate for phobias since it requires specifying the stimuli involved in anxiety hierachies. On the other hand, Anxiety Management Training is suitable for general anxieties since the treatment does not rely on immediately specifying the stimulus conditions. It should be cautioned, however, that it is more important to behaviorally understand the client's presenting problem and less important to finalize whether it should best be categorized as "anxiety" or "phobia." Instead, it is essential to determine the antecedent conditions which prompt the tensional responses, to determine the nature of the tensional responses as indicated in the preceding paragraphs, and to determine the consequences of these responses and the actions taken by the client in attempts to cope.

Since the behavioral patterns associated with the phobia may vary, the assessment methods should similarly be comprehensive. Self-report measures tap the degree to which the client believes himself/herself to be fearful. In some self-report measures, the client is asked basically to guess about the level of emotional arousal or behavioral disruption that will occur under anticipated conditions. These are basically "if" questions, and simply represent what the client thinks will happen if faced with certain circumstances. There may or may not be congruence between these self-reports and reality. In some instances, the discrepancies may lead the therapist to emphasize reality testing with the client, or discrimination training, or clarify misconceptions about emotional states. However, most clinicians accept that self-report scales have some validity. The Fear Survey Schedule (Wolpe & Lange, 1964) represents a general inventory of fears across several stimulus objects. Scales such as the Suinn Test Anxiety Behavioral Scale (Suinn, 1969) and the Mathematics Anxiety Rating Scale (Suinn, Edie, Nicoletti, & Spinelli, 1972) are measures aiming at assessing the stress experiences in delineated stimulus circumstances.

Measures of autonomic reactivity may confirm the actual physiological response to phobic stimuli. As directed earlier, this could involve measures of heart rate, palmar sweating, and so forth, and may be obtained through highly sophisticated instrumentation to simple direct pulse taking. The clinician may want to obtain indirect measures of autonomic change, such as observations or self-reports about involuntary excretion, nausea, throat dryness, breathlessness, a sense of constriction in the throat, changes in muscle tone, and the like.

Somatic–behavioral observations can be obtained through situational sampling. The client is presented with a phobic situation, for example, the presence of a live snake, a sound movie of flying, moving screens for reducing the size of an enclosure to simulate claustrophobia conditions. Behaviors that could be observed might include the distance the client is willing to approach the feared object, the latency before the client withdraws from the object, signs of distress such as speech interferences, fidgeting, agitation, inability to concentrate on the conversation with the therapist, and so on.

Fear responses may develop through a variety of mechanisms. Direct classical conditioning may lead to a neutral stimulus acquiring fear properties through association with an unconditioned fear response, for example, fear promoted by a sudden, high intensity stimulus. Experimental studies have proved that such conditioning will occur through repeated associations. It is likely that the conditioned phobia will be reported in the diagnostic interview as autonomic/physiological indices of fear. Eysenck and Rachman (1965) hypothesize that a phobia is more likely to develop in those persons who are introverted and higher on their neuroticism dimension, inasmuch as the neuroticism is reflective of a more emotionally labile autonomic nervous system. Acquiring phobic behavioral patterns through modeling is another possibility. Bandura (1969) has shown that observational learning in children does occur. Fear behaviors might also be developed or maintained through operant reinforcement mechanisms. Avoiding fear stimulus circumstances, discontinuing assignments, refusing to participate in certain activities, seeking sympathy for expressions of fright, might all lead to reinforcements which strengthen these fear behaviors. It is possible that these fear behaviors may be discrepant from the client's emotional state, such that severe avoidance behaviors occur but with an absence of emotional distress. Finally, fear reactions may occur as a reality reaction to helplessness, threat, or loss of control. A student who is inadequately prepared for an examination may well experience a fear of being tested, a client faced with an avoidance–avoidance situation may well become disrupted and anxious, a person with a behavioral deficit in coping skills may well be subject to perceiving situations as frightening.

Eysenck and Rachman (1965) have proposed a three-stage theory of the development of a phobia. In the first stage, a single or a series of traumatic events produces strong unconditioned autonomic reactions. Second, associated neutral stimuli may become conditioned to produce the same fear response. Finally, the avoidance behaviors adopted to protect the person from the stimuli act also to prevent extinction of the fear from occurring. These authors also delineate additional learning principles related to the acquisition of a phobia.

HISTORICAL OVERVIEW

This section briefly discusses treatment for phobias, a later section discusses general anxiety. Among methods for dealing with phobias are anxiety relief, self-reinforcement for approach behaviors, cognitive control methods, cue-controlled relaxation-only methods, and experimental and vicarious extinction. Desensitization still remains as perhaps the most popular treatment modality. Desensitization owes its development to Salter (1949) and Wolpe (1958). Although some discussion has taken place regarding the actual mechanism underlying the technique, Wolpe proposes that it is a form of counterconditioning. Fundamentally, the belief is that the client acquires a relaxation response which counters the anxiety response previously conditioned to the cue condition. Reviews have been published by Bergin and Suinn (1975), Paul (1969), Mathews (1971), Rachman (1967), Wilkins (1971), and Wilson and Davison (1971).

Two research directions have contributed results relevant to this chapter: automated or self-administered desensitization, and group desensitization. In the former, a number of therapists have used either special equipment or unmodified tape recorders for automated desensitization (Aponte & Aponte, 1971; Baker, Cohen, & Saunders, 1973; Donner, 1970; Migler & Wolpe, 1967; Suinn, Edie, Nicoletti, & Spinelli, 1973). The unique contribution of such works is in demonstrating that the individual attention of the therapist to the unique needs of each client is not crucial for all clients. Many phobic clients eliminate their fear reactions, and seem able to maintain their improvement after therapy with minimal therapist contact.

The group desensitization data were collected nearly concurrent with the automated studies. Although the original desensitization method demanded an individual therapy format because of the need for individualized anxiety hierarchies, questions were soon raised about the feasibility of group treatment. The hierarchy is composed of a set of situations involving the feared object, and arranged in an increasingly higher order of anxiety arousal. Individual hierarchies may have items with no overlap between one client and another; on the other hand, the standard hierarchies or group anxiety hierarchies have items shared across the clients seen together. Lazarus (1961) employed this solution with a group of phobic clients. This early study reported on the success of group desensitization and concluded " . . . that this method can be effectively administered . . . [and it] provides greater availability with little loss in economy or effectiveness for phobic sufferers" (p. 510). Others confirming such results include Anton (1976), Cohen (1969), Mitchell and Ingham (1970), and Paul and Shannon (1966).

Suinn, Edie, and Spinelli (1970) have also resolved one other methodological issue limiting the use of desensitization in groups, that is, the need for signals. A standard part of the desensitization method is having the client hand-signal anytime during scene visualization if anxiety is aroused. In re-evaluating the theory, Suinn et al. (1970) pointed out that " . . . this signaling may be superfluous [since] counterconditioning theory simply requires that the newly conditioned responses, e.g., relaxation, be stronger than the undesirable response, e.g., anxiety" (p. 309). Yet, the practice of signaling used by many clinicians seemed to assume that the client should signal at *any* appearance of anxiety. Results with an accelerated desensitization method supported the stance that signaling can be eliminated from the desensitization procedure without impairing its effectiveness. Emphasis is instead shifted to ensuring that the clients are well trained in relaxation such that counterconditioning may take place.

THE DESENSITIZATION MODEL

Desensitization may be viewed primarily as a counterconditioning process. The phobia involves the prompting of a fear response by an originally neutral stimulus, this learned reaction being strengthened to such a degree that any real or imagined presentation of the stimulus will precipitate the fear response. Desensitization basically attempts to attach a different response to the phobic stimulus, and specifically a response which is contradictory to and hence which can eliminate the fear response. Additionally, the procedure is aimed at setting up a learning condition which favors developing this new stimulus–response association (phobic stimulus–relaxation response), rather than precipitating the phobic reaction. This is accomplished through practice in relaxation to ensure overlearning and progressive exposure to phobic stimulus in a hierarchical sequence. Although relaxation training usually relies upon a direct muscle exercise, the exposure to the phobic stimuli during relaxation is usually achieved through the use of imagery. In vivo exposure is possible, but not considered necessary since recovery takes place without live exposure. In the approach described here, a traditional treatment model is used, rather than a self-control model. The client's fear is actually extinguished by the end of treatment, hence it is not essential to train the client in a self-management method. However, it is possible to expand the desensitization model to include self-control training. This basically provides the client with the theory for desensitization, and training in using relaxation is a systematic way under in vivo fear conditions.

Desensitization may be divided into three steps: relaxation training, hierarchy construction, and desensitization proper. Relaxation training may be achieved through a variety of methods, including modifications of autogenic training, hypnosis, and direct suggestion. However, the most straightforward method relies on an adaptation of the Jacobsen deep muscle relaxation technique (Jacobsen, 1938; Wolpe & Lazarus, 1966). The instructions involve an isometriclike tensing followed by relaxing of muscle groupings, such as the hands, the biceps, the eyes, the shoulders, the chest, and so on. The focus of the client's attention during the exercise should always be on the contrasting sensations between muscles as they are tensed and then relaxed. The setting for relaxation training should be generally quiet and private, lights may be dimmed, recliners or couches are suitable. Clients should understand how the relaxation fits into the total treatment program and be made comfortable about fears regarding hypnosis, loss of control, and so forth. A simple display by the therapist of what muscle groups will be used, and how to tense such groups, will be helpful. The pace of the instruction can be gauged by the time needed to attend to the muscle changes without a sense of rush. Although some writers recommend about 10 seconds of tension followed by about 15 to 20 seconds of relaxing, another useful technique is for the therapist to tense his/her own fist as a subjective pacer. Since the clients all have their eyes closed, this can be done without distraction. Clients are never taken into desensitization proper without practice; relaxation control is a skill and is improved with additional practice at home. One rule of thumb is for the client to practice 3 out of every 5 days. Behavioral evidences of successful relaxation observable by the therapist include slowed respiration, facial droop, motionless eyelids, body stillness, no reflex swallowing, flaccid muscles giving an overall impression of "sinking" into the chair, and the absence of controlled movements such as nose-scratching. Involuntary jerks may occur in the early phases of relaxation induction.

Hierarchy formation is extremely important. The aim is to obtain descriptions of realistic phobic events, and a sampling of events raising different levels of anxiety. Depending on how much acceleration is planned, the number of items may be as low as 6, and range as high as can be fit into the number of treatment sessions planned. The following is a useful instruction: "Describe the worst situation that has or could happen to you . . . a very concrete experience . . . pretend that I'm listening to you on the telephone and I'll have to describe the scene to an artist who will then draw it in detail." Once the high item is complete, then the client is shifted to selecting a low anxiety item. Assigning a rating to these scenes is often helpful, for example, the highest item being 10 and the lowest being 1. From here on, selecting the in-between values for the next scene to describe is useful, for example, a scene arousing anxiety rated about 5, then one between 5 and 10, and so on. It is instructive for the clinician to be aware of certain stimulus dimensions which can be introduced to affect the anxiety level within scenes. Among these are the size of the phobic object in the specific scene, its proximity, movement toward or away from you, barriers between the object and yourself, restriction of your freedom to avoid the object, and actions of others nearby (do they emit fear cues). In some phobias, the cognitive set may be an important parameter; for example, in public speaking, higher fear may be associated with perceiving the audience as evaluative or unfriendly, lower fear may be related to interest or the presence of a familiar face. Putting the scenes on index cards, and writing the anxiety values on the back, then arranging the cards from high to low based on these values, allows cross-checking on the adequacy of the hierarchy. If, upon looking at the narrative descriptions of the now-ordered cards, there appears to be some discrepancy, then the clinician should further discuss the item with the client.

Desensitization proper involves the use of imagery to enable the client to experience the scenes from the hierarchy. After relaxation induction, a relaxing scene may be introduced, then the lowest anxiety scene is described by the clinician, with the instruction that the client "actually be there, involved in the situation." Emphasis is on being in the scene while still experiencing the relaxation. The clinician may wish to have the client give a hand signal "when any part of the scene has developed," then retain the scene for about 5 seconds. Relaxation instructions are repeated, prior to re-presentation of the first scene. Each time a scene is presented for the first time, it should be long enough to permit clarity, but brief enough to prevent tension arousal. With repeated presentations of the scene, the exposure duration may be extended. Behavioral signs of anxiety being aroused should be followed by an increase in relaxation instruction, and a shorter duration when the scene is again presented. Such signs of tension include swallowing, irregular breathing, rapid respiration, return of muscle tone and tenseness in the hands or facial area, delay in returning to relaxation scenes. Some tension is acceptable and informative during the first presentation of a scene since this is an index of the clarity and reality of the scenes. Desensitization sessions normally last 30 to 40 minutes, with an additional 20 minutes for pre- and postinterviewing to determine progress, scene clarity, aspects that appear to be useful in enhancing treatment, and so on. The total number of sessions varies with the intensity of the phobia combined with the ability of the client to develop skill in relaxation and in experiencing scenes. Accelerated treatments have been as short as 1 day under special conditions.

SPECIAL CONSIDERATIONS

Preparation for termination is crucial. Because of the seeming lack of feedback on change (many clients report, "I don't feel any different") since such feedback will not occur until a phobic situation is again experienced, it is useful to deal with this. Once the therapist is convinced that therapy is complete, he/she might indicate only that "It's time to check on our progress. Between now and the next meeting, will you seek out one of those situations, see how you do, and report your improvement?" By not specifying that this was the last treatment session, and by offering another meeting, the clinician can avoid having to deal with the reluctance of the client, while instead using an in vivo proof of recovery. Most clients will simply telephone about their results, and suggest themselves that treatment be terminated.

Cautions in desensitization include the importance of stressing practice in relaxation, the need to allay any fears about the method or clarify misconceptions, the value of helping the client to understand in simple terms the principles involved, and the importance of careful scene construction. Diagnosis, of course, must be accurate to determine whether desensitization is even appropriate. As indicated earlier, phobic conditions may well be better treated by other behavioral methods, depending on the characteristics of the phobia. Regarding imagery, it should be mentioned that the purpose of imagery is to enable the client to *experience* the stimulus conditions in a realistic way. Ordinarily, clear imagery is needed. However, imagery may not be required where the client is still able to experience the tensional reactions through either thinking-recall or through listening to the clinician describing the scene. Finally, it might be mentioned in passing that some older clients seem to take longer in learning the relaxation skill and in progressing through desensitization. This is sometimes due to hearing losses, attentional difficulties, failure to understand the practice requirements, and so forth.

INTRODUCTION TO ANXIETY MANAGEMENT TRAINING

Anxiety Management Training (AMT) was designed to meet the deficiencies of desensitization and other anxiety management methods. Desensitization requires that the client be able to identify and specify the cue conditions prompting the tensional state. Where impossible, hierarchy construction and scene exposure are unfeasible. Also, where there are a number of different phobias, desensitization may be exceptionally long as each hierarchy is desensitized session by session by session. Implosive therapy has the advantage of being shorter, but still requires some knowledge of the stimulus conditions prompting the stress. Furthermore, implosion typically leaves the client emotionally fatigued and hence is somewhat aversive. Both desensitization and implosion do not provide for generalization of the recovery to fears different from those treated.

Anxiety Management Training (Suinn & Richardson, 1971) was primarily aimed at the so-called free-floating or general anxiety, but is considered applicable to single or multiple phobias. It is not necessary to design hierarchies, and since the client is trained in anxiety control, then each session ends with a controlled, low arousal state rather than tension or fatigue. Basically, AMT aims at training the client in changing the anxiety/fear *response* into *cue* conditions.[1] Thus, the client learns his/her own specific ways of experiencing stress, for example, neck and shoulder muscle tightening, clenching of hands, throat dryness, stomach motility. As this is noticed, the client then uses these cues to prompt tension-reduction coping reactions. At this stage, AMT relies heavily on relaxation as the coping reaction. It is believed that the primary step is first

---

[1]Further elaboration in the theory of AMT can be found in the chapter by Suinn (1975).

controlling the emotional correlates of anxiety, since this may prevent the client from acquiring or emitting other adaptive behavioral skills. Hence, the current AMT method offers relaxation as the first skill to learn. By using the relaxation when tensional cues are felt, the client is able to break the vicious cycle whereby the small arousal of tension cues off increased arousal, until the person is overwhelmed by the anxiety responses. AMT involves a self-control model whereby the clinician increasingly trains the client in self-initiation of management of anxiety. To achieve this, a variety of previous experiences of tension are used, but only as a means of arousing anxiety in the sessions so that the client may learn and practice anxiety reduction.

Anxiety Management Training was developed in 1971; research was conducted on single phobic (mathematics anxiety) subjects, using relaxation and competency responses for anxiety control. After therapy, subjects showed significant lowering of self-reported anxiety, and increases in performance on a mathematics test. Subsequently, other studies have reconfirmed the usefulness of AMT in dealing with stimulus-specific anxieties (Nicoletti, 1972; Richardson & Suinn, 1973a). Additionally, results support the belief that AMT can effect improvements similar to desensitization methods (Richardson & Suinn, 1973a, b; Suinn & Richardson, 1971).

Since a prime interest was in the application of AMT to free-floating anxiety, recent studies should be mentioned. Both Edie (1972) and Nicoletti (1972) found substantial reductions in general anxiety among university students. Edie also confirmed that the method described in this chapter seemed the most effective way of conducting AMT. Nally (1975) hypothesized that some adjudicated delinquents experience generalized anxiety, and that this anxiety prevented prosocial behaviors. Using AMT, he was able to reduce significantly the delinquents' level of anxiety, with corresponding increases in prosocial behaviors and self-esteem. Shoemaker (1976) conducted the first study using AMT with anxiety neurotics in a mental health center. He not only discovered that AMT was successful in comparison to implosive therapy and pseudotherapy, but that gains were retained over a 1-month follow-up.

THE ANXIETY MANAGEMENT TRAINING MODEL

Anxiety Management Training involves three basic phases: (a) introduction to AMT and relaxation training, (b) training in visualization of an anxiety-arousing experience, a scene associated with relaxation, and practice in switching from arousal to relaxation control, and (c) increased training in self-initiation of anxiety management. Phase 1 relies on the Jacobsen relaxation training, with training proper taking between 20 and 30 minutes. This phase also introduced the client briefly to the principles of AMT, its aims, and especially the concept of being able to utilize self-management in real-life events through practice in the sessions. Phases 1 and 3 are available on audio tapes[2]; however, Phase 2 should be conducted "live." In Phase 2, four objectives are sought. First, the clinician assesses the skill in relaxation achieved by the client by this meeting. Second, there is an assessment through observation and interviewing of the ability of the client to use scenes or other methods as a means of precipitating anxiety arousal or relaxation responses. Third, the sessions are used to begin training in controlling the anxiety responses by using relaxation skills. Fourth, the client is taught to identify early cues indicating the buildup of anxiety, such as muscle tensions and autonomic signals. Many clients soon recognize their own "stress profile," such as the one client who clenches his fist as stress begins, or another who can always tell because of tightening of the facial area. Most clients are unaware of these cues prior to training, experiencing their physical states only after anxiety arousal has reached an irreversible level. Phase 3 involves more complete training during which the client is relaxed, anxiety is aroused through visualization, followed by termination of the anxiety through a deep breath signal and an immediate shift to relaxation. Phase 3 actually proceeds with the clinician initially establishing the control, instructing the client when to develop anxiety arousal, when to terminate the arousal scene, and detailing the relaxation control sequence. With further sessions, the clinician gradually withdraws from direct instructional control, requiring the client to assume more and more responsibility for anxiety management. These three phases are discussed in more detail next.

Except for remarks regarding AMT principles and usage, Phase 1 involves relaxation training utilizing the same general rules outlined in the earlier section under desensitization. It is important to emphasize practicing relaxation skills, and particularly to be able to initiate relaxation without the tensing format as soon as the client is able. Additionally, training usually pairs the use of deep breath with relaxation induction to permit the deep breath to act as a cue for the future. Other cues can be used on the discretion or preference of the clinician, such as the word "relax"; it is wise to avoid multiple cues for relaxation.

The introduction to AMT in Phase 1 briefly emphasizes the need to become aware of the bodily cues signaling the onset of anxiety, the importance of learning a method for self-control and reduction of the anxiety, and the training steps in AMT to achieve such control. Becoming actively aware of early signs of anxiety arousal and actively self-initiating control are key concepts. Clients are also informed of the distinction between the emotional/physiological responses associated with anxiety arousal, versus behavioral skills such as problem/solving or conflict resolution to remove the sources of the anxiety or stress. AMT is aimed at providing control over anxiety responses, which may then permit the client to better acquire other adaptive skills.

[2]An AMT audio tape program is distributed by the Rocky Mountain Behavioral Sciences Institute, P.O. Box 1066, Fort Collins, Colorado, 80521.

Phase 2 comes after relaxation practice through homework (similar to that for desensitization). During Phase 2 sessions, clients are asked to identify a relaxation scene and an anxiety-arousal scene. The relaxing scene is later used as one mechanism for focusing attention on a stimulus condition which may enhance the retrieval of relaxation after anxiety. Other conditions include refocusing on the muscle groups, using the deep breath to trigger relaxation, and so on. In previous AMT work, a competency scene had also been used. However, some clients are unable to recall occasions when they felt competent, and hence relaxation training is currently emphasized more for use in group treatment. The anxiety-arousal scene involves recalling "an experience when you felt quite anxious, it may not be necessary to know what you were responding to that made you anxious, only how you were feeling, what was happening, what the general circumstances were. . . ." The emphasis is on retrieving a single event. For those rare clients who cannot immediately remember the locale, the interaction, the individuals, and so on, the clinician can start them instead by saying simply "Recall the last time you felt quite anxious. Focus on those anxious feelings, and let them return."

Under the direct control of the clinician, the client is instructed to take steps in becoming relaxed, in switching on a relaxation scene, using the scene to further relax, using deep breaths as a relaxation cue, switching off the relaxation scene, switching on an anxiety-arousal scene, momentarily using the scene to recapture the anxiety reactions, then switching off the scene and returning to relaxation activities. Later in the session, the anxiety-arousal scenes are held longer with the instruction to "notice how you react to anxiety. . .the ways your body reacts to stress. . .perhaps through tenseness in the neck and shoulders, or reactions in the throat or stomach area, or the face. . .the specific ways in which you tend to react." This aids the client in identifying their bodily "stress profile" that will serve as early warning cues to initiate future anxiety control responses. This phase of training is conducted at a pace which permits the client to understand the technique for anxiety arousal, identification of the ways in which the anxiety is expressed in the muscle stress profile, while keeping the anxiety under control in the sessions. Interviewing of the clients is conducted to determine how clear the imagery was, how well the clients were able to switch scenes, and the progress being made in responding to the anxiety responses as cues.

At the end of Phase 2 sessions, homework assignments involve continuation of relaxation practice and daily checks on stress. In the latter, the client does two things: (a) he/she spends a few moments in the morning and afternoon to attend to muscles in the stress profile to determine if they signal signs of stress building at the moment, and (b) he/she attends to the muscle groups during any period in which he/she is experiencing a stress. This homework exercise aids the client in confirming the muscle stress profile, and provides practice in attending to these profile cues as early warning signals.

Phase 3 continues the basic methods introduced in Phase 2, but emphasizes the anxiety arousal. After relaxation is achieved, the client is directed to initiate an anxiety scene, and to use the scene to trigger heightened anxiety arousal: "Let the anxiety develop, as high as possible, permit yourself to really experience the anxiety again, noticing how you react." Relaxation control is then initiated upon instructions by the clinician. As Phase 3 sessions continue, the role of the clinician shifts from directly guiding the clients throughout the relaxation activity, in the starting and stopping of the anxiety scene, and in the retrieval of relaxation control. Instead, the clinician begins to require the clients to take on more and more responsibility. For example, the clinician may first transfer the relaxation induction by saying, "Close your eyes, now use whatever relaxation method works best for you. . .and signal me when you are reasonably comfortable" (clinician then becomes silent). Later, the clinician transfers the anxiety-arousal activity, "Start the anxiety scene, and use it to again become more and more anxious. . .signal me when you're again experiencing that high level of anxiety." During the earlier part of Phase 3, the clinician will still wish to follow the *client*-directed anxiety arousal by *clinician*-directed return to clinician-directed relaxation control. Later, the relaxation control itself is transferred to the client, for example, through the instruction, "All right, while still staying in that anxiety scene, regain controlled relaxation, using whatever method has worked for you. . .signal when you're reasonably comfortable again." Finally, the clinician simply has the clients "switching on the anxiety scene" and "sometime after the anxiety arousal, when you are ready, reestablish the relaxation control" and "signal when the whole sequence is done." Homework emphasizes using the relaxation control to prevent anxiety from developing, by initiating relaxation whenever the clients perceive anxiety as building, as evidenced by the muscle stress profile early warning signals. Also, anytime the clients experience stress to a serious level, the anxiety management system (relaxation control) is to be used, thus applying the practice from the treatment sessions to real life.

The anxiety management training program may be completed in 6 to 8 sessions of 45 to 60 minutes each. Phase 1 can be achieved in one session with homework practice for about 5 to 7 days before the second meeting. Phase 2 can often begin with the second meeting, and can be completed in two sessions. The remaining 3 to 5 sessions can be devoted to different aspects of Phase 3. The rate of progress is, of course, determined by the ability of the clients to acquire the skills in relaxation, in experiencing anxiety arousal, and in developing relaxation control. By interspersing homework assignments during Phase 3 sessions involving use of AMT principles in vivo, generalization is achieved and application of the training to real-life circumstances is enhanced. In fact, as indicated earlier, a primary objective of AMT is self-control. In this sense, AMT is more nearly *training* rather than treatment, and the role of the clinician is more that of a consultant or trainer than therapist. Of course, the results of the training do involve therapeutic gains and recovery from tensional conditions.

SPECIAL CONSIDERATIONS

Since many clients perceive their meetings as therapy sessions, they may need special encouragement in completion of homework assignments, and in recognizing the importance of applying AMT in daily life. Rather than being "treated," they should become aware that the training of AMT is in coping skills and these skills need to be practiced and utilized.

Since AMT involves coping with anxiety arousal, it is less important what the source of the anxiety may be. Thus, it may be used with single phobics or multiple phobias. Unlike desensitization, a separate hierarchy is not needed, only a scene that enables the anxiety to be experienced in sessions in order for relaxation control to be developed. Unlike implosive therapy, AMT also has the advantage of ending each session with controlled relaxation, and a sense of achievement and progress, rather than emotional fatigue.

There is a note of caution in regard to Phase 2. In a few cases, clients have experienced extreme levels of anxiety during training; therefore, it is recommended that this phase be under the direct supervision of a trained therapist. Although this has not occurred with anxiety neurotics involved in AMT research programs, a few clients in university samples have needed therapist guidance to retrieve relaxation control. The simplest method is to return to muscle relaxation instructions, focusing on each muscle group in sequence, but without tensing these groups. The instructions should be given by the clinician to enable the client to focus in on a specific set of activities, as well as using the voice of the clinician as the stimulus for each stage of relaxing.

Again, the importance of sound behavioral diagnosis is essential. Is anxiety actually involved? Occasionally a client mislabels the emotional state as tension or anxiety, when it may really be other forms of arousal, such as anger, irritability, excitement, resentment. A complaint of anxiety may actually be a response operant to achieve gains. That is, a client may be using the complaint as a mechanism for achieving reassurance, for justifying inhibitions or dependency behaviors, for explaining ambivalences, and so forth. Assessment is also desirable throughout training to determine whether homework assignments are being accomplished, and if not, then the diagnostic reasons.

As indicated previously, AMT has now been used with anxiety neurotics. Furthermore, the treatment format involved the use of audio recorded treatment, although a clinician was physically present during all sessions. Results have been favorable and show promise for the use of AMT as a means of quickly providing such patients with a means for remaining out of hospitals. An interesting by-product of the AMT treatment has been in helping the patients in self-understanding. In behavioral terms, what seems to be happening are two things. First, the AMT procedure has helped patients to pinpoint the stimulus conditions which precipitated the tensional responses. For example, a patient will suddenly say, "I know what was crucial in my anxiety scene; when the other person started to say evaluative things about my work, *that* made me anxious and upset.'' In addition, once the anxiety reactions are under control, this seems often to permit a patient to refocus attention on identifying the sources of the tension. For example, a patient may become aware that social skill deficits exist, and ask for treatment/training for this area. It is as if the previous anxiety condition prevented the client from examining his/her own personal characteristics. Additionally, perhaps the patient can now confront deficiencies, without this confrontation leading to anxiety reactions that then remain uncontrolled.

CONCLUSION

The treatment of phobic conditions appears to be well in hand. Of all the varieties of human suffering, this area seems most amenable to control through desensitization. It is true that the actual theoretical explanation for the effectiveness of desensitization seems to be still open for discussion. However, fears of flying, of dentists, of heights, of snakes, of blood, of closed spaces, of public speaking, need no longer be considered untreatable. Standard individual desensitization, accelerated desensitization, group desensitization, even automated desensitization[3] techniques have been researched and tested on clinical samples and found effective. The key still does seem to be the level of skill in relaxation which the client can achieve, and the client's ability to experience the stimulus conditions during treatment. There is some controversy regarding whether imagery as such is essential, if the client can experience the phobic stimuli some other way, for example, through controlled thoughts, detailed descriptions by the clinician, photographs, or in vivo presentations.

General anxiety, or the so-called free-floating anxiety, may be conceptualized as a tensional condition that is subject to some control. AMT seems to be a promising approach not only for the community client but also for the more severe person often diagnosed as anxiety neurotic. Although desensitization is more straightforward for single phobias, anxiety management training can be applied for multiple phobias or more ambiguous tensional conditions. Since AMT involves training in self-control, it is likely to have more generalizability for the client than desensitization for specific cue conditions. An interesting by-product of anxiety management training for general anxiety appears to be in enabling clients to more accurately assess the sources of their tensions, and possible personal deficiencies associated with such anxieties. Although a semiautomated treatment tape has been in use, this approach still involves some clinician presence. It may be possible that complete automation can be achieved, if the clinician can be assured of a high skill in relaxation control among clients, and a more gradual approach to anxiety arousal and control.

[3] A Test Anxiety and a Mathematics Anxiety Desensitization program is distributed by the Rocky Mountain Behavioral Sciences Institute, P.O. Box 1066, Fort Collins, Colorado, 80521.

REFERENCES

Anton, W. An evaluation of outcome variables in systematic desensitization. *Behaviour Research and Therapy*, 1976, *14*, 217–224.

Aponte, J., & Aponte, C. Group preprogrammed systematic desensitization without the simultaneous presentation of aversive scenes with relaxation training. *Behavior Research and Therapy*, 1971, *9*, 337–346.

Baker, B., Cohen, D., & Saunders, J. Self-directed desensitization for acrophobia. *Behavior Research and Therapy*, 1973, *11*, 79–89.

Bandura, A. *Principles of behavior modification*. New York: Holt, 1969.

Bergin, A., & Suinn, R. Individual psychotherapy and behavior therapy. *Annual Review of Psychology*, 1975, *26*, 509–556.

Cohen, R. The effects of group interaction and progressive hierarchy presentation on desensitization of test anxiety. *Behavior Research and Therapy*, 1969, *7*, 15–26.

Donner, L. Automated group desensitization—A follow-up report. *Behavior Research and Therapy*, 1970, *8*, 241–247.

Edie, C. *Uses of AMT in treating trait anxiety. Unpublished doctoral dissertation, Colorado State University, 1972.*

Eysenck, H., & Rachman, S. *The causes and cures of neurosis*. London: Routledge & Kegan, 1965.

Jacobsen, F. *Progressive relaxation*. Chicago: University of Chicago Press, 1938.

Lazarus, A. Group therapy of phobic disorders by systematic desensitization. *Journal of Abnormal and Social Psychology*, 1961, *63*, 504–510.

Mathews, A. Psychophysiological approaches to the investigation of desensitization and related procedures. *Psychological Bulletin*, 1971, *76*, 73–91.

Migler, B., & Wolpe, J. Automated self-desensitization: A case report. *Behavior Research and Therapy*, 1967, *5*, 133–135.

Mitchell, K., & Ingham, R. The effects of general anxiety on group desensitization of test anxiety. *Behavior Research and Therapy*, 1970, *8*, 69–78.

Nally, M. *AMT: A treatment for delinquents*. Unpublished doctoral dissertation, Colorado State University, 1975.

Nicoletti, J. *Anxiety management training*. Unpublished doctoral dissertation, Colorado State University, 1972.

Paul, G. Outcome of systematic desensitization. 11: Controlled investigations of individual treatment, technique variations, and current status. In C. Franks (Ed.), *Behavior therapy, appraisal and status*. New York: McGraw-Hill, 1969.

Paul, G., & Shannon, D. Treatment of anxiety through systematic desensitization in therapy groups. *Journal of Abnormal Psychology*, 1966, *71*, 124–135.

Rachman, S. Systematic desensitization. *Psychological Bulletin*, 1967, *67*, 93–103.

Richardson, F., & Suinn, R. A comparison of traditional systematic desensitization, accelerated massed desensitization, and anxiety management training in the treatment of mathematics anxiety. *Behavior Therapy*, 1973, *4*, 212–218. (a)

Richardson, F., & Suinn, R. *Effects of two short-term desensitization methods in the treatment of test anxiety*. Unpublished manuscript, 1973. (b)

Salter, A. *Conditioned reflex therapy*. New York: Creative Age, 1949.

Shoemaker, J. *Treatments for anxiety neurosis*. Unpublished doctoral dissertation, Colorado State University, 1976.

Spielberger, C. Theory and research on anxiety. In C. D. Spielberger (Ed.), *Anxiety and behavior*. New York: Academic Press, 1966.

Suinn, R. The STABS, a measure of test anxiety for behavior therapy: Normative data. *Behavior Research and Therapy*, 1969, *7*, 335–339.

Suinn, R. Removing emotional obstacles to learning and performance by visuo-motor behavior rehearsal. *Behavior Therapy*, 1972, *3*, 308–310.

Suinn, R. Anxiety management training for general anxiety. In R. Suinn and R. Weigel (Eds.), *The innovative psychological therapies*. New York: Harper, 1975.

Suinn, R., Edie, C., & Spinelli, P. Accelerated massed desensitization: Innovation in short-term treatment. *Behavior Therapy,* 1970, **1,** 303–311.

Suinn, R., Edie, C., Nicoletti, J., & Spinelli, P: The MARS. *Journal of Clinical Psychology,* 1972, **28,** 373–375.

Suinn, R., Edie, C., Nicoletti, J., & Spinelli, P.: Automated short-term desensitization. *Journal of College Student Personnel.* 1973, **14,** 471–476.

Suinn, R., & Richardson, F. Anxiety management training: A nonspecific behavior therapy program for anxiety control. *ehavior Therapy* 1971, **4,** 498–510.

Wilkins, W.. Desensitization: Social and cognitive factors underlying the effectiveness of Wolpe's procedure. *Psychological Bulletin,* 1971, **76,** 311–317.

Wilson, G., & Davison, G. Processes of fear reduction in systematic desensitization: Animal studies. *Psychological Bulletin,* 1971, **76,** 1–14.

Wolpe, J. *Psychotherapy by reciprocal inhibition*. Stanford: Stanford University Press, 1958.

Wolpe, J., & Lang, P. A fear survey schedule for use in behavior therapy. *Behavior Research and Therapy,* 1964, *2,* 27–30.

Wolpe, J., & Lazarus, A. *Behavior therapy techniques*. New York: Pergamon, 1966.

James Gormally
and Clara E. Hill

Chapter 3
Treatment of Overweight and Eating Disorders

Numerous experimental demonstrations of the effects of behavioral treatment procedures for obesity have appeared since Stuart's (1967) pilot project. Reviews of the behavioral obesity treatments particularly seem optimistic about the effectiveness of self-control techniques. In our experience, these techniques work well with clients who are willing to engage in self-monitoring and habit change tasks. However, some of our clients have not been so motivated and have dropped out or failed to comply with tasks when presented with a traditional behavioral model. We feel modifications in present procedures are needed to accommodate client differences.

The major premise of this chapter is that the etiology of obesity and overeating is highly individualistic, which suggests that no single treatment will be effective for all individuals. Thus, therapists need to be familiar with assessment techniques to determine which treatments are suitable for different types of clients. Very little attention has been given in the weight control literature to the role of assessment, and unfortunately research has focused on manipulating treatments rather than examining the influence of subject characteristics.

This chapter contains a brief overview of the history of obesity treatment approaches. The following section discusses various assessment procedures for determining important clinical features of an individual's weight and eating problem. Based on these assessment considerations, three group treatment programs are outlined. Finally, special considerations for conducting obesity treatments in groups are presented.

HISTORICAL OVERVIEW

Behavioral techniques, in contrast to earlier psychodynamic treatments, have used learning principles to change eating responses. These techniques emphasize the identification and modification of problem habits and situational cues which are antecedent to problem eating behavior. Although the history of behavioral applications to obesity has been recent, a vast number of experimental studies have been reported. Ferster, Nurnberger, and Levitt (1962) discussed concepts such as stimulus control and ultimate aversive consequences to modify problem eating habits. Stuart's (1967) case study data on eight overweight females still rank as one of the most effective treatments in the literature. His approach involved a three-pronged treatment: stimulus control procedures and changing the eating response (e.g., eating more slowly, a balanced nutritional diet, and increasing physical activity levels). Wollersheim (1970) conducted the first well-controlled factorial design to test the effects of group therapy, based on learning principles. The major elements of her behavioral group included stimulus control techniques, relaxation training, group discussion and support, and a group weigh-in with therapist and group reinforcement for weight loss.

Stuart and Davis (1972) described a three-pronged approach to weight control: situational control, decreases in intake using a sound nutritional diet, and increases in exercise. This book, and its companion client version, is essentially an elaboration of Stuart's (1967) procedures. Situational control involves the use of techniques as stimulus narrowing, for example, eating in one place in the house, and in general, focusing on the antecedent stimuli which serve as cues for inappropriate eating. The second element of their approach involves the use of a food exchange program to systematize dieting efforts. This approach is recommended because it is nutritionally well balanced and relatively easy to utilize over a long period of dieting because of the variety of foods allowable on the diet. The third component, exercise, emphasizes teaching clients the importance of increased calorie expenditure through increased exercise (calisthenics, jogging), or changing daily routines to increase caloric expenditure. The most sound weight control program, according to Stuart and Davis, is one in which caloric intake is decreased moderately and caloric expenditure is increased moderately.

The discovery of the importance of the environment in controlling eating responses has provided support for behavioral treatments. Schachter (1971), in a summary of several studies, found that obese persons were more sensitive to external cues than were nonobese persons. He showed that the sight or smell of food and time of day could be more powerful cues to the obese person for eating than internal, physiologically based hunger cues. Thus, a major component of the behavioral approach has been the emphasis on teaching persons the principles of stimulus control. However, Wooley and Wooley (1975), review some theoretical alternatives to Schacter's work, which may ultimately effect the relative importance of stimulus control procedures now utilized.

The most current development in behavioral approaches has been training overweight clients to modify their eating behaviors through self-control skills. Hall, Hall, Hanson, and Borden (1974), Jeffrey (in press), Mahoney and Mahoney (1976), and Stuart and Davis (1972) have all developed treatment programs which teach self-control skills (environment manipulation and reinforcement of habit change). Several reviewers (Abramson, 1973; Hall & Hall, 1974) have asserted that self-control techniques seem to be the most promising of all the behavioral techniques.

Mahoney and Mahoney (1976) described a sequence of steps for implementing self-controlled behavior change. In summary form, these steps include specifying a target problem, data collection, devising and implementing ways to resolve the problem, evaluating the change procedures by further data collection, and revising or continuing the change project. This sequence is applied to a number of problem areas, which are essentially the same as the three components in the Stuart and Davis program. In addition, Mahoney and Mahoney describe the pitfalls of "perfectionistic thinking" and suggest ways of adapting more realistic dieting attitudes. We view this emphasis on cognitions as an important area to include in behavioral treatment.

Even though systematic application of self-control techniques has some appeal, the overall treatment impact on weight loss has been meager. Generally, inadequate attention has been given to clinical vs. statistical significance for determining the effectiveness of behavioral treatments (Gormally, Note 1). In addition, there has been little effort to determine which treatment works best for different types of clients. The underlying principle for this chapter is that a variety of approaches are necessary for treating obese clients. The choice of treatment depends largely on careful assessment of client problems.

DESCRIPTION OF THE MODEL

We will first describe an assessment procedure for obese clients. Based on assessment information, we see three possible treatment approaches: a 20-session behavioral self-control skills training group, a 40-session behavioral group counseling, and an on-going insight-oriented therapy group. Major emphasis is placed on describing the first two treatments.

The initial assessment interviews, conducted individually with each client, are a crucial component to all the treatment programs. The assessment interview can be used to assess the severity of the overweight, determine the motivational reasons for wanting to lose weight, and to observe the attitudes and cognitions of the client about dieting.

Body Measurements

Although weight is often used as the major criterion for inclusion in a weight control program, assessment should also include the measurement of body fat. A simple instrument, called skinfold calipers, is commonly used to measure subcutaneous (directly beneath the skin) body fat. Seltzer and Mayer (1965) have established a table of skinfold thicknesses (according to age and sex) for determining whether a person's skinfold at the triceps is indicative of obesity.

Nature of Eating Problems

A difficulty in assessment is the confusion between obesity and overeating. Even though a person may not be obese, he/she may have severe problems with compulsive eating. For example, one middle-aged female seeking treatment for her overeating, was approximately 20 pounds overweight with 25% body fat, thus not clinically obese. However, she reported severe difficulty controlling hunger urges, such that she was unable to keep any food stored in her house. Her binge behavior could be categorized as compulsive eating in the sense that she would consume an exessive amount of calories at one sitting with no awareness of satiety cues. She ate foods that were not inherently enjoyable in excess, for example, brown sugar, honey, natural cereals. Interestingly, she controlled her body weight by "compulsive dieting" and by frequent jogging and hiking. The proper focus for assessment for such a client is primarily the compulsive eating, and only secondarily, weight.

In our experience, some persons with less severe overweight have a "fat mentality" toward eating, and regulate their weight only by tenuous controls. Hence, major reliance on physiological indices of obesity in assessment lacks clinical precision. The assessment interview should also focus on inappropriate eating habits, such as binge eating, snacking behavior, secret eating, and eating in response to emotional cues.

Motivation and Attitudes Toward Dieting

Many persons entering weight treatment have a strong initial resolve to lose weight. However, this resolve seems to have little correspondence to persistence in treatment. In several groups, where we have investigated these phenomena, there has been no correlation between self-reported motivation and either weight loss or persistence. In fact, most clients showed high motivation at the beginning of treatment, by initiating contact, completing inventories, and self-monitoring their behavior. The danger with this initial desire to lose weight is that often, high expectations for some cure are followed by rigid conformity to highly depriving diets, which end quickly and are followed by binges and feelings of guilt and failure. This cycle of failure, which is repeated over and over by many obese persons, seems to reinforce low self-confidence and low self-esteem.

The key to assessing motivation involves careful probing into the clients' attitude toward the weight loss program. One cognitive style that frequently leads to premature termination is "magical thinking," in which a client believes that something simple and magical will instantly relieve him/her of fat. This style is reinforced by diets which result in large amounts of fast weight loss. Unfortunately, many behavioral techniques with novel sounding labels can also reinforce this thinking. The problem with magical thinking is that the client adopts a passive role in the treatment process. The therapist becomes the "sorcerer" with a bag of tricks. The client's cooperation with assignment of tasks is actually passive compliance. If the treatment program does not produce immediate changes in weight, which the client desperately wants, this sets the occasion for resistance, anger and/or premature termination.

Weight Loss and Dieting History

The history of weight loss and dieting behavior is an excellent indicator of dubious motivation; for example, persons who have lost substantial amounts of weight through extreme dieting programs such as drugs, diet farms, hospitalization, or injections, are very likely to adopt a passive role in future treatments. Frequently, it is not enough to admonish clients that a behavioral weight control program demands more active involvement, simply because this thinking may be well engrained. In addition, client behavior toward most helping professions is shaped so that the client expects to be a passive recipient of some treatment.

Analyzing the reasons for failing previous diets may be enough to help expose inappropriate attitudes toward dieting. Mahoney and Mahoney (1976) describe how perfectionistic thinking often leads to dieting failures. A person who approaches a diet thinking he/she will never be able to have a pizza again is unrealistic and setting up a failure. These "never again" thoughts seem to set off obsessions about the denied food.

Another method to assess motivation is to examine the reasons a client states for wanting to lose weight. Typically, reasons generally fall into two categories: cosmetic or health concerns. Clients often have a specific event, such as a Bar Mitzvah or wedding, for which they want to be thin. In the past, we felt that health-related reasons would be more indicative of a longer term motivation to lose weight and that weight loss efforts which were motivated for superficial reasons or upcoming events did not translate into persistence in treatment. However, our experience has shown that this hypothesis simply is not true. For example, one client who was 235 pounds at the outset of treatment and had developed diabetes as a result of overweight had not been able to use very serious health problems to motivate her to make permanent changes in eating habits.

It may be that important reasons to lose weight are difficult to articulate during the initial phase of treatment. For example, in one group session 3 months into treatment, a 230-pound woman in her late twenties indicated for the first time that losing weight would bring a decrease in her sexual frustrations, because she would be more appealing to men. A useful probe for delving into this kind of material is to ask the client for a fantasy of what would be different if he/she lost weight.

Related to reasons for dieting is the issue of whether weight loss is internally or externally motivated. External motivations are often experienced as pressures, threats, or subtle demands imposed on the client by significant others (e.g., spouses, parents, friends). Even though these pressures may result in some motivation to begin a weight loss program, the client often has residual feelings of anger and resentment, which can undermine the treatment. Several clients, often realizing how useless it is to respond to external pressures, have offered the alternative of internal motivation, such as, "I have to do it (diet) for myself."

Although it is difficult to determine if a person is thinking properly about a weight loss program, we have determined some indicators which are helpful. The most important factor is a realistic sense of the effort involved in losing weight, including the length of time, caloric intake decreases, activity changes, and the difficulty involved in changing habits. The person should also be able to anticipate problems that may occur from changes in routine; for example, fixing separate foods or meals for dieting, changes in the frequency of eating in restaurants, and so on. Jeffrey (in press) alludes to the importance of "client readiness" for starting a self-control weight loss program. This concept of readiness is very useful in assessing proper motivation and seems related to commitment to change. The meaning of commitment varies from client to client, but generally commitment is manifested when a client is able to realistically appreciate that he/she has to give up something in the struggle to lose weight. For example, a female client in her mid-twenties was discussing the great difficulty involved in trying to lose weight after several weeks in the treatment program. The therapist, after providing some empathy and encouragement, also confronted her with the statement, "Whoever said dieting was going to be easy?" In the discussion that followed, the client was able to realize how little she focused on the hard work involved in losing weight.

Realism also involves setting attainable weight loss goals. The typical weight loss rates for clients in behavioral treatments average 1 to 2 pounds a week. Many of our clients, however, report goals of 4- to 5-pound losses, which are difficult to reach on a sensible diet and again sets them up for disappointment and failure.

Because realistic attitudes are difficult to develop, it may be best not to start a structured program immediately for a client without proper attitudes. It is extremely difficult to suggest to a desperate-sounding client that more preliminary work needs to be done on developing proper attitudes. Two procedures are useful in dealing with client desperation and unwillingness to put off active weight control. First, gathering baseline data on circumstances surrounding eating can give the client a specific task while avoiding attempts at changing eating habits. This task also gives valuable information regarding a client's readiness to engage in simple self-control techniques. Second, a therapist can strongly assert the value of waiting by stating that the client should avoid another "false start." If the therapist is aware that a client's history is replete with many false starts at dieting, he/she is in a good position to assert that attention to changing attitudes in the beginning of treatment makes it more likely that the program will be completed and successful.

In summary, assessment should provide information on four variables: degree of obesity and weight, nature of eating problems, motivation and attitudes toward dieting, and weight loss and dieting history.

Based on these variables, it is possible to roughly categorize clients who are appropriate for three treatments: skills training in behavioral self-control techniques, integrated treatment of group counseling and behavioral skills training, and group/individual psychotherapy with little or no behavioral techniques. There may be a group of clients who are unsuitable for any psychological treatment, because of the severity of the obesity. A thorough medical examination is useful to help determine whether a client is appropriate for a treatment involving increased activity and decreased caloric intake. At this stage of development, this category system is based on our clinical successes and failures but does not have empirical support. Thus, our current knowledge does not allow us to assert that a particular treatment is the treatment of choice for a certain client type.

In our discussion of treatment procedures, we first provide a description of the kind of client who is most suitable for the treatment being described. Following this description, treatment procedures are outlined. Each of the three treatments is summarized in terms of therapist behavior, client behavior, and group process.

BEHAVIORAL SELF-CONTROL SKILLS TRAINING GROUP

The format for this group is a presentation and discussion of behavioral self-control skills. It is a 30 hour program, ideally suited for 20 weeks, with a 1½ hour session per week. This is followed by the longer term maintenance phase of the treatment described below. The typical client for this treatment can be characterized in the following manner: age range from college age up to the early thirties; reactive obesity (weight problems are the result of some situational trauma); the weight and eating problems are fairly discrete and not part of a constellation of other disturbances; is relatively free of any compulsive rituals such as secret eating, nighttime eating, or induced vomiting. The client's weight loss history is not marked by extreme weight fluctuations, wherein substantial weight losses have been regained. This client is committed to the idea of the importance of data collection and to a relatively objective approach to habit change. Most importantly, the client has a realistic attitude about the effort needed to lose weight and senses the importance of his/her active involvement in the treatment.

A case example should illustrate the kinds of characteristics which make a client suitable for behavioral self-control skills training. A 20-year-old college female was 15 pounds overweight when she requested weight control treatment. She had a relatively brief history of overweight and her eating habits became a problem when she started college. One of the major problem eating habits which contributed to her overweight was eating in her dorm room while studying for courses. She did have realistic career plans, a satisfying relationship with her boyfriend, and generally exhibited a good deal of interpersonal skill. At the onset of treatment, she fully cooperated with data collection tasks and exhibited a realistic sense of how much effort and time it would take to lose 15 pounds. Her attitude toward treatment was such that she adopted a "personal scientist" role. She seemed objective about her problem rather than angry, disgusted, and ashamed with herself because of the problem habits. She viewed her therapist more as a teacher and source of support rather than as a person to whom to confess weekly her dieting mistakes.

Adequate descriptions of self-control techniques have been presented by Stuart and Davis (1971) and Mahoney and Mahoney (1976), although methods for applying these techniques in a group setting have not been thoroughly discussed.

In outline form, we will present the major elements of a 20-week training group. At least 20 weeks is recommended because a shorter program does not provide the continued support needed to institute the major changes in life-style necessary for permanent weight loss. However, this period only includes the active treatment phase, so that added sessions are necessary to continue the maintenance phase.

Pretreatment

After it has been determined that a person is appropriate for behavioral treatment, several pretreatment measurements should be taken individually. Measurements optimally should include a full range of body dimensions: size (in inches) of chest, waist, hips, right thigh, bicep of the dominant arm (unflexed); skinfold thicknesses (Seltzer & Mayer, 1965) of the tricep (dominant arm), subscapula (near the backbone), and suprailiac (above the hipbone); and body weight. Particularly when exercise programs are used, changes in body measurements usually result from treatment, providing another source for measuring success. Skinfold thicknesses give a direct measure of subcutaneous body fat and the percentage of body fat relative to the weight can be calculated before and after treatment. Because skinfold calipers, which are used to measure skinfold thickness, are somewhat expensive (approximately $120) and brief training in their use is required, the resources of a health education department in a university may be helpful.[1]

Each client should also specify a weight loss goal for the 20-week program, because the client's estimate of a weight loss goal for a given period of treatment offers the therapist a chance to assess realistic thinking. Attention to the total amount of excess weight is important to document the clinical significance of treatment which requires the calculation of an ideal weight. However, it is difficult to determine ideal weights, especially when the popular Metropolitan Life Insurance table of ideal weights is utilized. This table requires some estimate of the client's body frame and gives wide ranges of acceptable weights for males and females at given heights. More importantly, the Metropolitan table was based on actuarial data with ideal weight based on longevity. Because clients often seek weight loss for cosmetic reasons, the ideal weights in the Metropolitan table may seem too high to a client.

An alternative for determining ideal weight are formulas described by Mahoney and Mahoney (1976). Ideal weights can be calculated for males and females for a given height. For males, the formula is $(4.0 \times \text{height in inches}) - 130$, and for females $(3.5 \times \text{height in inches}) - 110$. Unfortunately, no allowance is made in these formulas for the natural trend of increased weight with increasing age. In general, older clients typically adopt weight loss goals which would have been appropriate during their early twenties.

The best alternative, in our view, is to help the client come to his/her own realistic ideal weight, based on tables, formulas, cosmetic factors, and personal preferences. The therapist can use this opportunity to emphasize the importance of realistic goal setting to minimize discouragement and premature termination. Finally, the therapist can assert to the client the importance of developing a "winning" self-concept by setting and achieving realistic goals. In our practice, we have repeatedly seen that chronic dieters are the most desperate and because of this, set the most unrealistic weight loss goals. These same persons also seem to view themselves as failures at weight loss and have ample opportunity to reinforce this "losing" attitude by setting themselves up for another failure by setting goals too high.

Treatment should include weekly weigh-ins, but great caution should be used to prevent a competitive group atmosphere during the weigh-ins. Competition among group members may motivate some clients to lose weight; however, these weight changes are probably the result of trying to save face rather than the result of acquiring self-controlling responses. If pressure is created to report weight loss weekly, the client is given the expectation that only success is

[1]See Wilmore and Behnke (1969) and Sloan and Weir (1970) for procedures on calculating the percentage of body fat.

acceptable, which prevents the client from using the resources of the group for help when the inevitable relapses occur. Our clients, who have often been failures in the more popular diet programs available to the public, have frequently reported quitting these programs because of intense resentment over the pressure to lose weight. To minimize competition, the group should decide whether weight changes should be openly reported in the group.

Session 1

This session begins with introductions and an explanation of the groups. The major lesson for this session is a proper method for counting calories. A helpful book is Kraus' *Calories and Carbohydrates,* which lists calories for name-brand foods. The therapist can also educate clients as to the calorie costs of items typically obtained at fast-food restaurants. This can be done by providing a list with the amount of calories for fast food (550 calories for a ''Big Mac'') and the amount of walking or jogging necessary to burn it off. In this task, the clients are expected to record the calories consumed daily, although they do not have to alter their caloric level. This data should be used to provide a baseline prior to dieting. The goal of this task is to give the client the opportunity to experiment with the amount of calories with which they feel satiated and to assess the motivation of the client to engage in self-monitoring tasks. If the client is unable to record calories for 1 week, the therapist should reevaluate the client's readiness to profit from the behavioral skills training group. Since clients who self-monitor their behavior at the beginning of the treatment rarely behave as they normally would when not on a program, this task is not a true baseline. For example, the clients sometimes engage in ''last supper'' behavior, where they have one last binge before the diet begins. Discussion of group norms (reporting weights, attitudes toward successes and relapses, importance of being task oriented) should also be conducted by the therapist.

Session 2

During the second session, the calorie data should be discussed briefly with the goal of selectively reinforcing appropriate self-monitoring. However, the therapist should stress that no caloric reduction has to be undertaken unless it comes naturally. The rest of the session shoild be used to introduce clients to the concepts of situational control, which they will practice in the potluck supper during the third session. In describing situational control, the therapist should point out that eating problems are not the result of some inherent weakness, but the client's lack of awareness as to the ways situations influence eating behavior and food urges. Schacter's (1970) research can be used to explain how obese individuals are highly responsive to situational cues, such as sight of food, time, location, and events.

The group needs to decide who brings what to the potluck supper, which can generate valuable cognitive material about the social self-consciousness of most dieters. Self-monitoring of calories should also be assigned as the task for the week.

Session 3

Covert rehearsal before the meal should focus on creating a success experience of controlling the thoughts and urges to eat. Simple instructions can be given to the clients to fantasize each aspect of their eating behavior, and generally controlling the urge to eat just because the food is present. During the meal, instruction and practice can be given for techniques to use to slow down eating. Some helpful techniques are placing the fork on the table after each mouthful, increased talking as a substitute for eating; pauses in eating during the meal. Many clients will be able to offer other techniques which they find helpful. The purpose of the session is to provide each person with alternative methods of controlling inappropriate urges to eat when food is present. Attention can also be paid to other habits, such as the quantity of food consumed, placing food on the table versus in other rooms, and offering food to others. The purpose of this meal is to provide an opportunity for clients to practice and get feedback and reinforcement on specific habit changes. By observing themselves and each other, they will begin to see other modes of behavior.

Session 4

Further discussion should be held on the importance of bringing eating under stimulus control. Stimulus narrowing, or reducing the number of cues associated with eating, is a helpful technique for decreasing bad eating habits. Specifically, clients can be instructed to reduce the number of places they eat in the house, as well as the number of activities they engage in while eating.

At this point in the program, clients should be ready to begin their first self-change project, which should last about 3 weeks. Each project entails the following steps: (a) problem identification, (b) data collection, (c) intervention, and (d) reassessment and modification through further data collection. We view these steps as the core component of training in self-control skills. Each person will be individually helped to choose a project, based on personal difficulties with situational control problems. These target problems may range from eating too quickly, eating while watching television, snacking behaviors, and so on. By this time, group members will hopefully know each other well enough to help each other identify problem areas (Step 1). The main guideline here is to pick a target which is likely to be changed to ensure success. Each client will be asked to record data on the problem (Step 2) for the next session.

Considerable resistance to data collection seems to be the rule rather than the exception in our experience, so prior to such assignments, clients should be reminded that the data provide the only objective method for determining the success of the intervention strategy. The importance of the active involvement of the individual in the project for permanent weight control should also be stressed. The expectation should be given that each group member will collect a full week of data on the target problem for the next session, as well as maintain the record of the daily caloric intake.

Session 5

This session will serve as an opportunity for examining each individual's data on the target problem and deciding on intervention strategies (Step 3). Again, the entire group should be encouraged to become actively engaged in the problem-solving task for each individual, but the ultimate decision about intervention strategies should be up to the individual because it must be something the person is able to do. An intervention program may be beautiful on paper, but if it is not designed to the individual's life-style and behavioral patterns, it could easily fail. A good technique is to provide the client with several alternative interventions and instruct the client to choose the best one for him/her. Each group member should be given a prescribed amount of time to discuss his/her project, so that equal attention is given to all members. The task for the week is to implement the intervention and to maintain the record of the daily caloric intake.

Session 6

In the beginning of this session, each group member should be given the chance to report on the change project, with others providing comments for reassessment and modification of the intervention strategies (Step 4).

The core skill for training in self-control is self-reinforcement. Our experience has been that clients, at the outset of treatment, engage in few reinforcing activities besides eating and have little realization of other potential pleasurable activities. In fact, we suspect there may be a relationship between eating problems and meager self-reinforcement menus for clients. When a person can successfully decrease inappropriate eating, they can often begin to find substitutes for pleasuring themselves. Thus, there may be considerable resistance to using self-reinforcement to maintain behavior. Another difficulty in training in the use

---

Fig. 1. Calorie focusing chart. *Note:* Client marks by an × the amount of daily intake on the chart and records the amount of calories on the bottom of the chart as well. The caloric intake goal is marked in the middle of the sheet and each line can be used to indicate 50 calories away from the goal. Thus, if the goal was 1,350, the next line above would be 1,400, and the next line below the middle would be 1,300.

DAYS

GOAL

CALORIES

45

of self-reinforcement is an unwillingness to administer reinforcements on a contingency basis. Frequently, clients will claim that they can do the reinforcing activity anyway even if they do not earn it.

The goal for this session is to help clients identify both current and possible reinforcers which could be used in conjunction with their self-change projects. The therapist should emphasize the need to maintain motivation by using self-reinforcement. Since this skill is difficult to acquire, very simple self-reinforcing procedures may be best to use at first. The discussion of various reinforcers by the group can be helpful in generating alternatives so that each person will have a few reinforcers that can be used interchangeably. Tharp & Watson (1971) is a useful reference for the therapist in preparing for this discussion of self-reinforcers.

The assignments for the week will be to carry out the modified project and to maintain the caloric intake record.

Session 7

In the next three sessions, each person will choose and initiate a new self-change project focusing on decreasing caloric intake. By this time, the clients will have 6 weeks of caloric intake data, so that they will have a reasonably accurate picture of their fluctuations and averages and the necessary caloric level for feeling nourished. During this session, clients should be taught a more simple method of recording the amount of food they eat. The food exchange system is recommended (explained by Stuart & Davis, 1972), since it enables the person to keep track of the calories in a simpler and quicker manner and is also helpful in planning a nutritionally sound diet.

After the explanation of the food exchange system, the calorie focusing chart can be introduced as a convenient way to record the daily caloric expenditure (see Figure 1). This chart has three purposes: (a) it provides on one sheet a convenient record of the entire week's caloric intake, (b) it teaches clients flexibility in goal setting by the use of upper and lower limits, and (c) it graphically demonstrates the importance of avoiding extremes while restricting the caloric intake. Flexibility is important since many clients enter a weight control program feeling that they have to be "perfect," that is, eat 500 calories a day, never have another sweet, etc. By setting upper and lower limits on daily intake, the therapist can help to teach clients to avoid perfectionistic standards.

Two techniques which may be helpful for some clients in becoming more flexible are the caloric savings bank and the "day off." In the caloric savings bank, the client keeps records of the difference between the daily caloric intake and the amount actually consumed. An entry in the passbook can be made when the calories consumed are less than the target goal. Thus if the goal was 1,350 and 1,200 was consumed, 150 is entered into the passbook. The entries can be saved up and used for special events when the client chooses to eat in excess of the target goal. The "day off" strategy involves allowing the client to choose a certain number of days a week not to count calories, thus building in days when the client does not have to be completely concerned with dieting. The usefulness of either of these strategies, or others, will depend on the individual client, who should choose which strategies he/she wants to try.

For the first week on the caloric intake self-change project, each person will record their caloric intake via the food exchange system and the focusing chart, with no attempted intervention.

Session 8

During this session, intervention strategies for the caloric intake self-change project can be discussed. A daily caloric intake goal should be chosen, at a level which avoids excessive deprivation. Some nutritionists have suggested that no dieter should consume fewer than 1000 to 1200 calories a day, and this range should be kept in mind. However, for an occasional dieter, much lower levels are necessary to lose weight, due to metabolic difficulties. This type of person, however, should have a thorough medical checkup prior to going on such a low intake level. The group members should give each other feedback about the appropriateness of the goals selected.

Clients should also select appropriate self-reinforcements to reward attainment of realistic caloric intake goals. For example, a reinforcement could be earned for achieving caloric intake goals 5 out of the 7 days.

Session 9

The main focus of this session is to review the progress of the caloric intake self-change project, engaging in problem-solving for those difficulties brought up by clients. Attention should not be provided for noncompliance or rationalizations for not completing projects, as this tends to reinforce such behavior. Perhaps a better way of dealing with this is first to discuss achievements and successes in the self-change projects. Those clients who have attained at least five of seven daily caloric goals should be praised and encouraged to maintain this level for an additional week, to ensure that this new caloric level is learned. Clients who have not achieved their goals for at least 5 days should be questioned about the reasons for their difficulties and helped to modify their project, aiming for more attainable goals.

Session 10

This session should be used for a second potluck dinner, to review and reestablish proper eating habits, and also to reinforce progress in these changes.

During this meeting, the progress on the caloric intake project should be discussed. Appropriate modifications in intake goals can be made if necessary, based on group discussion. This project will continue throughout the remainder of the program, with checks made each week on the achievement of caloric intake goals. Each person should be able, by this point, to determine exactly how many calories are needed to lose ½ to 1 pound a week. It should be noted that generally more calories are needed to burn off a pound of fat as dieting progresses.

Sessions 11–13

The focus of the next three sessions is on increasing caloric expenditure through activity and planned exercise. Although it is possible to lose weight merely through decreased caloric intake, the combination of decreased caloric intake and increased caloric expenditure is probably the most healthy and efficient method. Exercise not only burns up more calories, making marked decreases in intake less necessary, but it also aids in maintaining muscle tone and feelings of greater energy and fitness if instituted gradually.

Many clients have strong resistances to exercise. Often, strenuous exercise programs are begun after long periods of relative inactivity, leading to aversive muscle aches and pains. Or sometimes, exercise programs are begun which require a lot of time and disruption of schedules. Both of these factors decrease the probability of a person's beginning and maintaining an exercise program. Therefore, exercise should be instituted gradually, with as little disruption in the daily routine as possible. Activities such as calisthenics, jogging, tennis, etc. are considered planned exercises. Walking upstairs, parking in a corner of the parking lot and walking, and daily housework chores are examples of unplanned activity, because they essentially involve changing daily routines to burn additional calories. Both planned and unplanned activities should be instituted for this self-change project. Useful references for this section include Stuart and Davis (1972), Cooper (1970), and the Royal Canadian Air Force Exercise Program.

Session 11 will be spent discussing exercise and teaching clients to record a baseline of activity data for the week. During Session 12, these baseline activities will be analyzed and intervention strategies can be formulated for each individual. And finally, Session 13 will be used as a time to assess and modify the intervention program. Hopefully, at this point, clients will have instituted various planned and unplanned activities that intrude minimally into their daily routines. As with the caloric intake project, this project should be continued and checked throughout the remainder of the program, to enable the clients enough time to learn these changes and to integrate them into their lives.

Sessions 14–16

The final self-change project involves modifying some aspect of the clients' interpersonal environment which impacts on their eating behavior. As Stuart and

Davis (1972) suggested, spouses sometimes reinforce inappropriate eating habits through excessive criticism or by offering food. Since a person is affected by others in the environment, who may do things which serve to defeat progress in the weight program, clients will need specific help in dealing with significant others.

An example might be a person who eats rather than expressing angry feelings to his/her spouse. A self-change project which might be used could include increasing assertive responding to the spouse (after first ascertaining the baseline for assertive responding). Another example of such a target problem might be criticism by the spouse of dieting behavior (e.g., "Should you eat that on your diet?"; "You sure don't look like you've lost any weight; what good is that program doing?"). The intervention for this problem will need to be focused both on the spouse (e.g., decreased criticism) and the client (e.g., increased reinforcement of the spouse's noncritical behavior).

Session 14 should be spent in identifying problem areas. These areas will be more ambiguous and complicated than the previous target problems, simply because more persons are involved and the behaviors often are less specific. Care should be taken by the group to help each person identify the target problem in operational terms so that baseline data can be recorded. Specific examples for each target problem should be found, including both the client's behavior, the spouse's behavior, and the consequence of the behavior. Once the baseline has been collected, session 15 can be used to devise possible intervention strategies, based on the individual's particular situation. Session 16 can be used to analyze the effectiveness of the intervention strategies and to modify the components to account for difficulties.

Although the influence of another person's behavior on the dieting client can be crucial for successful weight loss, it is beyond the scope of this behavioral program to focus exclusively on relationship difficulties. If eating behavior represents just one facet of a generally distressed relationship, it is unlikely that simple intervention strategies in a self-change project would effect changes. The therapist's assessment of the marital difficulties can help to guide realistic change programs. Alternatively, the therapist may choose to refer the client and spouse for marital counseling.

Session 17

This session will serve as a review and summary of the client's progress on the four self-change projects. Areas which still present problems will require further modification. Additionally, clients can be asked to think about possible future problems in maintaining their achieved levels on these projects. By planning for the future difficulties, the client can more adequately handle them.

Individual clients may choose, during this session, to develop another self-control project to be carried out on their own. The group can be used to give them feedback about its feasibility.

Sessions 18–20

These three sessions constitute the preliminary portion of the maintenance phase of the program. By this time, group members who have not lost at least 8 to 10 pounds will most likely have dropped out. Successful weight losers will be confronted with one of two tasks at this stage of treatment: maintenance of weight losses or continued weight loss. The therapist may decide to divide the members into two groups, based on this distinction. One group of persons who either have lost their goal weights or who want to stay on a plateau of their current weight, will need to learn maintenance skills. A second group, those who have not achieved goal weight, may want to continue to a fairly regular program, instituting new self-change projects.

A maintenance program would consist of these three sessions, spaced at 2-week intervals. During these sessions, time would be spent reviewing the maintenance of the self-change projects. On the caloric intake project, clients would raise the level of calories to a maintenance rather than dieting level (e.g., 1,800 rather than 1,200 calories) and reinforce themselves for attaining these goals. The eating habits and exercise programs would be maintained as before. Many treatment programs do not emphasize these maintenance skills, nor do they give continued attention after the basic skills are learned, which is needed to ensure permanent weight loss. Following the completion of the 20 sessions, this group can meet again at intervals of 1 month for a year to reinforce the maintenance of the losses.

The clients who need to achieve additional weight losses would continue in a behavioral group. Their task is very difficult and arduous. Many of these persons have a great deal of weight to lose and the novelty of the behavioral program and the self-change projects has worn thin. Further, such a client typically needs a larger caloric deficit during extended periods of caloric deprivation, which leads to more feelings of discouragement and hunger. Inevitably, weight loss plateaus also occur, which add to the discouragement. The role of the group at this point is to provide help in troubleshooting for the problem areas and to provide continued reinforcement. For each client, new self-control projects can be instituted, as well as modifying the old projects. Weekly meetings are probably still necessary, until such time as the group decides to begin the maintenance phase. The length of this group is open-ended.

The therapist in this treatment can best be described as highly directive and reinforcing. He/she is primarily a teacher, describing techniques, analyzing data, assigning tasks, and providing positive feedback for accomplishments. The weight problem for these clients is viewed as a behavioral excess, rather than as symptomatic of underlying disturbances. Clients are expected to be actively engaged in between-session tasks and projects. The task of the group is learning and practicing skills, with minimal emphasis on acquiring insight into the dynamics of the problems. Thus, the group focuses on successful completion of self-change projects, with individuals presenting data and problems, and group members giving feedback and suggestions. The process is task-oriented, with little emphasis on group interaction and/or discussion of feelings.

BEHAVIORAL GROUP COUNSELING

The format for this group treatment is a combination of group discussion in conjunction with the behavioral self-control skills training. This group would contract initially to meet 20 weeks, with one session on skills training and one session on group counseling. Whereas the purpose of the training sessions is to learn specific self-control skills ("how to do it"), the purposes of the group discussion/counseling sessions are to understand the emotional significance of eating and weight problems as well as to develop a proper attitude toward dieting ("why I do it"). The goal of counseling sessions is limited to discussing feelings and attitudes, not to effect deep-rooted personality reorganization. Client expectations regarding these limited therapeutic goals should be clarified at the beginning of treatment.

This form of combined discussion/counseling and behavioral skills training seems most appropriate for clients presenting two major characteristics during the assessment interviews: First, attitudes toward dieting give valuable clues regarding the appropriateness of the treatment. Clients with a long history of repeated failures at dieting often need to gain insight into their failures before they can adopt a "winning" attitude toward a new weight control program. Additionally, perfectionistic goal-setting and magical thinking (described in assessment section) are indicators that a person may not be able to persist in a long-term behavioral treatment without being given some opportunity to discuss and modify these attitudes. The second characteristic can generally be described as eating for emotional reasons, such as anger, anxiety, boredom, or sexual frustration. The client who eats in response to emotional arousal needs help in differentiating the various stimuli so that each can be dealt with appropriately. The major focus in the counseling group is to identify self-defeating cognitions about dieting and to help the client learn more effective coping strategies to deal with emotions.

The atmosphere in the discussion/counseling session should be supportive and relaxed. Rather than dealing with behavioral data, therapists should encourage group members to discuss their feelings related to weight, eating, and the weight control program. At the end of each session, group members pick a topic for the coming week, based on some of the issues they are currently facing. During the week, they can then be thinking about the topic.

So that each client gets equal attention, it may be helpful to structure the "talk time", giving a person 5 uninterrupted minutes to discuss their feelings followed by 5 minutes of questions and comments from the group directed to the person. Remaining time can be spent discussing the issue in general.

The following list contains three areas of topics which have been useful in stimulating discussion in our groups: attitudes and cognitions about weight loss, social self-consciousness about overeating and overweight, and reasons for emotional eating. These topics have been recurrent themes in our groups, but they are certainly not exhaustive.

Attitudes and Cognitions about Eating

1. Advantages of being overweight—exploring client ambivalence about weight loss.
2. Fear of failing on a diet—gaining insight into the reasons for previous failures.
3. Fear of being thin—understanding how fatness insulates the client from insecurities.
4. Exercise—exposing myths and resistances to exercise.
5. Resentment about being on a diet—discussion of feeling victimized and being different because of the weight problem.
6. Deprivation feelings—learning how to cope with feeling deprived.

Social Self-Consciousness and Overeating and Overweight

1. Body image—negative feelings about one's body and the resulting effects on overall self-confidence.
2. Significant others—discussing how the overweight affects relationships with others.
3. Clothes shopping—shame and embarrassment about buying clothes and attitudes concerning dressing up.
4. Eating in the presence of others—shame and anxiety with public eating; being able to have a "guilt-free" cookie.

Reasons for Emotional Eating

1. Childhood experiences with food and eating.
2. Parent–child interactions concerning food; importance of food in the family life.
3. Food as a reinforcer—examining how many pleasures a person has besides eating; discuss how food is used as a reinforcer.
4. Chain of events leading to emotional eating.
5. Binges and secret eating—probing the reasons for these problem behaviors.
6. Feeding others—attitudes and behaviors involving the feeding of others.

7. Sexual significance of eating—discussing how unmet sexual needs can lead to overeating.
8. Obsessions with eating, food, and dieting.

In addition to discussion of these topics or others introduced by group members, some attention can be given to periodic mood checks about client progress in treatment. This focus on client progress typically results in a group issue: how to deal with group members' progress or setbacks. Open discussion of the effects of each other's behavior can lessen competitiveness and foster a supportive group atmosphere.

The behavioral sessions in this treatment share the same characteristics as in the behavioral skills training. However, the group discussion/counseling is conducted in a different manner and has different characteristics. In the group counseling sessions, the therapist promotes self-understanding by probing underlying feelings. The therapist does not reinforce specific accomplishment of tasks but rather helps to create an atmosphere in which clients can explore the reasons for and feelings about success or failure in self-change projects. The weight problem for these clients could be construed as either a behavioral excess or symptomatic of an underlying disturbance, or both. For this reason, clients are helped to understand the nature of their problem and also to act on this understanding by acquiring self-change skills. The only between-session task assigned at the counseling session is to think about the topic for the coming week. The group process is oriented toward discussing feelings and insights which lead the clients to acquiring a self-understanding regarding their eating and weight problem.

CHRONIC DIETERS GROUP

For some clients, neither of the two treatments just described would be effective. Persons who are likely referrals for a chronic dieters group have a history of repeated failure at dieting, sometimes utilizing extreme measures of regulation (shots, diet farms, etc.). Their weight loss history often is marked by extreme fluctuations in weight, with some clients losing enough weight to be considered at normal weight and then regaining the weight. Because of the repeated failures at weight control, a person may feel overwhelmed by the uncontrollability of their eating behavior, perhaps leading to a learned helplessness phenomenon. This may account for the severe depression prevalent among chronic dieters. A history of dieting which has failed to produce permanent results seems indicative of self-defeating attitudes about diets. For example, we have noticed that such persons are highly susceptible to pressures and demands by others to lose weight. There is a corresponding lack of insight that dieting is something done for oneself. Thus, any dietary device is perceived as a demand which is met by only temporary compliance.

Since between-session tasks are core requirements for the other two treatments, clients who exhibit resistance to completing simple tasks during assessment should be considered for inclusion in this group. The noncompliance with assigned tasks often cannot be resolved by direct teaching of self-control skills. Thus, the lack of self-controlling responses for chronic dieters can be viewed as caused by underlying disturbances rather than due to behavioral deficits, although this is merely a clinical hypothesis.

The general strategy of the therapist should be to avoid giving specific weight control techniques. In addition, therapists should admonish clients to avoid another "false start" in a weight control program. Because these clients are understandably desperate to lose weight, the therapist may experience considerable difficulty abstaining from giving advice about dieting. The clients' role in this treatment is to discuss the reasons why previous diets have failed. In addition, relatively more attention is placed on controlling binges rather than losing weight.

The goal of the group is to promote fundamental changes in the clients' self-concept and increased awareness about food and dieting. As such, it is beyond the scope of this chapter to detail the procedures necessary to implement the group. The group should not be limited to a fixed number of sessions, because these goals may take considerable treatment to achieve. Therapist monitoring of specific targets such as weight may be countertherapeutic because of the implicit importance placed on weight loss, which may distract the client from gaining insight. The interested reader should consult Yalom's (1975) text on group psychotherapy, as well as Bruch's (1973) work on eating disorders.

SPECIAL CONSIDERATIONS

There are two special considerations for conducting weight control treatments in groups. First, the composition of the group in terms of age, sex, and severity of overweight is critical in the planning of a group. The age variable can be classified into three levels: adolescence, college-age or young single adults, and middle-aged and/or married adults. This distinction is important because these three groups probably engage in different patterns of behavior regarding food preparation, regularity of meals, eating, and food shopping. When the group is composed of members of a similar age grouping, the therapists can tailor the treatment to their particular behavior patterns. Building group cohesiveness by creating a homogeneous group is probably more important in the behavioral group counseling and chronic dieters groups, because these treatments rely more heavily on group interaction.

Our experience has been that same-sex groups are more desirable than mixed-sex groups. Discussion of weight issues with members of the opposite sex may be more difficult and unduly embarrassing, because such topics are highly emotionally laden. However, it may be more difficult to start a group for males because fewer males seem motivated to seek treatment for weight or eating problems.

Severity of overweight is probably the most important group composition variable. Treatment procedures may have to be substantially different for severely obese clients, particularly in the length of the treatment period. When a wide range of overweight is represented in a group, the severely obese client, because of self-consciousness, may openly resent or ridicule clients who are close to their ideal weight, thus distracting the group from its task. A simple categorization which may be helpful for female clients is grouping clients less than or more than 35 pounds overweight.

Clients inevitably lose weight at different rates and perform tasks at various quality levels. Since we believe that a supportive group atmosphere is desirable, these variable performances should be addressed by the therapist to prevent the countertherapeutic effects of competitiveness from developing. The therapist should actively reinforce a group norm which primarily praises any attempts at behavior change, with weight changes given only secondary emphasis. In addition, minimal attention should be given to group members who do not attempt between-session tasks.

The sex and body proportions of the therapist can be significant influences in the group treatment models. If the group has all female members, it is preferable that at least one of the therapists be a female. Additionally, a therapist of average body proportions, who has experienced previous weight problems, provides a good model of a person who has successfully coped with his/her weight problem. On the other hand, an overweight therapist who attempts to lose weight during the treatment can be a model for appropriate client behavior. Moderate amounts of self-disclosure by the therapist of a previous or current weight problem can enhance the therapist's role in the group. Although these therapist variables are not requirements, they may have an effect on the course of treatment. Actually, little literature on the therapist variable exists, although materials on countertransference may be applicable here.

When a therapist overemphasizes changes in eating habits and weight, it is easy for the client to misinterpret reinforcement as therapist overinvestment in the outcome of treatment. The client may then feel that he/she has to lose weight to make the therapist feel good, thus undermining the purpose of a self-control program. The most appropriate role for the therapist is to facilitate client self-controlling behavior. For this reason, the therapist should avoid being cast as the source of external reinforcement. Operationally, this suggests that the therapist should respond in a neutral manner to reported weight losses or gains, by simply asking the client how she/he feels about the weight change. Praise by the therapist should be given out very carefully.

CONCLUSION

This chapter suggests several possible programs of research which are needed in weight control treatment. Ample experimental evidence has accumulated that documents the effectiveness of behavioral self-control procedures for promoting weight loss. However, Gormally, Moscati, Clyman, and Forbes (Note 2) in their review of this literature cautioned against excessive optimism about behavioral treatments. They noted that most treatments were too brief to help clients attain goal weights. In addition, follow-ups produced mixed results, especially for longer (over 12-week) periods. Outcome research on longer term treatments, such as the models described in this chapter, need to be done, paying careful attention to client attainment of weight loss goals. Our clinical experience regarding the suitability of different treatments for different clients also needs empirical testing. The goal of both programs of research should be to develop treatments which produce permanent changes in weight by taking into account the important needs of various types of overweight clients. We now know behavioral treatments do "work," but we need to know how to increase the reliability of the outcomes produced by behavioral treatments. As a final note to future practitioners of weight control treatment, we have found that the work is long and frustrating, demanding much patience.

REFERENCE NOTE

1. Gormally, J. Determining the effectiveness of behavioral obesity treatments. Unpublished manuscript, 1977.
2. Gormally, J., Buese-Moscati, E., Clyman, R., & Forbes, R. R. *Research design issues for behavioral treatment of obesity.* Unpublished manuscript, 1976.

REFERENCES

Abramson, E. E. A review of behavioral approaches to weight control. *Behavior Research and Therapy,* 1973, *11,* 547–556.
Bruch, H. *Eating disorders.* New York: Basic Books, 1973.
Cooper, K. *The new aerobics.* New York: Bantam Books, 1970.
Ferster, C. B., Nurnberger, J. I., & Levitt, E. B. The control of eating. *Journal of Mathematics,* 1962, *1,* 87–109.

Hall, S. M., & Hall, R. G. Outcome and methodological considerations in behavioral treatment of obesity. *Behavior Therapy*, 1974, *5*, 352–364.

Hall, S. M., Hall, R. G., Hanson, R. W., & Borden, B. L. Permanence of two self-managed treatments of overweight in university and community populations. *Journal of Consulting and Clinical Psychology*, 1974, *6*, 781–786.

Jeffry, D. B. Behavioral management of obesity: Learning principles and a comprehensive intervention model. In E. Craighead, A. E. Kazdin, & M. J. Mahoney (Eds.), *Behavior modification: Principles and applications*. New York: Houghton Mifflin, 1976.

Mahoney, M. J., & Mahoney, K. *Permanent weight control*. New York: Norton, 1976.

Mayer, J. *Overweight: Causes, cost, and control*. Englewood Cliffs, New Jersey: Prentice-Hall, 1968.

Schacter, S. Some extra-ordinary facts about obese humans and rats. *American Psychologist*, 1971, *26*, 129–144.

Seltzer, C. C., & Mayer, J. A simple criterion of obesity. *Postgraduate Medicine*, 1965, *38*, A101–A107.

Sloan, A. W., & Weir, J. Nomograms for prediction of body density and body fat from skinfold measurements. *Journal of Applied Physiology*, 1970, *2*, 221–222.

Stuart, R. B. Behavioral control of overeating. *Behavior Research and Therapy*, 1967, *5*, 357–365.

Stuart, R. B., & Davis, B. *Slim chance in a fat world*, Champaign, Illinois: Research Press, 1972.

Watson, D. L., & Tharp, R. G. *Self-directed behavior: Self modification for personal adjustment*. Monterey, California: Brooks/Cole, 1972.

Wilmore, J. H., & Behnke, A. R. An anthropometric estimation of body density and lean body weight in young men. *Journal of Applied Physiology*, 1969, *27*, 25–31.

Wilmore, J. H., & Behnke, A. R. An anthropometric estimation of body density and lean body weight in young women. *The American Journal of Clinical Nutrition*, 1970, *23*, 267–274.

Wollersheim, J. P. Effectiveness of group therapy based upon learning principles in the treatment of overweight women. *Journal of Abnormal Psychology*, 1970, *76*, 462–474.

Wooley, O. W., & Wooley, S. C. The experimental psychology of obesity. In T. Silverstone (Ed.), Obesity: Its pathogenesis and management. Acton, Mass.: Research Publishing Group.

Yalom, I. *The theory and practice of group psychotherapy*. New York: Basic Books, 1975.

Joel Block

Chapter 4
Treatment of Smoking

In this chapter methods are described for effecting changes in maladaptive behavior and emotion from a cognitive–behavioral viewpoint. Specifically,
cognitive–behavior therapy is discussed in regards to smoke cessation in a small
group setting.

Cognitive–behavior therapists notably stress the cognitive element in the
acquiring and the changing of emotional reactions in humans. It is a comprehensive system of psychotherapy that consciously and directly employs cognitive,
emotive, behaviorative modalities; but it uses the last two modes largely in order
to affect the first one significantly. Cognitive–behavior therapists are primarily
interested in helping clients to understand, get in touch with, and modify their
basic values, cognitions, attitudes, or philosophies; and they employ behavioral
techniques mainly as a means of aiding deep-seated philosophic changes rather
than solely for symptom removal. Further, when cognitive–behavior therapists
help clients to modify their beliefs regarding a certain phobia, obsession, com-
pulsion, or other symptom, the therapists usually try to induce them to make
more generalized changes in their belief systems, so that they will have, in the
future, considerably less of a tendency to disturb themselves with related self-
defeating philosophies. That is, cognitive–behavior therapists stress the importance of mediational processes, in relation to disturbance creation and disturbance removal. Since cognitive–behavior therapy practitioners adhere basically
to an educational rather than a medical or psychodynamic model, it is almost
inevitable that it be done in groups as well as individual sessions. Moreover,
frequently the cognitive–behavior therapist uses group processes as the method
of choice rather than because of practicality.

From the cognitive–behavioral point of view, conclusions such as Hunt's
(1970) regarding the failure of behavior modification approaches in regard to the
problem of smoke cessation become intelligible. Attempts to modify smoking
behavior through any technique that is aimed at habit modification but which

59

does not attend to the belief system of the individual will increase the probability of a resumption of smoking once the individual leaves the controlling environment. For example, sanitarium procedures such as the Seventh Day Adventist clinics offer a supportive environment in which the smoker may suspend for a brief period his customary roles. Without a change in his belief system, once outside this hospitable surrounding the person finds himself in the world of temptation assailed by all the internal and external conditions which initiate smoking behavior. Similarly, an individual subject to standard behavior modification procedures will likely resume characteristic modes of behavior once the reinforcement contingencies are no longer under extrinsic control, that is, when he returns to the demands of "Marlboro Country" (Sarbin & Nucci, 1973). Hunt and Matarazzo (1970), in their penetrating analysis of "habit," suggested that the traditional categories of behavioral psychology are inadequate and need to be supplemented by other concepts, such as attitude. In the language of cognitive–behavior therapy this is translated to a process through which a person acquires an ability to speak to himself in appropriate ways so as to conduct himself in a self-enhancing rather than self-defeating or maladaptive manner.

SMOKE CESSATION: A BRIEF REVIEW

Many writers (e.g., Greenwald, 1974) point out that the process of decision is basic to change. Clearly, decision-making is a cognitive process. Unhappily, the decisional patterns for smoke cessation are more like a messy bush, to use Raiffa's (1970) picturesque phrase, than a neatly shaped tree. We are aware that cigarette smoking, for many people, is an important source of ego strength. It not only yields a variety of pleasurable sensations, but, more important, helps the smoker cope with the demands of life, eases and promotes his or her social interactions, and is a valuable aid to the establishment of a sense of identity. As such, the activity of smoking is congruent with the achievement-oriented values of our society. However, even after smokers have officially "stopped smoking" it is difficult to describe the branches which led up to a presumed moment of decision. You get a neat tree only when you ask people to generalize about their reasons for smoking or stopping; however, retrospective data about the transition from smoking to nonsmoking status are unilluminating (Mausner, 1973).

We do know what does not work too well. For example, the wide variety of responses which have been reinforced for enabling smoking makes it unlikely that extrinsic extraction or punishment procedures can be sufficiently comprehensive to be efficacious in maintaining a reduced frequency of smoking (Hunt & Matarazzo, 1970). Similarly, the external restriction of stimulus situations in which smoking is permitted, although helpful, probably can only temper the control exerted by an otherwise multifarious and permissive stimulus environment. Moreover, although external self-control procedures, which attempt to alter the external stimulus condition under which smoking occurs (and hopefully generate self-produced reinforcing consequences for not smoking), do hold some promise of success, it is likely they will be insufficient (Ferster, 1970).

If external control proves to be insufficient, then additional help from internal control is necessary. Internal control has several possible meanings. What is intended here is control over those covert responses, that is, self-talk, produced by an individual in his head. In the context of self-control of smoking, the internal control rubric may include such notions as covert sensitization (Cautela, 1966), operants of the mind or coverants (Homme, 1965), covert self-punishment (Bandura, 1971), and several other cognitive–behavior techniques to be discussed later.

As an illustration of the potentially more efficacious cognitive–behavioral approach let us look at the phenomenon of aversive conditioning. The aversive conditioning paradigm typically involves showing the client a taboo stimulus or its representation (e.g., a slide) and when the client responds (as indicated by GSR, penile erection, etc.) he is shocked. Shock is terminated by the reduction of the autonomic arousal or by an instrumental response such as choosing another slide. In some paradigms the onset and offset of shock are made contingent upon the initiation and termination of an instrumental act such as smoking. A study was conducted in which the aversive conditioning paradigm was elaborated in order to modify what clients say to themselves. Steffy, Meichenbaum, and Best (1970) regarding the failure of behavior modification approaches in regard to the self-statements, thoughts, and images which accompany the smoking act. Termination of the shock was contingent upon the expression of self-instructions to put out the cigarette or such self-statements as not wanting "a cancer weed." In this way an explicit attempt was made to influence the chain of covert behaviors that control the smoking behavior. The clients reportedly were very inventive and serious in generating self-persuasive and self-rewarding self-statements which they could use to combat their urges to smoke.

This treatment approach is consistent with Premack's (1970) analysis of the self-control mechanisms which contribute to the termination of smoking behavior. Premack proposed that the decision to stop smoking results in a self-instruction that interrupts the automatic quality of the smoking chain. An increase in self-monitoring of one's smoking behavior sets the stage for such self-instructions. Thus, a treatment procedure that focuses on the development of such self-instructions should prove efficacious. Indeed, postassessment and 6-month follow-up of the Steffy study indicated substantial and significant improvement for the treatment group whose attention to covert verbalizations was accentuated as compared to a standard aversive conditioning group. The addition of having the clients verbalize an image while smoking and then making the onset and offset of shock contingent upon the verbalized covert processes was highly effective in modifying what clients say to themselves and in reducing smoking behavior.

Another interesting tack is suggested by the work of Cautela (1971). Cautela trains his patients to engage in mediating responses which are intended to reinforce, positively or negatively, desirable or undesirable behaviors. Actually, Cautela discussed smoking briefly, but like most clinicians he interpreted the problem as one of need for aversive conditioning. His solution, and he has apparently actually tried this, is to use a kind of "interior aversion" reminiscent of Premack's coverants. Unfortunately, as Premack himself pointed out (1970), the degree to which fresh negative feelings can continue to be aroused is very limited. And thus it is likely that aversive coverants will have little permanent effect on many smokers. A more hopeful cognitive–behavioral approach would be to teach smokers to fantasize success in not smoking. A procedure along these lines is discussed in the context of the cognitive–behavioral model described next.

THE COGNITIVE–BEHAVIORAL MODEL

The cognitive–behavioral therapy model to be emphasized in this chapter, rational–emotive psychotherapy (RET), has been developed by Albert Ellis (1957), over the past two decades. Ellis' form of cognitive–behavior therapy is in keeping with the collapse of behavioristic S–R theories which tried to bypass anything "mental" but finally had to be modified to account for those events which occur between the input of a stimulus and the emission of an overt response. Thus, S–O–R theories have gained prominence and the conception of stimulus–response bonds has given way to a mediation model. The rational––emotive approach, like Tolman's, may be conceptualized as a S–CM–R model (stimulus–cognitive map–response). Ellis (1962) refers to it as "the ABC theory of personality and of emotional disturbance," and stresses that it is not the activating events (A) that cause emotional consequences (C) but rather the individual's beliefs (B) about what occurred at point A. This aspect of the model was originally propounded by the stoic philosopher, Epictetus, some 2,000 years ago and is a cornerstone of the therapy approach.

RET builds on the pioneering emphasis of Alfred Adler (1929) that humans, quite unlike rats and guinea pigs, are uniquely valuing creatures. They consciously and unconsciously rate or evaluate, or attach significant importance to various things, events, and meanings, and, once attached to certain goals or ideals, they regulate an enormous part of their lives by these attachments. More specifically, RET posits that practically all people have in common a basic set of value assumptions and that once these assumptions are made or "given," the rationality and irrationality of their subsequent thinking and behaving can be examined and understood. It is reasonably assumed that almost all humans have the basic goals of wanting to survive, to be relatively happy and free of pain, to get along with members of their social group, and to relate intimately to a few selected members of this group. If it is assumed that these basic values are desirable, behaviors that abet them are rational and those that sabotage them are irrational. Rationality, then, is a method of effectively gaining certain values; it does not exist in an absolutistic sense.

In the main, there are perhaps 10 to 15 irrational beliefs that people hold to with costly results in terms of their emotions and behaviors. These can be reduced to three dictates that cause immense emotional difficulties. The first dictate is "Because it would be highly preferable if I were outstandingly competent, I absolutely should and must be; it is awful when I am not; and I am therefore a worthless individual." The second unrealistic belief is "Because it is highly desirable that others treat me considerably and fairly, they absolutely should and must and they are rotten people who deserve to be utterly damned when they do not." The third self-defeating dictate is "Because it is preferable that I experience pleasure rather than pain, the world absolutely should arrange this and life is horrible, and I can't bear it when the world doesn't."

Any number of clinical examples may be cited to clarify the ABC philosophy, but let us take one very typical case in point.

A man informs his woman friend that he is seeing another woman and wishes to end their relationship. The woman in the example may tell herself statements such as:

Since he doesn't want me, nobody possibly could.
This is terrible. Everything bad always happens to me.
I must really be a worthless person.
I can't stand the world for being so unfair and lousy.
The bastard. He shouldn't be that way.

These beliefs (B) will likely lead to the emotional consequence (C) of depression and/or hostility. Frequently, however, the client will erroneously state something similar to "losing him makes me depressed," implying that the activating event (A) caused the emotional consequence rather than more accurately stating "I am depressing myself about this loss." Although depression is an unnecessary and self-defeating reaction, it can be argued that when a person is rejected by someone he or she loves very deeply, it is "normal" for that person to react with intense emotion. Indeed, a sensitive and feeling person who is nevertheless a rational human being, may reason at point B as follows:

I am sad that Mark rejected me, because I enjoyed being with him, I liked his stimulating companionship. I had strong hopes that we could develop a more lasting relationship, but unfortunately it didn't work out. This certainly is unpleasant, but it is certainly not the end of the world.

In this instance the individual drew conclusions from the rejection that resulted in feelings of "normal sadness" rather than conclusions leading to depression, which as Beck (1967) has shown usually include unrealistic, invalidatable over-generalizations ending with the nonsequitor "therefore I am worthless."

The main goals of RET group therapy are essentially the same as those of individual therapy: namely, teaching clients that *they* are responsible for their own emotional upsets and behavioral excesses; that they can change their disturbed emotionality and behavior by changing their beliefs, values, and philosophies; and that if they acquire radically new and profoundly held belief systems, they can live with a minimum of self-defeating emotions and eliminate behavioral excesses such as smoking, overeating, and drug abuse. Some of the important group-oriented goals and methods used by the cognitive–behavior therapist are the following:

1. Since teaching the client how to accept the existence of grim reality and to try to change it by concerted effort rather than whining is essential to cognitive––behavior therapy, all group members are encouraged to reveal and discourage the presenting individual's perfectionism and dictatorialness. Group members are taught to parse logically and empirically contradict the disordered, disturbance-creating thinking of each of the other members.
2. The therapist is usually probing, exceptionally active, confronting, and directive. He teaches the scientific method to the group members so that they can apply it effectively in their daily lives.
3. Because they do not believe in "pure" cognizing, emoting, or behaving, cognitive–behavioral therapists use a wide variety of cognitive–educative, emotive–evocative, and behavioristic methods including, but not limited to, role-playing, assertion training, and in vivo risk-taking. These can frequently be done in individual sessions but are more potent in group. One procedure, rational–emotive imagery (Maultsby, 1971), alluded to earlier in the literative review, can be used to teach cigarette smokers to fantasize not smoking and feeling frustrated but not destroyed. Using rational–emotive imagery (REI), a woman in one of my groups who was terrified about not smoking anymore, particularly during demanding circumstances, was asked to imagine vividly, to fantasize as clearly as she could, being in a very difficult situation without cigarettes, not handling it well, and being negatively evaluated by onlookers.
   She was then asked her gut-level feeling as she imagined herself in this predicament. She replied:

"Utter panic! I feel very anxious and have an intense need for a cigarette."

"Fine!" I said. "You are reacting to this technique quite well. Now, see if you are able to change your gut feeling. Keep the same picture in your head—imagine yourself still in this demanding predicament. This time, however, change your feeling in your gut to one of mild disappointment and frustration in regard to not doing well in this circumstance and not having cigarettes to smoke. Not panic, not intense craving, only mild tenseness and frustration. Can you, if only momentarily, change your feeling to that?"

"It's hard! I still feel panicked and intense craving for a cigarette."

"I can appreciate that it's hard, but I'm sure, at least temporarily, that you can do it. Stick with it."

(After a long pause) "OK. Now my feelings have changed somewhat, now it is more like disappointment and frustration."

"Very good. Now, what did you do, what did you say to yourself to change your feelings?"

"I—uh, I managed to say to myself, I don't have to handle this situation perfectly. It is just a difficult circumstance, not a catastrophe and even though I would like a cigarette to 'help me,' I don't need one; I can stand feeling tense without having to reach for a cigarette!"

"Good," I said. "That's exactly what you might tell yourself when you are actually in this kind of situation. Now, what I want you to do is take 5 or 10 minutes every day, put the time aside, and practice just this kind of imagery during this time. Vividly imagine, just as you have just done, being in a difficult situation, a circumstance where you are likely to be tense. Let yourself feel panic, intense craving, whatever. Let yourself really experience what you would typically feel. Then, just as you did now, change that feeling to one of disappointment and frustration, using the same kind of thinking you just used. Do that for 5 or 10 minutes every day, for the next 2 weeks or so. Then we'll see how your smoking behavior and your anxiety are affected!"

As predicted, this woman's anxiety in certain situations and her smoking behavior decreased appreciably as she continued to do this imagery homework assignment. A few weeks later, she reported complete cessation of smoking even though she still experienced moderate anxiety on occasion. As she put it, "even though I still get nervous, I found out it's not that bad, I can stand the tension without cigarettes!"

The use of REI with regard to smoke cessation has been evaluated experimentally on a limited basis (Block, in preparation) and in conjunction with other procedures has high potential. Further, it has been my experience that REI is a useful technique for demonstrating to people that they can change their feelings by altering their cognitions about an event.

4. REI is part of a broader range of homework assignments that cognitive-
   -behavior therapists may use for a wide range of problems, including smoking. Both the therapist and the group consistently give homework assignments to group members. Homework assignments frequently include activities of a graded nature which slowly increase in difficulty—thus, they comprise an in vivo desensitization. For example, it may be suggested (by fellow group members, the therapist, or the client himself) that an individual increasingly cut down his smoking by a specified amount each day in particular circumstances. Occasionally, if the individual feels it necessary, a reward/penalty contingency based on Premack's model (1970) is set up and monitored by the group.

The theory behind homework assignments is that humans practice telling themselves all kinds of negative internalized sentences that create feelings of anxiety, depression, guilt, and hostility oftentimes leading to or at least maintaining self-defeating behavioral habits such as cigarette smoking. Instead of being externally conditioned—as we commonly condition rats in a laboratory experiment in psychology—we are mainly self-conditioned by our own thinking and imagining processes. The homework assignments are designed to challenge the disturbing, self-defeating cognitions while clarifying and reinforcing reality-based cognitions.

Moreover, since many of us are born short-range hedonists with high degrees of low frustration tolerance, we would much rather avoid almost any momentary discomforts, especially the discomfort of anxiety, even at the expense of foregoing all kinds of long-range satisfactions. Consequently, when we tolerate even a little discomfort which we really had better do in order to work through these feelings and eliminate defeatist habits, we make it feel so intolerable (mainly by telling ourselves, "I can't stand it!") that we conclude—"it's insurmountable!" Because people often react this way, homework assignments are used to encourage them to become longer range hedonists; to stick with their present pains—that is, their anxieties, guilts, and so on—and even temporarily exacerbate these feelings in order ultimately to diminish or eliminate them. Just as individuals practice telling themselves unrealistic ideas and practice feeling needless disturbances consequent to these ideas, homework assignments represent a method of helping them practice counterconditioning rational ideas, appropriate feelings, and behaviors which aid their survival and enhance their life.

To abet the learning process clients frequently fill out written homework report forms and give them to the therapist to go over. In group sessions, a few homework forms are often read and corrected so that all the members of the group, and not merely the individual handing in the form, may be helped to see specifically what self-defeating consequence was experienced, what irrational self-talk the individual engaged in to create the dysfunctional consequences, and what kind of disputing could be done to minimize or eliminate the irrational beliefs that led to the defeating consequences. By hearing about other group members' main problems and how they dealt with them on the homework report, clients are helped with their own problems.

5. The group provides a setting which is generally supportive, and which offers members a wider range of possible solutions to their problems than they might normally receive in individual sessions. Further, the individual gets valuable feedback from the group as to how he malfunctions and what he is probably telling himself to create and maintain this malfunctioning. He also learns to talk others out of their irrational beliefs and thereby weakens his own self-defeating belief system.

6. Group procedures can be especially helpful for rigidly bound individuals who

have a most difficult time modifying dysfunctional behavior patterns and establishing new, healthier ones. Individual therapists, for example, frequently have considerable trouble inducing compulsive smokers to experiment with smoke cessation for a sufficient length of time. In a group setting, however, most other members will unblamefully accept him with his difficulty while continuing to show him that he can change and that they intend to keep after him until he does. This supportive yet direct and persistent confrontation frequently encourages the individual to try new behaviors until he becomes accustomed to them and even learns to enjoy them.

For many reasons, of which the foregoing list is hardly exhaustive, group processes are exceptionally useful in attacking the client's irrational premises and illogical deductions and helping him reconsider and reconstruct his basic self-destructive philosophies and behavioral patterns.

RESEARCH RESULTS OF THE PROCESS

Little research has been carried on, to date, in regard to the specific process of rational–emotive and related cognitive–behavioral approaches to group therapy. A good many studies have been done, however, to show that self-verbalizations do indeed exert some control over the way we feel and behave. In one study (Rimm & Litvak, 1969), subjects from a normal college population were required to read to themselves triads of sentences that according to Ellis should lead to maladaptive responding (e.g., "My grades may not be good enough this semester. . .I might fail out of school. . .that would be awful."). As a control condition, other subjects were required to read neutral triads of sentences to themselves (e.g., "Inventors are imaginative. . .Edison was an inventor; therefore, he was imaginative."). As expected, subjects in the experimental group experienced significantly more emotional arousal (as measured by respiratory changes) than did control subjects.

In two studies (Meichenbaum, 1971; Meichenbaum & Goodman, 1969), it was found that young children whose approach to problem-solving was marked by impulsivity tended to engage in less self-regulatory speech than other children less impulsive in their problem-solving behavior. These findings, taken along with the results of a number of other investigations (e.g., Beck, 1967; Davison & Valins, 1969), support the view that cognitive activities such as self-verbalization exert a definite effect on emotion and behavior.

Although research concerned with the use of cognitive–behavioral group therapy has been scarce, data in this area are growing. Further, almost all the therapeutic experiments that have been done have helped validate its practice. Most notable in this respect have been the studies of Dr. Donald Meichenbaum and his associates in Ontario, Canada (e.g., Meichenbaum, 1971; Meichenbaum, Gilmore, & Fedoravicicius, 1971). Not only have these researchers shown, in a very ingenious set of studies, that cognitive modification works better than desensitization or other forms of behavior therapy which do not stress cognitive approaches, but they have also tended to prove that cognitive group therapy is often more effective than individual therapy along similar lines. The work of Dr. Maxie Maultsby, Jr. (Note 2), testing the effectiveness of group and individual cognitive–behavioral procedures with individuals suffering from psychosomatic ailments, also produced corresponding conclusions. The cognitive–behavioral group therapy research related to smoke cessation reported earlier has also been quite positive.

Other experiments testing the effectiveness of cognitive–behavioral group therapy have been carried out by Block and Knaus (Note 3), Burkhead (1970), Karst and Trexler (1970), and Sharma (1970). These, and a number of other controlled experiments which continue to be reported in the scientific literature, tend to show that cognitive–behavioral therapy not only works but that it works unusually well when used with groups.

LIMITATIONS AND SPECIAL CONSIDERATIONS

The impression may be gained from the foregoing that RET or related cognitive–behavioral group therapy is a simple process that merely involves showing clients that their "emotional" problems stem from their illogical internalized sentences, demonstrating how they can parse and challenge their self-verbalizations, and then after a short period of time there will be inevitable improvements. This is a gross distortion. The difficulty with the presentation of any method is that the presenter is almost exclusively interested in showing the *success* of the procedure without the complexities and failures. In reality, however, every system, be it of psychotherapy or anything else, has its limitations. Cognitive–behavioral group therapy is certainly no exception.

The cognitive–behavioral group therapy procedure does not work equally well for all persons under all circumstances, and for some individuals it may not even work at all. For example, some people are too afraid of group contacts even to try it; some are too disturbed to stick with it when they do try it; and some are so suggestible that they take all therapeutic suggestions, good and bad, with equal seriousness, and therefore may be more harmed than helped by group treatment. Although some clients are not ready for group treatment, others, such as compulsive talkers or hypomanic individuals, may benefit considerably from group work but are too disruptive to the group and require too much monitoring; hence it is better to exclude them and to have them work out their problems in a more compatible modality such as individual treatment.

Aside from individual differences which preclude cognitive–behavioral group therapy from being a panacea for all ills, the group therapy process has other limitations and disadvantages. In small group procedures, for example, the best intentioned members can waste time in irrelevancies; mislead the problem presenter; hold back because of anticipated disapproval from other group members; sidetrack the therapist; and bring out their own and others' unimportant rather than important difficulties. Group members can also introduce so many suggestions to a presenter that he or she is left overwhelmed and/or confused. If the therapist does not actively intervene, a shy inhibited group member can easily "get lost in the shuffle," that is, get away with minimal participation and quite likely minimal change. In addition, group members can become hostile and strongly condemn a participant for his symptoms and as a consequence, the individual finds himself with more unhappiness to contend with.

Just as group therapy is unsuitable for some clients, so is it strongly suggested for others. Many clients who have socializing problems are difficult to help in individual therapy, particularly when they refuse to increase their social contacts and work through their relationship problems under therapeutic supervision. These same individuals if they can be persuaded into joining a therapy group, frequently interact on a gradual basis (particularly when reinforced) and, after a time, they socialize better and begin to diminish their relationship difficulties. In the area of smoke cessation, the American Health Foundation, a research organization, has found that for most (though not all) of their clients, active–directive, cognitive-oriented group procedures are the treatment of choice.

As implied, serious consideration would best be given to the nature of the individual, his presenting problems, and circumstance in choosing a treatment modality. Thus, rather than the usual active–directive approach of the cognitive–behavior therapist, a minority of people might benefit by a passive, inactive, reflective, and noncommittal approach. This may be particularly true for certain college-age youngsters who can effectively resolve their own "identity crisis" with the assistance of a concerned listener. Or, as regards smoking behavior, one person might desire to quit smoking but lack the self-control necessary to accomplish it, whereas another person might have sufficient self-control but see no reason to exercise it. Although smoking behavior is involved in both instances, the issue of self-control and motivation may require different tactics. The point is, to minimize the limitations of any one approach the clinician would best maintain an attitude of flexible, technical eclecticism, and based on careful diagnosis, draw from various approaches that which has proven effective.

CONCLUSION

Considerable data are now available to show the relationship between smoking and ill health. Yet many scientists, psychologists included, in full knowledge of the facts continue to smoke cigarettes. When questioned about this, they will reply something like, "I know I should give it up. I once quit, but became so tense that I couldn't get any work done. All I could think about was a cigarette. I concluded that my work was more important than my giving up smoking."

This example furnishes an illustration of man's proneness to self-defeating thinking, short-range hedonism, and inappropriate emoting. That humans are predisposed in certain undesirable ways, or that they can significantly change their cognitions, emotions, and behavior, however, is not in dispute. However, the findings reported earlier indicated that the modification of human behavior in the area of behavioral excess (and elsewhere) will not likely be solved by a simple reinforcement paradigm. Indeed, given the findings available, it is also not possible to come to any firm conclusion regarding the cognitive–behavioral procedure in producing long-term cessation of smoking. However, although additional research is needed, many of the findings are suggestive and point to the cognitive–behavioral model as the treatment of choice. Thus, if an individual chooses a small group process and if he picks a cognitively oriented group that helps him attack his stubbornly held irrationalities by selected evocative–emotive and active–behavioristic techniques, he will avail himself of a multifaceted, comprehensive therapeutic procedure that, it is hypothesized, will most likely lead to an efficacious solution to many psychosocial problems, including cigarette smoking.

REFERENCE NOTES

1. Block, J., *The effects of rational emotive imagery on smoking behavior*. Unpublished manuscript, 1977.
2. Maultsby, M. C., Jr., *The implications of successful rational emotive psychotherapy for comprehensive psychosomatic disease management*. Unpublished manuscript, 1969.
3. Block, J., *The effects of rational emotive psychotherapy on the behavior of adolescents*. Unpublished manuscript, 1977.

REFERENCES

Adler, A. *Understanding human nature*. New York: Greenberg, 1929.
Bandura, A. Vicarious and self-reinforcement processes. In R. Glaser (Ed.), *The nature of reinforcement*. New York: Academic Press, 1971.
Beck, A. T. *Depression*. New York: Harper-Hoeber, 1967.
Burkhead, D. E. *The reduction of negative affect in human subjects: A laboratory test of rational-–emotive therapy*. Unpublished doctoral dissertation, Western Michigan University, 1970.
Cautela, J. R. Treatment of compulsive behavior by covert sensitization. *Psychological Record*, 1966, *16*, 33–41.

Cautela, J. R. Covert conditioning. In A. Jacobs & L. B. Sachs (Eds.), *The psychology of private events*. New York: Academic Press, 1971.

Davison, G. C., & Valins, S. Maintenance of self-attributed and drug-attributed behavior change. *Journal of Personality and Social Psychology*, 1969, *11*, 25–33.

Ellis, A. Outcome of employing three techniques of psychotherapy. *Journal of Clinical Psychology*, 1957, *13*, 334–350.

Ellis, A. *Reason and emotion in psychotherapy*. New York: Lyle Stuart, 1962.

Ferster, C. B. Comments on a paper by Hunt and Matarazzo. In W. A. Hunt (Ed.), *Learning mechanisms in smoking*. Chicago: Aldine, 1970.

Greenwald, H. *Direct decision therapy*. New York: Wyden, 1974.

Homme, L. E. Perspectives in psychology: XXIV. Control of coverants, the operants of the mind. *Psychology Record*, 1965, *15*, 501–511.

Hunt, W. A. (Ed.). *Learning mechanisms in smoking*. Chicago: Aldine, 1970.

Hunt, W. A., & Matarazzo, J. D. Habit mechanisms in smoking. In W. A. Hunt (Ed.), *Learning mechanisms in smoking*. Chicago: Aldine, 1970.

Karst, T. O., And Trexler, L. D. Initial study using fixed role and rational–emotive therapy in treating public-speaking anxiety. *Journal of Consulting and Clinical Psychology*, 1970, *34*, 360.

Maultsby, M. C., Jr. Rational–emotive imagery. *Rational Living*, 1971, *6*(1), 24–27.

Mausner, B. An ecological view of cigarette smoking. *Journal of Abnormal Psychology*, 1973, *81*, 115–126.

Meichenbaum, D. H. *The nature and modification of impulsive children: Training impulsive children to talk to themselves*. Research Report No. 23, Department of Psychology, University of Waterloo, Waterloo, Ontario, Canada, 1971.

Meichenbaum, D. H., & Goodman, J. Training impulsive children to talk to themselves: A means of developing self control. *Journal of Abnormal Psychology*, 1969, *77*, 115–126.

Meichenbaum, D. H., Gilmore, J. B., & Fedoravicius, A. Group insight versus group desensitization in treating speech anxiety. *Journal of Consulting and Clinical Psychology*, 1971, *36*, 410.

Premack, D. Mechanisms of self-control. In W. A. Hunt (Ed.), *Learning mechanisms in smoking*. Chicago, Aldine, 1970.

Raiffa, H. *Decision analysis. Introductory lectures on choices under uncertainty*. Reading, Massachusetts: Addison-Wesley, 1970.

Rimm, D. C., & Litvak, S. B. Self-verbalization and emotional arousal. *Journal of Abnormal Psychology*, 1969, *74*, 181–187.

Sarbin, T. R., & Nucci, L. P. Self-reconstitution processes: A proposal for reorganizing the conduct of confirmed smokers. *Journal of Abnormal Psychology*, 1973, *81*, 182–195.

Sharma, K. L. *A rational group therapy approach to counseling anxious underachievers*. Unpublished doctoral dissertation, University of Alberta, 1970.

Steffy, R. A., Meichenbaum, D., & Best, J. A. Aversive and cognitive factors in the modification of smoking behavior. *Behavior Research and Therapy*, 1970, *8*, 115.

Jonathan M. Chamberlain

Chapter 5
Treatment of Self–Defeating Behaviors

The general principles underlying the newly developed theory for group treatment discussed in this chapter focus on individual learnings in the social setting. These principles are that: (1) self-defeating behaviors (SDBs) are any recurring thoughts, feelings, or actions that create adverse consequences for the owner; (2) individuals are born without SDBs; (3) SDBs and accompanying erroneous self-concepts are learned in moments of felt pain, stress, anxiety, fear, or pleasure; (4) fear is the major source of energy used to maintain SDB patterns in current moments of living and is assisted by the use of choices, and disowning methods; (5) inevitable prices, that is, adverse consequences, are paid by the doer of the SDB; (6) an SDB can be eliminated when the doer of it understands and applies basic principles by (a) exposing to greater self-awareness the choices, maintenance techniques, and disowning methods used; (b) recognizing and feeling the prices paid; (c) facing the fears of being without the SDB pattern; and (d) imagining coping in reality without the SDB pattern.

HISTORICAL OVERVIEW

The eliminating self-defeating behavior (ESDB) theory has a very short history. It was developed by Cudney (1971) from his experiences with clients and the writings of Ross L. Mooney of Ohio State University. The ESDB theory contains trace elements of major psychological theories.

The author and other professionals who have applied the ESDB theory in one-on-one or group sessions with clients have been pleasantly surprised at its simplicity and power. Because of this its use is spreading to various parts of the country. It is currently a major group treatment procedure in the counseling centers at Ricks College, Rexburg, Idaho, at the Brigham Young University, Provo, Utah, and at Western Michigan University, Kalamazoo, Michigan. It is being used by many other colleges, school districts, and treatment centers located in Michigan, Utah, Idaho, and California. This method has been effectively adapted for the use of children as young as 8 and 9 years of age (Bills, 1973; Cudney, 1976, p. 155). It has been used successfully with substance abusers, prisoners in state penitentiaries, and homosexuals, and in marriage and family counseling (Chamberlain, 1973; Cudney, 1976).

Although the ESDB theory is currently being used by many psychologists and counselors in a variety of settings, it is still in the process of evolution and development. Its simplicity and ability to engender seemingly limitless possibilities for application may also be its greatest danger. That is, it can become watered down and less effective by the untrained and unskilled nonprofessional group leader.

The ESDB theory also lends itself to one-on-one therapy sessions. The author became aware of this theory from an unpublished paper presented by Cudney in 1971 and applied the theory to two private clients on a trial basis. The application of the principles brought about almost immediate and long-lasting relief to a client suffering from stammering and shaking when speaking in a class or a group. The second client was a minister who suffered from the consequences of a violent temper. These violent outbursts were eliminated after eight treatment sessions (Chamberlain, 1973, p. 100).

From this simple beginning, the author has conducted continuous ESDB group and individual therapy sessions in a variety of settings and has assisted in the completion of several doctoral studies regarding this method.

THE ELIMINATING SELF-DEFEATING BEHAVIOR MODEL

The following eight steps in this model can be accomplished by an individual or group in a flexible time schedule ranging from 1 day to 8 or 9 weeks. The typical schedule is approximately 4 weeks, depending on the self-defeating behavior that is under consideration. The longer time schedules are more effective. However, in many cases behavioral changes are observable and reported almost immediately. The group therapeutic sessions are typically called ESDB workshops and are individualized group experiences designed to give the participants specific tools with which to eliminate those self-behaviors which in some way are self-defeating.

At the beginning or prior to the first group session each participant chooses only one self-defeating behavior (SDB) on which to focus throughout the eight sessions. An SDB can be a feeling (e.g., depression) or thoughts (e.g., compulsive destructive thoughts or recurring, disturbing sexual thoughts) as well as actions, such as procrastination, compulsive eating, homosexuality, to name a few.

The unique design of this method provides treatment for a group with heterogeneous problems and at the same time enables each participant to keep confidential his/her SDB. Participants are required to keep a daily diary in which they are instructed to record their thoughts, feelings, and actions with regard to the particular self-defeating behavior they are trying to eliminate. In addition, homework is assigned and recorded on the homework summary forms at each step of the program. These writings are brought to each session and given to the therapist for private review and careful analysis. The therapist writes his/her impressions with confrontive straightforward comments and returns them to the group members at the next session. This method, although time-consuming to the therapist and sometimes taxing, forces the client to face methods he uses to maintain a SDB, and to challenge irrational ways of thinking about it. The written diaries get at the heart of the problem rather quickly and break through some of the social defense mechanisms that are maintained in many other group methods.

One of the beginning concepts presented to the group is the concept of their individual potentiality. Ways to defeat the change process are also discussed early. These are called "defeating-the-workshop behaviors," or "defeating-the-program behaviors," which, if allowed to continue, would result in the client's maintaining his self-defeating behavior rather than eliminating it. Thus, clients come to feel they have great potential at the same time resistance to change is predicted and immediately dealt with. These are presented to expose common and sometimes irrational excuses or ways of thinking that help to prevent change from occurring in the individual and to help the client to counteract the normal resistance to change. Fears of change are dealt with briefly at this time and more specifically in Step 6.

The client is taught how to eliminate his/her SDB in the group by applying the principles covered under each of the following topics: (1) what is my SDB and how do I do it; (2) psychological ownership of my SDB; (3) prices paid for doing my SDB; (4) choices I make to activate my SDB; (5) techniques I use to activate my choices; (6) fears I must face to drop the SDB; (7) facing my fears; and (8) living with my integrated self.

The first seven steps are presented in a didactic manner by the therapist, whereas the last one is a sharing session among the participants. The eighth step may be extended into more than one session and is a natural step in which to continue any additional therapy needed or to develop additional socializing skills and patterns of behavior.

A brief overview of the concepts presented in each of the eight steps follows and is written in a way that lends itself to the immediate use of the professional therapist. For a more complete description of each step along with many examples the reader should consult the book by Chamberlain (1977b), the handbook by Chamberlain (1976), or Cudney (1975).

Step 1: How Do I Do My Self-Defeating Behavior?

You are the doer of your self-defeating behavior. It is impossible for you to carry the SDB from one moment in your life to a future moment without your actively doing it. Until you really understand this at a deep level you will not eliminate your SDB.

A SDB is a behavior you have learned, something you *do* ; it is *not* something you are. It is a behavior you learned a long time ago to handle anxiety, loneliness, conflict, and so on. However, you are still using it even though the time of its original need and value has long since passed. At this point it is totally irrelevant to discuss *why* you do your SDB. The important thing is to know deeply *what* you do and *how* you do it. Dwelling on *why* you do it has only served to justify its continuation.

The following demonstration may help you to understand this principle. (This is usually demonstrated in the group by a group member and the therapist.) Hold an empty wastepaper basket in your hands. Let us suppose you are about age 4 and you have just emptied the basket into a large trashcan in the back alley. It has been snowing. Some rough boys decide to throw snowballs at you. Because you do not want to get hurt, the most logical thing to do is to use the wastebasket in some way to protect you, to defend yourself against possible pain. Now let us suppose that you used it as a shield and it worked. You did not get hurt. It felt good not to get hurt. Now let us imagine it is 6 months later in the summer and you have been carrying that wastebasket with you everywhere you go. There is no longer any apparent danger of being hit by a snowball; but every time you attempt to leave the wastebasket and go off without it, the original fear of getting hurt looms up within you and you reason, "Maybe, just maybe, someone saved a snowball in the deep-freeze and will hit me as soon as I put the basket down." That fear keeps you hanging on to the basket, which is now self-defeating. You take it to bed with you, you eat with it, you take it along with you every moment. Although it is cumbersome and in your way, as you mature you have learned over the years how to accommodate for it, and you actually begin to feel as if it were part of you or your personality. By now you have developed some very intricate and plausible rationale regarding why you still do it, but there is no way it can follow you from one moment in life to the next unless you take it. There is no way you can take it unless you make decisions to do it each time it is done. So it is with your SDB.

To accomplish the first step to eliminate a SDB you should (a) discover which behavior causes you the most problems, and (b) observe and list in writing specifically how you do it so you can see how you are choosing to get it done.

Step 2: Psychological Ownership of My SDB

All people who do SDBs (all of us) have ways to disown the responsibility for doing them. You have ways of thinking that help you to shift the blame to someone or something outside yourself, or even to part of yourself in such a way that you erroneously conclude that you are really not in control of the behavior. Therefore, you cannot be held responsible for the doing of it. You can bring about change in that moment when you realize deeply "I *am* in control of my SDB," and eventually, "I am in control, even when I am out of control."

You must assume the total ownership of the SDB before you can rid yourself of it. Otherwise, you will continue to expect father, mother, leaders, and others, to change as you hang on to the SDB. Their behavior will change in reaction to your changes.

One subtle disowning technique is to continue to live under a negative label, such as "I am depressed." You can begin by changing the wording of the label to either "I do a depression" or "I am not depressed over that," and so on, and remind youself very often of your new label. What you tell yourself about yourself is crucial. Telling yourself your new positive label constantly for about 14 days allows time for it to take root, like a seed that has been planted—if you nurture it, it will grow and eventually bring you good fruit.

In this step you should (a) identify a defeating label you have been maintaining related to your SDB and change the label to a more positive one to be maintained, and (b) identify all the ways you shift the responsibility for doing your SDB from yourself to someone or something else, and catch yourself about to blame in new moments of living. Write these down.

Step 3: The Price I Pay for Doing My SDB

You were created to perform as part of an integrated system. When you use SDBs to cope with your world, they interfere with the harmonious operation of your creative human system. The resulting consequences are defeating to your purpose and potential as an integrated being. As you continue to use SDBs, you pay some very deeply felt prices. SDBs kill and consume energy, joy, spontaneity, relationships, health, growth, and so on. Only after you let go of your SDB will you feel the release and freedom from the weight of your SDB as your life opens up, and as you truly see what the behaviors have cost you. The prices are inseparably linked to the doing of the behavior and will continue to be paid by you as long as you maintain the SDB.

Honestly facing the prices will help tip the scale so that the costs outweigh the gains from maintaining the SDB. The prices must outweigh the reasons for keeping the SDB going; otherwise, you will not have sufficient motivation to change. You are the only one who can deeply convince you that the SDB has *got* to go.

After you have faced all the prices you pay and cause others to pay (the adverse consequences) for doing your SDB and have felt them at deep levels, then you need to be aware of how you go about minimizing those prices to allow yourself to do it again. In order to do the SDB again, you must in some way minimize the prices.

To accomplish this step you should (a) identify and feel the prices you pay for using SDBs (i.e., actual negative results, plus positive experiences missed), (b) feel how much those prices hurt you, and (c) recognize how you minimize those prices. Writing a long price list will help you to recognize what you have been paying for doing your SDB.

Step 4: Choices I Make to Activate My SDB

A self-defeating behavior does not happen on its own. Each time a SDB is used a choice is required to activate it, and repetitive choices are needed to keep it going. To have full power over eliminating a SDB you need to control your choices fully.

Five major choices are needed to do your SDB: (a) *an inner choice* to react in the same old SDB way in a situation presented to you in a new moment of living; (b) *outer choices* you make to physically carry out the inner choice; (c) a choice *to minimize* the consequences or prices paid when doing your SDB; (d) a choice *to abandon* your best and most integrated self in that situation; and (e) a choice *to disown* the responsibility. By doing the SDB you are choosing to act irresponsibly in that situation.

A sense of control over your own life comes from recognizing and making non-SDB choices. *When you clearly see that you can make a SDB or non-SDB choice, you stand at the moment of behavior change.*

Preexperiencing (i.e., imagining) yourself at your best, most integrated non-SDB self in life situations which trigger off your SDB before they occur will give you added power over the choices to go the non-SDB route.

To take control over the choices, especially the inner choice, before momentum is gained in the direction of the SDB is like trying to stop a car by throwing away the key, as compared to waiting until it is coming toward you at 60 mph and then trying to stop it. (You will invariably get mashed against your price list—and that hurts!) Inner choices are easily identified by where you end up in each cycle of a behavioral pattern.

To do this step, you should (a) recognize the choices you make to do your SDB; (b) catch yourself as you are about to make the SDB inner choice, or any outer choices, and be aware of their alternative; (c) make a non-SDB choice in a situation in which a SDB choice was previously made; (d) become aware of the temptation to revert back to the SDB choice as a result of scaring yourself after responding with the non-SDB choice; (e) recognize the fears you create when a non-SDB choice is made in a situation in which a SDB choice was made before; and (f) practice preexperiencing yourself living self-enhancing behaviors as your integrated self.

In this step, the concept of two routes is presented and that in moments of time we are free to choose to go on either the SDB or the non-SDB route. We can discern which one we are on at any given moment and change directions (Chamberlaine, 1972).

Step 5: Techniques I Use to Activate My SDB Choices

You maintain your SDB by using certain techniques in such a way that you convince yourself you cannot cope without the SDB. In many ways the techniques you use are the SDB, since without certain techniques to keep a SDB going it would cease to exist. Techniques are to SDBs as fuel is to fire. When you stop using the techniques to keep it going, the SDB will die out and be eliminated. However, most people are unaware that they use specific techniques to maintain SDBs. In a deeper sense, techniques are ways of thinking which justify and lead to the doing of your SDB. A technique can be identified by its result. If it results in the doing of your SDB, you can be assured it was a technique.

Some common techniques used that help to activate the five major choices are discouragement, comparison, impatience, unrealistic expectations of self and others, and fear of the unknown when contemplating being without the SDB.

To eliminate your SDB you need to isolate the techniques you are currently using. This isolation tends to reduce the overwhelming nature of the problems that often accompany the fear of losing the SDB. It whittles the problem down to bite size. If you can identify and isolate the techniques being used and quit using them, you will stand face to face with the deep feelings from which the techniques have helped you to run. Then the battle is almost won. To stop using techniques to maintain the SDB is like the simple act of draining away the fuel from the car in the previous analogy so that you have nothing with which to activate the five major choices.

To take this fifth step, (a) identify and list the techniques you use to activate your choices to maintain your SDB, and (b) stop using them.

Step 6: Fears I Must Face to Drop my SDB

SDBs are kept functioning in your life because of fear. The greatest fear of eliminating a SDB is "How will I meet the world without it?" Since this fear is only the remembrance of a "real" fear experienced at the time the SDB began, you need to recognize this and bring to your awareness the fact that you may be afraid that without the SDB you will reexperience those same feelings you had when the behavior first started by continuing to hang on to the SDB rather than to let it go and risk yourself in a new moment of living. As you continue to avoid facing these fears, you develop a mythical fear of letting go of the SDB. Over time, the fear "balloons" out of proportion. (The snowballs in your memory are by now real killers—3 feet thick!)

Mythical fears seem to fall into two major categories: (a) fear that if the behaviors are not used you will find out negative things about yourself (e.g., I'll be dumb, I'll be all alone, I'll be nothing, I'll be obnoxious), and (b) a fear of what will happen to you (e.g., they will reject me, they will laugh at me, no one will like me).

When you are able to realize that the mythical fear is, in your present life, an unreal fear, you will be able to see the potential for feelings of creativity, competency, and joy that can come from dropping your SDB.

To do this step: (a) identify and list some felt fears you have about dropping your SDB and living without it; and (b) allow yourself to realize they are mythical in nature in your current life situation and created by you.

Step 7: Facing My Fears

Standing between you with your SDBs and the person you are without them is a barrier composed of mythical fears about what will happen to you and what you will be like if you risk facing life without your SDBs. Although you can identify a feeling of wanting to be without your SDBs, the fears you have may make it seem as though you are unable to drop them. You keep doing your SDB to avoid facing your mythical fear.

Having successfully internalized and applied basic principles and information from the preceding steps, you are now ready to face your mythical fears and move beyond them to become the healthy, happy, competent, and energetic person you really are and were created to be (these can all be done in a group in 15 to 25 minutes):

1. Close your eyes and imagine a physical barrier or obstacle with as much reality as you can. Keep your eyes closed until later when I tell you to open them.
2. Now notice the details of the barrier you envision. For example, what is its height, thickness, width, color; what might be on the other side of it?
3. Now you must find a way through, around, over, or under your obstacle. You created the barrier, and being the creator, you can also create anything you may need to help you to get to the other side of it.
4. After getting to the other side of the barrier, go back and destroy it. Get rid of it completely so that there is no way it can be a barrier to you again.
5. Now go back in time, perhaps when you were much younger, recall some incident when you were first made aware of the existence of your SDB.

This may be a specific experience or more than one. (Note: The therapist may later need to help the group member carefully to see the relationship between this early experience and the mythical fear and SDB. The therapist could point out how, with a childlike mind, the individual made an erroneous conclusion about himself or herself because of that earlier incident and others like it. Now with a mature mind the client can look back on that incident and see more clearly that it was an erroneous learning which was maintained by doing the SDB. It may have been an erroneous self-image that the client picked up from an early incident with a parent or teacher which the client has maintained by the use of choices and techniques over the years. Therapist, be prepared for anything at this point. Kleenexes are advised.)

6. Now that you have worked through your mythical fear and have seen the origin of your SDB, can you see more than ever that you have no further need for your self-defeating behavior? (Get affirmation of this before proceeding.) Let yourself feel deeply, "I no longer have a need to do this SDB."

7. Now see yourself as the person you are, totally free from the SDB. To help you do this, split yourself into two people, one with the SDB, and one without it. Notice those two images are incompatible. Now do away with the self-defeating image of yourself completely.

8. Now firmly fix an image of you as your true non-SDB self in the front of your forehead.

9. Now that you can see yourself as a person totally free from the SDB, integrate or merge that person into yourself so that you *feel* and *know* that the ideal person you imagined is *really you now!*

10. Imagine yourself coping with old SDB-provoking life experiences now as your integrated best self, then open your eyes.

The goal of this session is to have you squarely face your mythical fears and the barrier they represent and to experience the exhilarating strength and freedom that come from destroying your fears and negative feelings, ready to face life without your SDB as your most integrated, best self, the person you were created to be.

(The group members are able to indicate by raising a hand when they have successfully accomplished each of the 10 points in the guided imagery session. The therapist can then see that they are ready to go on. Some may need additional help getting through some of these points later either privately or in the group. The group members should be encouraged to share their experiences in this session.)

Step 8: Living with My Integrated Self

The guided imagery session in Step 7 was not magic; it will not eliminate the SDB for you. You must still continue to take control over the choices you make in order to avoid a relapse. But since breaking through the barrier, control over your choices will be much easier because you are operating from a new frame of reference—your integrated self.

After having let go of your SDB and because it feels new and different, there may be a lingering feeling of being vulnerable or exposed. As a result, 'there may be occasional tense moments when you want to revert back to your old SDB pattern or feel confused because you ''don't know what else to do'' if you do not use the SDB. If such is the case, you can trust yourself and know what you did to bring the behavior back and know that you have open to you non-SDB responses. You are the creator and doer of your non-SDB responses. You can do this effectively by continuing to make self-enhancing choices out of the integrated self in new moments of living. Keeping the price list handy to serve as a reminder of the consequences for traveling on the SDB route is also helpful.

(After working through the guided imagery session, the group members are allowed to engage in more free interchange of ideas and experiences. In this step they are encouraged to continue to share their experience so that they can realize everyone experienced something of significance to themselves that was unique. This step may be extended to more than one session in order for the participants to lend support to each other and to share successes and setbacks. Some therapists have found it helpful to allow a much longer time for this session so that each group member can gain the insights needed to understand the new self-image and to keep going on the self-enhancing route.)

In this step you can (a) understand your feeling of vulnerability; (b) trust yourself to become independently expert in recognizing relapses *before* they occur and knowing what to do to take control over them; (c) try out your new self-image in reality; and (d) support each other in this new experience.

The particular sequence of the steps of the ESDB as they are presented seems to follow a natural order of experience for most clients. However, not all group members are affected with equal impact by the same step in the method. Even though some are able to make changes in their behavior in the beginning sessions, all group members are encouraged to take all the steps to achieve a more complete and deeper change.

VARIATIONS IN THE METHOD

Although most of the ESDB groups are held 1 hour twice weekly allowing from 3 to 4 days between sessions over a 4-week period, some notable changes in behavior have been observed in a much shorter version of this method. Taking individuals or small groups through these eight steps in a 2- to 3-hour session has been done with some success. Also, all-day sessions have been found to be somewhat productive in which all eight steps are presented and worked through in an 8-hour session. Doing this in 2 days, 4 hours at a time, has also worked well for some. Shorter versions do not, of course, lend themselves for the keeping of and writing in daily diaries. Neither do they allow for time in which to catch oneself doing the behavior in question and to know whether or not changes have in fact taken place outside of the group. It is difficult at this time to specify the ideal duration of treatment for a specific problem. Generally speaking, conducting therapy sessions on a weekly basis allows for too much time between sessions in which to drift back into the SDB pattern. An exception to this general guideline seems to be the SDB of obesity which seems to require a longer time between sessions.

In a weekly prison group, reluctance, and in some cases inability, to do much personal writing demanded adaptations, for example, more time was needed for each participant to describe verbally those relevant self-observations which would have normally been written. Also, more explanations and illustrations were needed in order to convey the concepts intended in each step. After gaining trust in the therapist, later groups wrote much more.

The guided imagery session has been used by itself with individual clients who have been able to define some kind of specific problem. The author experimented with this technique on a middle-aged male at the Utah State Prison who had a compulsive hand-washing behavior. In a 20-minute guided imagery session, the man was able to recall, and to a degree, reexperience an incident that occurred when he was age 7. He described seeing his brother in that earlier incident covered with sores and scabs and scratching himself painfully. This client had concluded at the age of 7 that if he could keep his hands clean, he would not get the disease his brother had. In this short session, the client was able to recognize for the first time that he no longer needed to do this hand-washing behavior. In weekly visits during the 15 months that followed, he evidenced the maintenance of the remission of this problem.

The author used this method with a 19-year-old female client in a 40-minute session in which she was able to rid herself of a physically felt, black, pear-shaped core that she had imagined existed inside her abdomen since she was about age 3. This black blob symbolized the worthless feeling she had regarding herself. She was under treatment by a colleague for severe depressions and suicidal tendencies. She was able to look back on an incident of sexual molestation by her father which occurred at that early age and to see it more as his problem rather than her own. The guided imagery session was attributed to her changed outlook and observable growth in self-esteem.

Most group members are able to experience some growth-producing insight into their self-defeating behaviors through guided imagery. For some, it may serve to be the beginning of much more in-depth and meaningful therapy. For this reason the therapist should be prepared to invest additional time and emotional support either in the group or in one-on-one sessions with those who need it. This is especially true of those whose problem borders on a psychosis.

RESEARCH

There are no recorded studies regarding the ESDB model prior to 1972.

Does it affect grade averages and self-concept? Hendricks (1972) found no effects of this method on study effectiveness as measured by grade changes in university students enrolled in an effective studies class. He also found no change in self-concept and level of anxiety in these students. These findings varied with those of Coombs (1974), who found a statistically significant increase on the total scale of the Tennessee Self-Concept Scale for experimental subjects.

Does it affect locus of control? Parks, Becker, Chamberlain, and Crandall (1975) found a significant change from externality to internality in locus of control for experimental subjects using the ESDB model as the treatment intervention.

Are the diary and twice-weekly schedule of sessions important? Bohn's study (1975) indicated the importance of the daily diary concept in the maintenance of changes over a follow-up period, whereas Forsyth's (1976) pointed out the greater benefits derived from a spaced rather than a massed time schedule for the therapy sessions.

Is smoking affected by it? Johnson (1975) found the ESDB method to produce statistically significant results in the reduction of smoking behaviors in a small experimental group of smokers compared to a control group of smokers.

What are the effects of guided imagery? Preliminary studies are underway regarding the effects of a taped guided imagery session on regular counseling progress at a university counseling center.

Treatment by correspondence? An on-going study is being conducted to determine the effects of the ESDB model through a correspondence course developed by the author (Chamberlain, 1976a). The SDBs these home study "clients" chose to eliminate included compulsive eating and obesity, procrastination, lack of self-confidence, bad temper, depression, sexual deviancy, drug addiction, inadequate sexual relationship, and inferiority feelings. Of these, 44% chose compulsive eating as the SDB and accounted for 40% of the positive changes reported. Preliminary findings on 46 subjects, reported here for the first time, indicated that only 47% of those who initiated the first step completed the eighth step, but of those who completed the eight steps by correspondence, 94% reported change ranging from "very little change" (2%), "noticeable change" (9%), "considerable change but not completely eliminated" (52%), to "the self-defeating behavior is totally eliminated" (33%). These data compare favorably with those obtained from regular ESDB groups which ranged from 90 to 92% reporting change on a self-report scale.

What about long-range effects? A follow-up survey of 34 clients in ESDB groups in private practice indicated 74% reported that change had been maintained after 3 years. An additional 5% could not remember the SDB they had worked on. One totally eliminated a fear of suffocating in a room with people in it.

SPECIAL CONSIDERATIONS

Contraindications are seldom needed for this method because the clients who would be or could be damaged by it select themselves out of the process or are unable even to begin it. To assume more complete responsibility for one's self is too anxiety provoking for those few who are not ready for this much responsibility. These individuals usually drop out quickly. The results have been most positive when the group participants suffer from long-term habit disorders rather than situational crises.

Although the participants are requested to select only one SDB on which to focus, many report having eliminated or changed others as a beneficial side effect. Some SDBs support others. Parks (1976) found that those who have a high anxiety regarding their desire to eliminate the SDB make less change. He recommended that the overly anxious participant select an SDB to eliminate that is not the major one at first to allow some assurance of being successful before trying for a major one.

Murphy reported in Cudney's book (1976, p. 68) that substance abusers more than others develop substitute techniques when old standby techniques are exposed and dropped, and that they also disown responsibility for the consequences in different ways. For these reasons the focus for these particular clients should be on the prices, the search for identity as a person, and values clarification.

The major advantages of the ESDB model are that (a) it is highly focused on one behavioral problem chosen by the client; (b) it is capable of producing change in a very short period of time; (c) it gives the client a "handle" on other problems; (d) it places the responsibility for change on the client, as well as the responsibility for the behavior; (e) it is easily understood and immediately assimilable and applicable in the individual's life.

CONCLUSION

In the author's 12 years' experience as a psychologist, no other method has been as effective in producing the kind of change in the client in the amount of time that this method does. The ESDB theory cuts across and welds into one palatable therapeutic technique the salient features of several major theorists. There is in it something of Freud, Jung, Adler, Dreikurs, Rogers, Wolpe, Glasser, and Ellis. It gives the fairly normal client a way to take charge over those reoccurring behavioral patterns which are self-defeating. Its principles touch pointedly and deeply at the common elements in a variety of problem behaviors. This method helps the client to clarify values, take responsibility, face reality, change directions, and release a long-held mythical self-image.

"I'm a new person" is the typical client's concluding remark.

REFERENCES

Bills, C. C. *Effects of an eliminating self-defeating behavior workshop on self-concept and behavior of elementary students*. Unpublished master's thesis, Brigham Young University, 1973.

Bohn, R. F. *Effects of the eliminating self-defeating behavior workshop with and without the daily diary*. Unpublished doctoral dissertation, Brigham Young University, 1976.

Chamberlain, J. M. Eliminating self-defeating behaviors. In A. Mitchell & C. D. Johnson (Eds.), *Therapeutic techniques: Working models for the helping professional*. Fullerton: California Personnel and Guidance Association, 1973, p. 100.

Chamberlain, J. M. *Eliminating a self-defeating behavior*. A Brigham Young University Home Study Course (ED. 514Rx-1) (4th ed.). Provo: University Press, 1976.

Chamberlain, J. M. The choice is yours. *The New Era*. Salt Lake City, February, 1977, Vol. 7, #2, pp. 44–48. (a)

Chamberlain, J. M. *Discover yourself by eliminating your own self-defeating behaviors*. In press: Provo: University Press, 1977. (b)

Coombs, D. H. *The elimination of self-defeating behaviors and their relationships to self-concept*. Unpublished doctoral dissertation, Brigham Young University, 1974.

Cudney, M. R. *Elimination of self-defeating behavior*. Unpublished paper, Western Michigan University Press, 1971.

Cudney, M. R. *Eliminating self-defeating behaviors*. Kalamazoo: Life Giving Enterprises, 1975.

Cudney, M. R. *Implementation and innovation of the elimination of self-defeating behavior theory*. Kalamazoo: Life Giving Enterprises, 1976, pp. 68, 155.

Forsyth, R. D. *A comparison of change in locus of control for massed and spaced eliminating self-defeating behavior workshops*. Unpublished doctoral dissertation, Brigham Young University, 1976.

Hendricks, J. V. *The elimination of self-defeating behaviors and their relationship to study effectiveness, self-concept, and anxiety*. Unpublished doctoral dissertation, Brigham Young University, 1972.

Johnson, E. K. *The treatment of smoking as a self-defeating behavior and prediction of behavior change and maintenance*. Unpublished doctoral dissertation, Brigham Young University, 1975.

Parks, C. R. *Factors affecting performance in the workshops for elimination of self-defeating behaviors*. Unpublished doctoral dissertation, Brigham Young University, 1976.

Parks, C. R., Becker, M., Chamberlain, J. M. & Crandall, J. M. *Eliminating self-defeating behavior and change in locus of control. Journal of Psychology*, 1975, *91*, 115–130.

Martin Gittelman

Chapter 6
Treatment of Children's Behavior Problems

The setting is a child guidance center within a community mental health service. The children to be "treated" are generally of the type that, in Eisenberg's (1961) terms, have "exceeded the threshold of discomfort" for their parents and/or their teachers. The therapist's challenge is to try to reach these children in the briefest possible time, and to modify their behavior so that they can function adequately in their home and school milieux.

Ideally, such children should be "treated" in an ordinary school setting, in special classes conducted by teachers trained in behavioral techniques. And, ideally, the treatment should somehow encompass the youngsters' total environment and change those elements that are pathogenic: home, school, peer relations, and so forth.

Since both of these ideals generally remain simply that—ideals—the therapist must do the best he can in a clinic setting. The most he can hope for is some measure of teacher or parental cooperation (preferably both) in his attempts to improve the individual child's behavior. All too frequently, however, he is required to work in relative isolation with the child, or with a group of children. To achieve any practical results,, he must in some way mimic the child's daily life; he must try to re-create as authentically as possible the situations that produce inappropriate responses, so that he can teach the child better means of coping with the situations he must face.

Growth in the application of behavioral techniques in community mental health outpatient settings has been slower with children than with adults. Ross (1972) in his extensive review of the literature on behavior modification with children has shown that relatively more progress has been made in adapting such methods to the severely disturbed and mentally retarded in both inpatient as well as classroom settings. Much of the work with children has utilized the method of operant conditioning. Clinicians with this orientation have assumed that the behavior of the child is primarily maintained and under the control of reinforcing contingencies supplied by the environment (Skinner, 1953). The efforts of these clinicians have been directed toward the manipulation of reinforcement by those who constitute the social environment of the child, based on the view that they shape and maintain deviant behavior. In practical terms they have aimed to introduce procedures designed to alter the behavior of the parent, the teacher, the peer, and siblings.

Behavior rehearsal also differs from operant procedures such as the token economy. With the token economy the child is rewarded for desired behavior. In practice, many children begin to discriminate under what circumstances they will be rewarded and when not. In a sense, some children learn to contract, "If I do this, you give me that." When the reward is not given, they stop the desired behavior. (Levine & Fasnacht, 1974). In behavior rehearsal, the goal is to teach the child behaviors which he can obtain reinforcement even from those who "don't know the game," e.g. to behaviorally modify those in his surroundings, peers, teachers, etc.

The work of Patterson (1973) exemplifies the use of operant procedures in training parents in the control of aggressive, overactive behavior. Parents are trained in the collection of baseline data and to identify and modify current contingency patterns which maintain the undesirable consequences of aggressive behavior. Operant procedures of this type have been used with a wide range of conditions of childhood, including encopresis (Neale, 1963), bronchial asthma (Lukeman, 1975), deviant sibling interaction (O'Leary, O'Leary, & Becker, 1967), and hyperactivity (Gittelman-Klein, 1976). In dealing with behavior disorders, Lazarus (1960) was the first to describe the use of desensitization, especially in the treatment of phobic disorders. The method involves the construction of a hierarchy of fear-provoking stimuli, teaching the child to relax, and progressing from the least to the most feared situations by the use of imagery. For younger children and those who are not easily able to use imagery Gittelman (1965, 1967) has used the method of introducing the child to a facsimile or the feared object itself.

THE CHILDREN

The youngsters I am discussing have failed to adapt in one way or another. The largest group is made up of aggressive children, many of them products of a ghetto environment. They fight readily when provoked; some of those who fight almost never win. But they are limited in their ability to respond to stress in other ways.

Many of these children are identified by their peers as somewhat different or peculiar. They may be hyperactive, or have odd physical features, such as epicanthal folds, poor teeth, or large ears. Often they become scapegoats or are teased. Unsuccessful at responding adaptively to such stressful stimuli, many become shy, sullen and withdrawn, anxious, or aggressive. Habit disturbances may begin to appear: tics, nail-biting, restlessness, enuresis. Some of the young-sters may reach the point of refusing to attend school or, when in school, be so disruptive as to be suspended.

THE TREATMENT

Early intervention is paramount in treating these children. They must learn, as quickly as possible, how to "make it" in the give-and-take of the school and street environment. In treatment they are taught skills so that they may cope more effectively with the demands of their environment. Hopefully, they also learn when to inhibit responses and gradually increase their repertoire of responses to a wide range of environmental stimuli. I have found behavior rehearsal a very effective means of achieving these goals.

PRINCIPLES OF BEHAVIOR REHEARSAL

The term "behavior rehearsal" was first suggested by Wolpe (Note 1) to describe a procedure used in assertive training with adults (Wolpe & Lazarus, 1966). It was subsequently applied by Gittelman (1965, 1967) to techniques with aggressive children and with phobic and effeminate children.

The theoretical basis for the counterconditioning implied in behavior re-hearsal was laid down by Guthrie (1935), who noted that behavior could be modified if one could "find the cues that initiate the action and . . . practice another response to these cues" (p. 37).

Unlike systematic desensitization, behavior rehearsal does not rely on the subject to reproduce in imagination only the problem or affect-arousing situation; instead, an attempt is made to reenact, in as lifelike a manner as possible, the deficient or maladaptive behavior responses of the patient. Like systematic de-sensitization, behavior rehearsal employs a hierarchy of situations in the counter-conditioning.

Behavior rehearsal resembles psychodrama, but differs from it in a number of important ways. It is an attempt to synthesize psychodrama into a systematic behavioral framework in which a variety of complex behavior problems can be explored; maladaptive responses can be elicited; and stimulus, response, and reinforcement sequences can be ordered. Psychodrama is most often used as an uncovering device, helping the patient to act out his attitudes, conflicts, and patterns of responding, so that either catharsis or insight, or both, may occur. Behavior rehearsal goes beyond self-understanding: it attempts to refine what has been essentially an intuitive procedure by providing a more precise means for ordering the stimulus–response–reinforcement steps in each case. It is, moreover, an habilitative technique for teaching new responses and life skills to the patient. Children so often have "insight" into their difficulties but lack the skills to put new behavior into practice. Behavior rehearsal relies not only on restructuring cognition and insight, but also on teaching new behavioral skills.

APPLICATION IN TREATING CHILDREN

Behavior rehearsal as used in treating children has been described in detail in an earlier paper (Gittelman, 1965). Initially, role-playing is employed to elicit from the child the situations that are causing him stress. The therapist attempts to get a clear picture of particular situations and to determine how the child perceives the stimuli to which he responded, how he responded to them, and in what other ways he might have responded. During this stage the therapist and the child may frequently alternate roles, so that the therapist can "experience" both the stimulus and the response components of the situation.

Once the stressful situations have been made clear, they are then reenacted, in a hierarchical manner, the mildest situation being presented first. As the child develops tolerance for the milder situations, those that are more stressful are gradually introduced. The child is thus progressively "immunized" to stress and taught to respond more adaptively.

In practice, the patient is usually seen first in individual, that is private, sessions. This is particularly the case with a child whose major problem is withdrawal, shyness, or schizoidlike behavior. When a child is, in effect, "mute," he is not required to respond verbally at all: the therapist questions him gently and requests that he simply respond with blinks of the eyes (one blink for yes, and two for no). A number of private sessions are generally required before a child is seen jointly with another child. Then, once the child has adapted to being seen in joint sessions, he is introduced into a group.

The composition of the group that each child eventually enters can vary greatly, but the number in the group should be comfortably managed by the therapist. The group should be balanced: it may include children of different ages, racial and ethnic background, and both aggressive and shy, withdrawn children of both sexes. Also, it is important that it contain a number of "experienced" members who have already successfully learned new responses through behavior rehearsal. These children, functioning as "adjunct therapists," can often demonstrate the essential aspects of behavior rehearsal more effectively than the therapist.

The nature of the treatment is explained, in simple terms, to every child. The explanation is in itself reassuring to the child, who may feel he has been referred to a mental health clinic because he is "mental," that is, "crazy."

Explaining the treatment in terms of a learning process helps to make the child feel that he can learn to control his behavior, that he will eventually be in control of himself.

Aggressive children are told that the aim of the treatment is not to stop them from ever being aggressive, but to teach them when an aggressive or assertive response is the proper one, and the different forms that response can take—from verbal aggression to physical fighting. They are informed that it is hoped they will resort to self-defeating aggression as little as possible. This type of aggression is defined as fighting in school, striking out at teachers, and fighting when an alternate response can be successfully employed. They are assured, and quickly comprehend, that not fighting can often be braver than allowing oneself to be provoked into physical aggression. In brief, it is explained to them that their problem is not fighting per se, but the inappropriate expression of aggression. This point is strengthened when the aggressive children's skill in fighting is used in a therapeutic manner to teach the shy, withdrawn members of the group how to box, particularly when it comes to allowing the learners to practice their newly acquired boxing skills on their aggressive partners while the latter only defend themselves.

During rehearsal sessions, every attempt is made to help the child differentiate between adequate and inadequate responses by reinforcement of the former. The reinforcement varies with the age of the child; it may, for example, be material rewards, candy, the social reinforcement of therapist and/or group approval, or checks on a score sheet. Modeling, as described by Bandura and Walters (1963), may also be used to accelerate the child's acquisition of new responses. The therapist or other group members (if the child has advanced to group therapy) may take turns enacting their conceptions of adequate responses.

As the children learn to resolve their difficulties in new ways, they must leave the group to test their recently acquired skills on their own, in their daily lives. They may be discharged, or they may begin coming to the clinic at more widely spaced intervals—for example, every other week, or every month. Eventually they return to the treatment sessions only from time to time. But their presence when they do come adds a rich dimension to the group spirit, and their teaching and their accounts of successful adaptation are invaluable to the newer members of the group.

CASE ILLUSTRATIONS

Case 1

Dwight, 11 years old, was referred to the clinic because of "disruptive" school behavior. He was almost a nonreader, did not respond to most of his teacher's demands, and was constantly engaged in fights with his classmates. Dwight lived with his mother and four siblings in the most deplorable of living conditions. Shortly before his contact with the agency, his mother was reported to be an alcoholic. Tests revealed that Dwight's IQ was 74. When initially seen, he had been expelled from school and was receiving home instruction. He generally saw his home teacher on an average of 1½ hours a week.

Our initial interview went somewhat like this:

T: How come you're here?

D: (No reply; averted gaze.)

T: Things were bad in school?

D: (No reply.)

T: There was fighting?

D: (No reply.)

T: The kids fought with you?

D: (Looking at me for the first time, but not replying.)

T: They picked on you (affirmatively).

D: (Nods assent.)

T: How did they do it? Let's act it out. You be the other kid and I'll be Dwight, OK?

D: (Brightening, but speaking almost inaudibly) They told me, "Get out of here; you don't belong in this class!"

T: No, act it out.

D: "You don't belong in this class, you retard!"

T: Umm. OK. Now I'll be the other kid. What was his name—the worst one, I mean?

D: Michael.

T: OK. I'll be Michael. "You don't belong in this class, you retard!"

D: (Becoming genuinely angry) I'm not! You're a retard yourself!

T: You are retarded!

D: (Becoming angry and pushing me) You are retarded yourself!

T: OK. So that's what happens. You get angry easily.

At that point, the second step in the procedure was explained to Dwight—how he could be helped to inhibit his anger. Later he was made aware of how aspects of his behavior provoked his classmates and his teacher.

Other principles of behavior modification were also employed in Dwight's treatment. To encourage reading, he and another child who was a nonreader were taken on walking trips in the community and given candy rewards when they could read simple words they saw during their promenade: bus stop, no parking, restaurant, barber shop, and so forth. On his return to school, Dwight seldom behaved disruptively. He is now 14 years old and functioning adequately at his grade level.

Case 2

Robert, a frail 7-year-old, was brought to the center at the suggestion of another therapist who was treating the child's mother. The mother had been diagnosed as a schizophrenic and had been hospitalized for a brief period following Robert's birth. He was said to be an unhappy child; he spoke much of death and monsters, and was generally fearful.

At the second session, Robert entered the treatment room and flung himself on the floor to play with the dolls.

T: What's the matter?
R: I'm sad.
T: Why?
R: I hate the children in my class.
T: How come?
R: They call me retarded, and I'm not retarded. I get 100's in all my tests.

Following this brief discussion, we set about to find out why his classmates responded to him as they did. At this stage a situation was enacted to discover whether Robert knew what retarded meant and how he habitually responded.

T: I'll be the teacher and you be the student. I'll ask you a question and you answer as if you're retarded. How much is 6 and 3?
R: Zero.
T: Right. Now let's suppose you are "silly." How much is 6 and 3?
R: Frank says that question is a question that's a foolish game.
T: That's right. That would be a silly answer. Now how would you answer if you were just an average kid? How much is 6 and 3?
R: Ahhh, Niaaah (in a sing-song manner).
T: No, wrong. You ask me how much is 6 and 3—and sit up in your chair. (Role reversal. It should be noted that for this the therapist and the child should change seats so that the child doesn't become confused.)
R: How much is 6 and 3?
T: 9.

Following this interchange, it was explained to Robert, in simple terms, how his behavior resulted in unpleasant consequences for him. He was provided, through behavior rehearsal, with examples of "silly" (e.g., speaking in a babyish manner, sitting curled up in his seat, responding to questions in a tangential way) and "nonsilly" behavior. He was thus helped to discriminate among the behaviors that resulted in negative responses to him.

Case 3

Cary, an 11-year-old, was referred for treatment because of withdrawal. He never spoke in class and seemed not to comprehend directions. Psychological tests revealed that his IQ was within the normal range.

After four sessions of individual treatment, Cary was transferred to a group. In one of the group sessions, he introduced the problem of being picked on by a bully in his class. During behavior rehearsal it became clear that he characteristically responded to aggression by either withdrawal or fighting. He was taught several alternative responses: ignoring the provocation, threatening to tell the teacher, staying "cool," or using verbal aggression to humiliate his antagonist before his friends.

This last technique is well known to many ghetto children, both black and white, and is currently called "ranking out." It is also known as "the dozens," "slipping," and "putting down." The procedure generally involves verbal insults, which, if skillfully used, avoid actual fighting. A typical interchange casts aspersions on the antagonist's social class, parentage, or some other personal attribute, as the following example shows:

— Hey, I went to the zoo last week!
Yeah (guardedly).
—Saw your mother there.
—At least I have one.
—You call that a mother?
—Well, your mother was born in a sewer.
—How do you know? You must have been there.

And so it goes . . .

Although such an exchange might be expected to lead quickly to physical fighting, experience has shown that if certain taboos are observed (e.g., a white child may not use racial slurs in taunting a black child), "ranking out" rarely leads to fighting. Frequently, middle-class children with no experience in this "game" are provoked into fighting because they do not know the rules or the standard insults.

In addition to learning "ranking out," Cary was given instruction in the rudiments of boxing—as are most of the shy, withdrawn children. This was done according to standard learning theory principles. Initially the child is taught how to punch. He practices jabs and hooks by striking the extended palms of the therapist or of the more aggressive children. Subsequently he learns to shadow-box with the therapist or with other children. The child is eventually permitted to "fight" a stronger child, who only defends himself. Both children can "win" rewards, the timid child by being aggressive, and the aggressive child by defending himself properly and enabling the timid child to overcome his fear.

Case 4

Bernard, 8 years old, was brought to the center because of increasing unwillingness to attend school; he complained often of stomach complaints and frequently could not fall asleep. His teacher felt that he was an unhappy child and suggested that he receive counseling, which his parents delayed until his mother found him trying on her bra. A good-looking boy with freckles and auburn hair, his overweight, prominent breasts, and high-pitched voice immediately set him off from his peers. In the initial session of behavior rehearsal he revealed that his classmates constantly called him names—"fag," "homo," "sissy"—and that no one would associate with him, perhaps fearful that they too would be scapegoated.

Treatment was explained in terms of helping him to learn skills in order to avoid punishment (scapegoating) and get along well with his classmates. He entered eagerly into the group sessions where with the other children he was given exercises, boxing sessions, and behavior rehearsal. In the behavior rehearsal sessions he was taught how to respond competently to insults and provocation. He practiced ignoring low level provocation but when a confrontation was necessary he was taught to respond: for example "Look, I don't like being called a fag. I don't want to fight you but if I have to I will. And I'm not sure if you will win or I will . . . but I know this—you're going to be hurt." With other group members to advise him, he learned appropriately pugnacious body and facial gestures. He also learned how to move, to stand tall, and to carry himself as if unafraid. By the third session, Bernard was a clearly happier child. His mother reported no difficulties in getting him to school, he was enjoying his exercises (his dad was teaching him boxing), and he was on a diet. In school, his teacher reported that he was becoming too aggressive, "bullying" some of the smaller children. After a session in which he was helped to modulate and differentiate his aggressive responses to assertive ones he continued to progress. Bernard was discharged (or "graduated") from treatment after only seven sessions. At 1-year follow-up he continued to show satisfactory adjustment.

Case 5

Jay, 13 years old, is the only son of older parents. Severe acne and protruding teeth set him apart as unattractive. His parents brought him for treatment because of his increasing seclusiveness and inability to relate to other children. Jay is a bright child and does moderately well in school, but he spends most of his time reading or watching television.

Following an initial period in individual treatment, Jay was introduced to group therapy. During the group sessions, he was able to relate moderately well to other members. He learned to box fairly well and, through rehearsal sessions, acquired skill in dealing rather effectively with teasing, even when it was rather pointed. He became particularly adept at "ranking out," leading the group in this skill.

Each group member is permitted to suggest hierarchical tasks for the other members of the group. It was decided that Jay was ready to join his local Boy Scout troop. He had previously joined the Youth Group of his synagogue and was a member of the choir. Jay expressed fear about joining the Scouts and it was decided to desensitize him through acting, in a hierarchical manner, to many of the possible reactions that his entry into a Scout patrol would evoke. Various acting assignments were given to the group members in a succession of scenes:

1. Jay is a passive member of a Scout patrol. Another group member pretends to be Jay entering his first patrol meeting. Jay is greeted in a friendly fashion. The talk centers on what school each boy attends, what activities the patrol is engaged in, and the like.
2. Jay plays himself entering the patrol meeting. The response is friendly. Jay relaxes considerably. Token reinforcement in the form of points on an index score card is assigned to the best "actors."
3. Other scenes are enacted, different children playing the part of Jay and "modeling" alternative behaviors. The atmosphere of the "patrol" remains congenial and friendly.
4. Now the aversive stimuli of the situation are increased. The group is asked to become somewhat less friendly in greeting Jay. Jay is to try to "win them over." They warm up and accept him.
5. The group is told to be positively unfriendly. Jay is to try to win them, but succeeds in making only one friend.
6. The patrol is hostile. The children ignore Jay, then turn on him with "We've got enough kids already in this patrol." "You don't live in this neighborhood." (It should be made clear that, as in traditional desensitization, the intensity of the stimulus is not increased until the subject is relaxed and can muster the appropriate responses. In practice, the group sometimes tends to "run away with the script" and to skip steps in the hierarchy. Reinforcement of "good acting" tends to reduce this. Otherwise the activity is changed.)
7. In a hypothetical scene, Jay enters the patrol meeting and, following several insults, one of the patrol members tries to provoke a fight.

Although only seven steps are listed, it should be noted that each scene is enacted several times, the different roles being taken alternately by various group members.

This is not a paper on the outcome of behavior rehearsal, but it may be worth mentioning that Jay benefited considerably from treatment. He now has a number of friends and engages in community and social activities. He returns every several months to the group and undergoes another trial of behavior rehearsal.

This technique is also useful for teenagers who habitually cut class and fear to return and face ridicule from teachers and peers.

Case 6

Brett, a 13-year-old, was referred by his school because of stealing, fighting, poor schoolwork, and discipline problems. An analysis of his stealing reveals that it is almost always done with a group. He admits his gang will think him "chicken" if he does not steal.

A hierarchy of scenes is arranged in which Brett is provoked to steal. He is rewarded for responding to these stimuli verbally. Underlying this procedure is the hypothesis, from propaganda analysis, that an argument will have less persuasive power if the person has already heard counterarguments.

The following interchange is an example of this procedure. The scene is a department store. The parts of the "friends" are played by the other group members and the therapists.

Friend: Hey Brett, dig that shirt!
Brett: Yeah, I see it.
Friend: Let's take it.
Brett: Huh, uh, you take it, not me.
Friend: You chicken?
Brett: Uh huh.
Friend: What's the matter, afraid to get caught? You weren't afraid last week when you took the candy.
Brett: I'm reforming.
Friend: You mean you're scared. You lost your nerve.
Brett: Uh uh. I'm just beginning to think I might want that civil service job. (This remark is a double entendre since Brett feels that the civil service is staffed by Uncle Toms, and he wants to be identified as a militant.)

This is a technique that might well be used as a preventive or "immunological" device to help children resist smoking, drinking, or using drugs.

DISCUSSION

Behavior rehearsal can be a very useful technique in working with maladjusted children in a child guidance center or similar treatment setting, as these cases indicate. It is essentially a learning process that enables the child to broaden his or her behavioral and coping repertoire and respond more appropriately to various stressful stimuli. The child, in effect, is more able to control his or her own reinforcement.

Behavior rehearsal is not true counterconditioning (which perhaps is the ultimate, but difficult to arrange, therapeutic modality) which would require the setting up of real life experiences. Recently, more rapid learning has been accomplished when the children have been asked to bring in their peers, for example, gang members, siblings, friends. However, because it relies on simulations of the patient's actual life problems, this technique presumably results in greater general applicability than desensitization based on emotive imagery Yates (1970), for example, has suggested that behavior rehearsal seems to approximate actual problem material effectively enough to have considerable general application for the patient; and further evidence of this has been provided by Rachman (1962, 1966). Graham (1976) has recently noted that while nonspecific treatment methods have demonstrated equivocal results (Shepherd, Oppenheim, & Mitchell, 1971), treatment which is specific for a defined condition has provided more positive results (Eisenberg, Conners, & Sharpe, 1965; Gittelman-Klein, 1976). The subject is certainly one that warrants further, careful study.

Behavior rehearsal is, in any case, a technique most children find interesting and enjoyable. And that, in itself, is reason enough for at least trying it.

CONCLUSION

Behavior rehearsal is a rapid and effective technique for modifying the behavior of children who have become too disruptive for comfortable handling by parents and/or teachers. Each child is initially seen in individual, private sessions in which the therapist uses role-playing to elicit the stress-causing situation(s) and then begins to teach the child alternative behavior responses, building up from situations causing minor stress to those arousing considerable disturbance. Eventually the child is introduced into group role-playing sessions in which other children help to expand and reinforce the learning process. In behavior rehearsal an effort is made to mimic life and to afford the child opportunities to learn and practice a variety of behavior responses and to test the effects of these responses on others by acting out problem situations with other children and the therapist.

REFERENCE NOTES

1. Wolpe, J. Personal communication, 1964.

REFERENCES

Bandura, A., & Walters, R. H. *Social learning and personality development.* New York: Holt, 1963.

Eisenberg, L. The strategic deployment of the child psychiatrist in preventative psychiatry. *Journal of Child Psychology and Psychiatry,* 1961, *2,* 229–241.

Eisenberg, L., Conners, K., & Sharpe, L. A controlled study of outpatient psychiatric treatment for children. *Japanese Journal of Child Psychiatry,* 1965, *6,* 125–132.

Gittelman, M. Behavior rehearsal as a technique in child treatment. *Journal of Child Psychology and Psychiatry,* 1965, *6,* 251–255.

Gittelman, M. *Behavior modification approaches in childhood neurosis and psychosis.* First Annual Meeting, Association for the Advancement of Behavior Therapy, New York, 1967.

Gittelman-Klein, R. Relative efficacy of methylphenidate and behavior therapy in hyperactive children. *Journal of Abnormal Child Psychology,* 1976, *4,* 361–379.

Graham, P. Management in child psychiatry: Recent trends. *British Journal of Psychiatry,* 1976, *129,* 97–108.

Guthrie, E. R. *The psychology of human learning.* New York: Harper, 1935.

Lazarus, A. The elmination of children's phobias by deconditioning. In H. J. Eysenck, *Behavior therapy and the neurosis.* New York: Pergamon, 1960.

Levine F. M., & Fasnacht, G. Token rewards may lead to token learning, *American Journal of Psychology,* 1974, *29,* 816–821.

Lukeman, D. Conditioning methods of treating childhood asthma. *Journal of Child Psychology and Psychiatry,* 1975, *16,* 165–168.

Neale, D. H. Behaviour research and encopresis in children. *Behaviour Research and Therapy,* 1963, *1,* 139–149.

O'Leary, K. D., O'Leary, S., & Becker, W. C. Modification of a deviant sibling interaction pattern in the home. *Behaviour Research and Therapy,* 1967, *5,* 113–120.

Patterson, G. Reprogramming the families of aggressive boys. In C. E. Thoresen (Ed.), *Behavior modification in education* (72nd yearbook). Chicago: University of Chicago Press, 1973.

Rachman, S. Learning theory and child psychology: Therapeutic possibilities. *Journal of Child Psychology and Psychiatry,* 1962, *3,* 149–163.

Rachman, S. Studies in desensitization. III. Speed of generalization. *Behaviour Research and Therapy,* 1966, *4,* 7–16.

Shepherd, M., Oppenheim, B., & Mitchell, S. *Child behavior and mental health.* London: University of London Press, 1971.

Skinner, B. F. *Science and human behavior.* New York: Macmillan, 1953.

Wolpe, J., Lazarus, A. *Behavior therapy techniques.* Oxford: Pergamon, 1966.

Yates, A. J., *Behavior therapy.* New York: Wiley, 1970.

PART II

Treatment of Antisocial Behaviors

David C. Rimm

Chapter 7
Treatment of Antisocial Aggression

This chapter is concerned with a treatment approach to antisocial aggression, which stresses the teaching of alternative modes of responding. More specifically, the focus is on teaching persons who typically or frequently act out in an antisocial aggressive way to behave assertively instead. The layman does not usually distinguish between the terms *aggression* and *assertion*. For those involved in assertive training, and certainly for the purposes of this chapter, this distinction is absolutely critical. Aggression, whether verbal abuse or physical violence is employed, involves the expression of one's needs or desires, independent of the rights, prerogatives, or feelings of the target or victim. Assertion similarly involves the expression of one's needs or desires (in the present context, it might be best to say standing up for one's rights). The fundamental difference is that an assertive act reflects a basic positive concern for the needs and the welfare of the other person (Lange & Jakubowski, 1976). To illustrate, the reader should imagine that he or she is in a theater and that a nearby couple are chattering in a loud, distracting manner. The following verbalization would illustrate aggressive behavior: "Why don't you stupid asses shut up?" An assertive response might be "You may not realize it, but you are talking loudly. Could you keep it down?"

Unfortunately, antisocial aggression is not limited to verbal abuse. Acts of violence, such as murder, aggravated assault, and rape are on the increase in the United States (and in almost all technologically advanced societies; Wolfgang, 1976). Frequently it is possible to conceptualize acts of violence in terms of a lack of a repertoire of assertive verbal behaviors, or an unwillingness to use them. For example, the author recalls a former mental patient who had been AWOL from the hospital for 1 year. While on a weekend pass he had sought lodging in a hotel. He was standing in the lobby when another man inadvertently jostled him. The patient might have said "Hey, please be careful," which could be described as assertive. Instead he said nothing and stabbed the man with a knife, receiving a year in prison for this needless act of violence. It is probably more than a coincidence that the words "mute" and "violence" have a common root (Wolfgang, 1976).

BACKGROUND

Present-day assertive training procedures derive, to a large degree, from the writings of Wolpe (Wolpe, 1958; Wolpe & Lazarus, 1966) and to a lesser extent from those of Salter (1949). The procedures were developed principally to deal with problems associated with timidity, and indeed, almost all the research (most of which has appeared in the past 5 years) focuses on timorous rather than aggressive behavior. Although group assertive training has become an immensely popular clinical tool in recent years, published reports, wherein group assertive training has been employed with *aggressive* clients or patients, have not been numerous (e.g., Rimm, Hill, Brown, & Stuart, 1974; Sarason, 1968; Rimm, Keyson, & Hunziker, Note 1). Sarason provided juvenile delinquents with a total of 6 hours of behavior rehearsal (the principal treatment component of assertive training). The situations dealt with were not ones which would necessarily give rise to aggression (e.g., applying for employment). In terms of staff ratings and ratings of review boards, behavior rehearsal was superior to merely describing the behavior appropriate to the situation, which was superior to no treatment. Rimm and co-workers (Note 1) used assertive training with a small group of adult males institutionalized because of antisocial aggressive behavior. The 6 hours of treatment included a variety of "warm-up" exercises, which are discussed briefly in a later section, as well as behavior rehearsal; the latter dealt with situations which typically provoked anger (e.g., a patient being denied a pass he believed he deserved). In terms of ratings of assertiveness (as opposed to aggressiveness) treatment subjects showed significantly greater improvement than a group of placebo controls. Informal follow-up observations by ward personnel and relatives tended to suggest that assertive training resulted in less hostility and aggression. Rimm and colleagues (1974) worked with a group of nonhospitalized males who volunteered because of a troublesome history of antisocial aggression. The experiment was similar to Rimm et al. (Note 1). Subjects who had received 8 hours of group assertive training were rated significantly more assertive (and less anxious) than placebo control subjects when presented with anger-eliciting laboratory situations.

A MODEL

Writers in the area (e.g., Feshbach, 1970) make a theoretically and clinically useful distinction between *instrumental* and *drive-mediated* aggression.

Instrumentally aggressive behavior is a means to an end, for example, boxing one's way to an Olympic gold medal, or shooting a perfect stranger for a large sum of money. If a drive such as anger is present, it is presumed not to be the primary motive, and in fact (as any successful prizefighter and presumably any successful "hit man" knows) high levels of anger may be self-defeating. In drive-mediated aggression, the behavior is not acted out in a relatively dispassionate manner. Instead, it is driven by intense emotion and the most plausible drive or emotion is anger, or hostility, that some characterize as an angerlike state with a gradual onset. In anger-induced aggression, injury of a physical or psychological nature is an end in itself rather than a means to an end.

The treatment procedures outlined in the section to follow are not presumed to be applicable to antisocial aggression that is purely instrumental. Instrumental aggression is, after all, maintained by powerful external reinforcements (money, recognition) which, presumably, would not be forthcoming were the individual taught to substitute assertion for aggression. An individual who kills for money would hardly be expected to receive similar remuneration for asserting himself vis-a-vis his victims rather than shooting them! One could argue that childhood instruction in assertion might reduce the probability that anyone would end up being forced to ply such a dangerous and antisocial profession (i.e., because the person would be in a position to obtain important reinforcements by engaging in prosocial behaviors). However, given a pattern of socialization that has consistently and powerfully rewarded antisocial aggression, assertive training would not seem to be the answer, especially if the reinforcements for antisocial aggression are likely to continue.

It is clear, however, that a great many acts of aggression are, at least in part, motivated by anger. What maintains or reinforces such behavior is not entirely clear, although it is likely that anger reduction consequent to aggressive behavior plays an important role. The work of Hokanson (1970) suggests this, but it also suggests that nonaggressive behaviors may substitute for aggressive behaviors in reducing anger. In the present context one might say that whatever satisfaction a person experiences by behaving in an antisocial aggressive manner may also be experienced by behaving in a socially appropriate assertive way. Admittedly this is an assumption, but it is one that has some empirical support, both clinical and experimental. Certainly, in the long run, there is more external payoff for behaving assertively rather than aggressively.

In relation to the reinforcement associated with anger-induced aggression, there is a second possibility: people become angry and aggressive in the presence of events which are threatening, that is, initially give rise to anxiety. Presumably the anger or aggression (or both) is antithetical to anxiety, so that the locus of reinforcement, rather than being anger reduction, is anxiety reduction. But if Wolpe (1958) is correct in his contention that assertion also inhibits anxiety, and there is some experimental support for this, then one might logically substitute assertion for aggression as a means for reducing anxiety.

Thus, whether drive-mediated aggression is rewarding per se, or whether its reward value is associated with anxiety reduction, assertive training would seem to be a reasonable treatment.

CLINICAL IMPLEMENTATION

There is nothing in this formulation which requires that assertive training be carried out in a group setting. However, group assertive training, as opposed to one-to-one treatment, has several obvious advantages (Rimm & Masters, 1974; Lange and Jakubowski, 1976). Clearly, one can treat more individuals in a shorter period of time in a group setting so that from the therapist's perspective it is more efficient and from the client's viewpoint it is less expensive. This advantage would accrue to virtually any type of therapy conducted on a group as opposed to an individual basis.

However, there are advantages to a group format that are more specific to assertive training. First, there are certain warm-up exercises which can only be carried out in a group setting. Second, assertive training involves a good deal of role-playing and a group provides multiple models for any particular group member to emulate. Similarly, the group setting provides a large number of "target persons" toward whom a member may direct his assertion. Assuming the group members differ with respect to age and other personal characteristics (physical appearance, type of dress, manner of speaking) it is likely that at least one member may realistically substitute for the real-life person to whom some other member wishes to direct his assertions. Third, in role-playing one must first decide what behavior or behaviors are appropriate for a particular situation, and the group may act as a forum for reaching such decisions. It is worth mentioning that assertive training, although it may be the most interesting of the many behavior therapies, is probably also the most difficult to implement, principally because one must decide what behavior is socially appropriate. What is appropriate in one setting or subculture may be inappropriate in another. In this regard, input from various group members is invaluable. Fourth, it is assumed that social reinforcement for more assertive (and in this context less aggressive) behaviors is important, and the group is in a position to provide such reinforcement, en masse. It is one thing for a single therapist to say "the way you came across that time was much more assertive and less threatening" but quite another for seven or eight individuals to communicate this same message; whereas a client may discount the praise he receives from one person, it is difficult to ignore reinforcement from an entire group. Finally, the group may engender an esprit, not possible in individual treatment, that may serve as an impetus for attending sessions and for improvement.

Although there are no hard and fast rules, experience suggests that an ideal group comprises 7 to 10 members, not including the group leader or leaders.

Assemblies much smaller than this tend not to maintain a group identity and the result may be, in effect, individual therapy in the presence of a few spectators. Numbers much in excess of 10 or 12 members result in an unwieldly situation which may bear a closer resemblance to a class than a group. A client or patient, viewing himself as a "student" rather than as a group member, may well perceive himself to be in a one-down situation, which would be counterproductive.

It is recommended that whenever possible the group be led by two therapists. They may provide a consensual basis for judgment regarding the appropriateness of a response and they may model interchanges, and in the face of an especially hostile or aggressive group, provide mutual support (although care should be taken so that a "we–they" dichotomy does not develop; one way to prevent this is for the leaders to disagree with each other openly when disagreement exists). Although this may not always be possible, it is suggested that one therapist be male and the other female. This is recommended when the clients or patients are timid, but even more so when their problem is one of antisocial aggression. More often than not group members of an antisocial aggressive group are all male. Some will have problems dealing with anger around authority figures, and the male therapist may readily assume such a role during behavior rehearsal, although hopefully at other times he will not assume an authoritarian posture. Others will report problems in relating to women (usually girlfriends or wives) and in an all-male group, the female cotherapist will be the only person present who can realistically assume the role of the woman in role-played troublesome situations.

Unfortunately, it is necessary to stress that the therapists be professionally dedicated and experienced persons. In the case of cotherapists, it is likely that one will be the more experienced, but it must be presumed that both have at least some appreciation for the complex theoretical and empirical issues involved in assertive training, and a keen awareness that if this (or any) treatment is to maintain a scientific footing, the therapists must make some effort at keeping abreast of the literature. At the very least one should read a scholarly text from time to time. At this writing, there are many paperbacks on the market dealing specifically with assertive training. They vary immensely with respect to quality and professionalism. Lange and Jakubowski (1976), aimed at practitioners rather than laymen, is clearly one of the better books. All too often, as in the case of sex therapy, would-be practitioners of assertive training have nothing even approximating reasonable professional credentials or an awareness of the issues raised herein. Instead, they have had some personal experience that has "turned them on" to assertive training and they mistakenly believe that this is sufficient to qualify them to lead assertive groups. Let the reader be so forewarned!

As a behaviorist the author is not especially comfortable with typologies. Nevertheless, the distinction that Megargee (1966) points out between aggressive individuals who are overcontrolled and those who are undercontrolled is considered useful in relation to decisions regarding group membership. Simply stated, the overcontrolled person has been taught not to express anger. Characteristically, he keeps his anger to himself until it reaches a level that literally cannot be controlled, at which time an outburst occurs, possibly violent in nature. Sometimes such individuals have difficulty acknowledging the presence of anger, because they have been taught that it is wrong even to experience this emotion, let alone act out on it. The following statement suggests such a learning history: "It really takes a lot to make me angry but when I blow, I really blow!" The undercontrolled aggressive individual has been socialized in a manner wherein the slightest instigation to anger elicits acts of aggression. One may infer undercontrolled aggression from frequent acts of verbal or physical abuse, especially in the absence of apparent guilt or remorse. Statements such as the following may also provide a clue: "Hell, I don't take any shit from anyone."

Although there is no experimental evidence bearing on the following recommendation, experience and common sense suggest that it would be unwise to attempt to work with overcontrolled and undercontrolled aggressive persons in the same group. The undercontrolled members intimidate or frighten the overcontrolled members, who may be as uncomfortable with the anger of others as they are with their own anger.

A group setting is certainly appropriate for members whose problems stem from overcontrol, assuming of course that each member is reasonably comfortable in a group. However, a word of caution is in order. Group leaders in their efforts to model spontaneity and directness, may engage in verbalizations that "polite" society considers profane. It is important to realize that overlycontrolled individuals not infrequently come from conventionally religious backgrounds and they might be quite disapproving of or threatened by profanity. Such an individual is likely to be "turned off" by the experience and may drop out of treatment.

Although a group setting, with all its aforementioned advantages, may be appropriate for undercontrolled individuals, it does present certain problems. There is some risk of physical abusiveness on the part of one or more members. If such behavior does occur, it is more likely to be directed toward another member than toward the therapist or therapists; in view of the damage that such behavior would do to group functioning, this is small consolation! Clearly, at the very outset the group must be informed, gently but firmly, that such behavior is strictly forbidden and will result in the perpetrator being dismissed from the group. A less drastic but somewhat more likely happening, is that the members form a kind of implicit alliance, wherein they reinforce each other for verbally abusive behavior. At such times the therapist will have the feeling things are "out of control" or that the members are "ganging up" on the therapist (and will be thankful for the presence of the cotherapist!). This situation is obviously counterproductive. At such times a relatively straightforward confrontation may be helpful, wherein the group is reminded that they have gotten themselves into trouble in the past because they were aggressive rather than assertive, a pattern that is evident at that moment. Following this, one of the therapists might say: "Let's see if we can express the same thoughts and feelings, but this time let's try to be assertive and not aggressive."

Implicitly, at least, the focus of this chapter has been on the treatment of antisocial aggression in males. Although acts such as spouse beating and certainly forcible rape are more commonly perpetrated by males, males certainly have no franchise on aggressive behavior. For example, for every 100 cases of spouse killing in the United States, 46% involve wives murdering their husbands (Uniform Crime Reports, 1970). In dealing with a group of females or a group of males and females, the aforementioned comments are assumed to be applicable. It is especially recommended that two therapists, a male and a female, be employed and that the female be sensitive to problems which, in our society, are somewhat unique to females (e.g., inequities in professional opportunies, sexual exploitation by males).

While behavior rehearsal is the principal method of assertive training, certain warm-up or preliminary group exercises seem to facilitate group functioning. The exercises that the author and his colleagues regularly employ are presented below.

Before commencing the exercise, the group should be encouraged to provide feedback and reinforcement for each member's participation. The group should be asked to be as effusive or enthusiastic as possible in providing praise for responses or interchanges that are deemed appropriate, while being tactful and gentle in providing negative or corrective feedback. The group should be encouraged to reinforce good eye contact (but not staring, which many take as aggressive), verbalizations that sound direct and genuine, and good body language (e.g., leaning toward someone when you address them).

Initially, the group will probably show considerable reluctance to provide the desired feedback, deferring instead to the identified therapists. Early on, the therapists will model when and how to provide feedback, while actively encouraging members to emulate such behavior. Questions such as, "I wonder how Joe's response came across to you people . . . what do you think?" are helpful, and when one or more members do react, they should be praised for their contribution.

1. *Exchanging introductions.* This is an icebreaker. It also serves to help members get acquainted. A member (perhaps a therapist) begins by turning to another member, let us say, to his right, with "Hi, I'm Dave . . . what is your name?" (Second member) "I'm Ed." (First member) "How are you Ed?" (Second member) "OK, Dave . . . about you?" (First member) "Not bad." The second member then turns to the person on his right, and the process continues until each member has participated.
2. *Exchanging compliments.* Many people have difficulty giving and/or re-

ceiving compliments; this exercise is a good deal more challenging (and stimulating) than the first exercise. One member begins by selecting any other member and provides a sincere compliment such as, "Hey, Joe . . . I really dig that belt." Replies such as, "What . . . this old thing?" are gently discouraged. Obviously a more satisfactory reply would be, "Thanks. I like it myself,-- or simply, "Thanks a lot." The recipient is then required to compliment another member of the group. The process continues until each member has received a compliment.

3. *Positive self-statements.*   Here, each member says something positive about himself, for example, "I like the way I say what's on my mind," or "I like the fact that I work hard." Were a member to say, "I like that I can beat the shit out of anybody in here," a chorus of humorously delivered "boos" would be a good group response, but any response to the effect that this is an aggressive, threatening response should suffice.

4. *Small talk.*   Initially, certain members may adopt a disdainful attitude toward this exercise, viewing small talk as silly or trivial. It should be pointed out that engaging in light conversation is usually a necessary precursor for more intimate interchanges. Although it may seem boring, it is important. One member designates two other members, and gives them some mundane, noncontroversial topic to discuss, for example, "Joe and Harry . . . talk about trees." The assumption is that if they can talk about trees, they can talk about anything! After a few minutes, preferably by the time the conversation is proceeding comfortably, one of the participants selects two other gorup members and provides then with a small-talk subject. The process continues until each member has participated.

These are not intended to exhaust the possibilities with respect to warm-up or preliminary exercises. The reader is free to add or delete exercises at his or her own discretion. The aforementioned exercises do facilitate certain social skills, as well as create an atmosphere favorable to behavioral rehearsal, but other exercises may be equally effective.

As has been suggested, the principal method of assertive training, whether it be for shy or aggressive individuals, is behavior rehearsal. Although implementation varies somewhat from therapist to therapist, the author has found the following steps or guidelines to be useful.

1. *Assessment.*   The group member (Mr. X) who wishes to change his behavior in a specific situation is asked to behave the way he typically behaves in that situation, in as realistic a fashion as possible. Mr. X designates another member to be the target person, usually providing that person with a brief script, to which he responds. The therapist asks how uncomfortable or angry Mr. X felt when making the response.

2. *Feedback.*   The group is asked to evaluate the response, providing as

specific a feedback as possible. The therapists participate in the feedback process. Special care is taken to point out *positive* features of the response.
3. *Modeling.*   Someone (either another group member or a therapist) models what is presumably a better response. Care is taken that there is some consensus that the response is indeed appropriate.
4. *Rehearsal.*   Mr. X substitutes the newly modeled response for his original response in a second interaction with the target person.
5. *Reinforcement.*   The group provides generous reinforcement for any observed improvement.

If, at this point, there is consensus that the resopnse was appropriate *and* if Mr. X reports having felt comfortable in making the response, the group may move on to another problem. If the response is judged inadequate and/or discomfort is reported, rehearsal is continued until the two criteria are met.

ILLUSTRATION OF THE MODEL

Assume that the group has participated in the preliminary exercises and are now reasonably well acquainted with each other. Bob, a 23-year-old construction worker, has volunteered to participate in behavior rehearsal. During the past 2 years he has lost six jobs. He has never engaged in physical violence, but reports that he has "come close" several times. He does not condone his own behavior, but believes that it is something that he simply cannot control.

Therapist:	OK, Bob, why don't you tell the group what happens.
Bob:	Well, I'll get this job, see, and everything is fine for a couple of months. But then I start feeling like the foreman is picking on me. Like, he accuses me of being late to work all the time, when I'm not. I'll tell him off, and he fires me.
Therapist:	Let's act out that situation to see how you come across. Pick somebody out to play the foreman, and tell him what the foreman said so he can play the part realistically.
Bob:	(Looks around the group) Art, you kind of look like my last foreman (laughingly). You be him. He walks up to me and says "You better start getting your ass to work on time."
Art:	(As foreman) You'd better get your ass here on time.
Bob:	(With intense anger) Get off my back you ignorant son of a bitch!
Therapist:	Bob, how do you feel right at this instant?
Bob:	So mad I could shake. (Turning to female cotherapist, apologetically) I don't usually cuss, but when I get mad I can't help it.
Therapist:	Well, people, what's your reaction to Bob's response?
Jim:	I kind of admire you for standing up to him.
Cotherapist:	Yeah, Jim. But that's how Bob keeps losing those jobs.

Steve:	I agree. I mean, it seems like you could stand up to your foreman without blowing your top.
Cotherapist:	I was thinking the same thing. Steve, do you think you could show Bob a better way to handle this situation? In other words, play-act, asserting your feelings without being aggressive. Maybe Art can be the foreman again.
Steve:	I can try . . . give me a second to think (pause). OK.
Art:	(As foreman) You'd better get your ass here on time.
Steve:	(As Bob) Goddammit, I *am* always on time!
Therapist:	Well, it was better than Bob's, but I still think it was pretty aggressive. Besides, I don't think Bob likes to swear. Right?
Bob:	That's right.
Therapist:	OK. Steve? Art? Want to try it again? Let's go through it one more time.
Art:	(As foreman) You'd better get your ass here on time.
Steve:	(As Bob) Man, I'm *always* on time.
Alice:	That was really good, Steve. Right on!
Jim:	Yeah, I guess I agree. You wouldn't get canned for saying that.
Therapist:	I agree. But what do you think, Bob?
Bob:	I wish I could be that cool.
Cotherapist:	Maybe you can. Why not role-play what Steve said? Art, one more time.
Art:	(As foreman) You'd better get your ass here on time.
Bob:	I'm always on time (slight tremor in the voice).
Therapist:	How did that feel, in comparison to the first time? Say, on a 10-point scale where 10 is like you feel like blowing up, and 1 is like you feel cool and relaxed.
Bob:	Better, not as angry. Maybe a 4 or a 5. The first time . . . heck, that was 10 for sure.
Jim:	I thought it sounded really good.
Art:	Real cool, man.
Therapist:	I thought that was very good Bob. But let's practice one or two more times, so that we can get you to feel more comfortable. Down to a 1 or a 2, maybe. (The group continues in this manner until Bob reports he is at a 2.)
Bob:	But if I say that, what if he calls me a liar?
Art:	I don't think he would. But maybe. . . .
Cotherapist:	I don't think he would either. But we can practice how to handle that if you like.
	(The group deals with the ''escalated'' interaction in the same manner.)
Therapist:	Before we leave this, I'd like to say something. Bob, I kind of get the feeling that you let your emotions bottle up. I mean, that the foreman accused you of being late several times before you finally blew up. Am I right?
Bob:	Yeah, I try hard to control my feelings.
Therapist:	Well, maybe you try *too* hard. What I'm getting at is, the first time, the very first time you think the foreman is making an untrue accusation, it would be good to assert yourself, like what you've learned to do this evening. In other words, say what is on your mind *before* your emotions build up to the point where you don't think you can control them.

Steve:	I was thinking the same thing. Man, you keep those feelings to yourself, and you end up like a volcano ready to blow.
Bob:	That's just what I do. I don't . . . I mean I didn't know what to say, so I didn't say anything and just kind of sulked. Now I'll know what to say. At least I hope so!
Cotherapist:	I think you'll do all right. Remember what you've learned in here and it may be easier than you think.

In the preceding, Bob was portrayed as an overcontrolled individual. Suppose, instead, that his aggression has been characteristically undercontrolled. The Bob we are about to present is actually rather proud of his acts of aggression and the group (now assumed to be undercontrolled aggressive persons also) is inclined to reinforce this. The new script might begin as follows:

Therapist:	OK, Bob, why don't you tell the group what happens.
Bob:	I've been on this construction job for 2 months, OK? And the foreman comes up to me and says, "You better get your ass to work on time!" Well, I don't take any shit, see, and I told him what I thought of that. Hell (laughing) he just walked away with his old tail between his legs!
Therapist:	Let's play-act the situation. But remember, no actual fighting or you are out of the group. Bob, pick out somebody to play the foreman.
Bob:	Art, old buddy, you look like enough of a turd to be the foreman (said playfully).
Art:	Well, screw you! But what the hell, OK.
Art:	(As foreman) You'd better get your ass to work on time.
Bob:	(In a very threatening voice, with clenched fists) *You* get off my back, you dumb bastard, 'fore I bust your ass!"
Therapist:	How did you feel just after you said that? Angry? Uptight?
Bob:	Good. Maybe kind of pissed off.
Cotherapist:	OK, group, what do you think about Bob's response?
Jim:	Right on, Bob. You scared the pee out of that uppity mother!
Bob:	You're damned right. You know, I was *never* late on that job.
Steve:	These foremen think they're God almighty.
Therapist:	Well, maybe they do come on that way. But let's face it. Bob has lost six jobs in the last 2 years. And sooner or later nobody in this town is going to hire him. Doesn't look like the foremen are going to change.
Cotherapist:	I think it is kind of up to Bob.
Art:	I think Miss Goody-Two-Shoes over there is telling you you gotta learn to be an ass kisser, Bob.
Bob:	The *hell* with that noise! Sure, I don't like losing jobs . . . who does? But I'd rather not work than take crap.
Therapist:	I don't think you have to. Remember, the main purpose of this group is to teach people how to stand up for themselves, *without* getting into trouble. Like losing your job.
Bob:	Well, what *am* I supposed to do when this bastard picks on me?
Therapist:	That is a very reasonable question. We will show you.

The behavior rehearsal format is now employed, much as it was in the first script. In contrast to overcontrolled Bob, undercontrolled Bob is not upset by his aggressive behavior; in fact, he associates it with a feeling of satisfaction. The trick is to teach Bob to become aware of the fact that feelings of satisfaction may also be consequent to assertive responses, and with little risk of reprisal. As for the group's general belligerence, it will tend to subside as the members "get the idea"!

SOME LIMITATIONS AND CAUTIONS

Much of this chapter has dealt with the presentation of a set of clinical procedures for dealing with antisocial aggression. It has already been suggested that the treatment is not really applicable to individuals who engage in antisocial aggression of a purely instrumental nature. Further, as the reader may have surmised, some individuals may be so aggressive (they would usually fall into the undercontrolled category) that their presence in a group can only be disruptive. For such persons, individual treatment is suggested, possibly involving the use of drugs and other behavior therapy techniques such as progressive muscle relaxation as well as assertive training. Finally, although a review of the pertinent literature is beyond the scope of this chapter, research tends to show that assertive training does not generalize greatly. Thus, teaching Bob to be assertive rather than aggressive vis-aà-vis his foreman might have very little effect, for example, on his tendency to abuse his girlfriend verbally or physically. The latter is a separate problem and should be treated as such. Naturally, if another member chooses to work on a problem involving abusing females, and if the specifics of the situation are similar to those experienced by Bob, observational learning would probably result in some amelioration of Bob's difficulty with his girlfriend. As has been suggested, the opportunity to learn vicariously from other members is one advantage inherent in a group setting.

REFERENCE NOTE

1. Rimm, D. C., Keyson, M., & Hunziker, J. *Group assertive traininging in the treatment of antisocial aggression.* Unpublished manuscript, Arizona State University, 1971.

REFERENCES

Feshbach, S. Agression. In P. H. Mussen (Ed.), *Carmichaels' manual of child psychology,* Vol. 2. New York: Wiley, 1970.

Hokanson, J. E. Psychophysiological evaluation of the catharsis hypothesis. In E. I. Megargee & J. E. Hokanson (Eds.), *The dynamics of agression.* New York: Harper, 1970.

Lange, A. J., & Jakubowski, P. *Responsible assertive behavior: cognitive/behavioral procedures for trainers.* Champaign, Illinois: Research Press, 1976.

Megargee, E. I. Undercontrolled and overcontrolled personality types in extreme antisocial aggression. *Psychological Monographs,* 1966, 3, Whole No. 611.

Rimm, D. C., Hill, G. A., Brown, N. N., & Stuart, J. E. Group-assertive training in treatment of expression of inappropriate anger. *Psychological Reports,* 1974, *34,* 791–798.

Rimm, D. C., & Masters, J. C. *Behavior therapy: Techniques and empirical findings.* New York: Academic Press, 1974.

Salter, A. *Conditioned reflex therapy.* New York: Farrar, Straus, 1949.

Sarason, I. Verbal learning, modeling, and juvenile delinquency. *American Psychologist,* 1968, *23,* 254–266.

Uniform Crime Reports. *Crime in the United States, 1969.* Washington, D.C.: U.S. Government Printing Office, 1970.

Wolfgang, M. E. *Crime, aggression, and social policy.* Paper presented at the International Conference on Psychological Issues in Changing Aggression. Warsaw, Poland, July 9–14, 1976.

Wolpe, J. *Psychotherapy by reciprocal inhibition.* Stanford: Stanford University Press, 1958.

Wolpe, J., & Lazarus, A. A. *Behavior therapy techniques: A guide to the treatment of neuroses.* Oxford: Pergamon, 1966.

Cole Barton
and James F. Alexander

Chapter 8
Treatment of Families with a
Delinquent Member

Behavioral approaches to producing change have been successfully applied across a wide range of settings, including highly constrained laboratory environments, relatively controlled environments such as hospitals and training schools,
and problems occurring in more open or natural environments such as outpatient
clinics. Empirical demonstrations of the utility of behavioral techniques coupled
with their seeming adaptability and relative simplicity, have enhanced their
status to the point that behavior modification now represents a predominant
clinical paradigm. This chapter describes one behaviorally derived family
therapy program, but in so doing will emphasize the assertion that the professional literature has failed to identify and disseminate adequately several major
facets of family behavior change. Most behavioral programs describe a range of
potential techniques, but may omit descriptions of salient client, treatment, and
therapist characteristics that constrain their utility (Kiesler, 1971). To use but
one example, contrasting behavior change efforts with parents and younger
children versus parents and older adolescents highlights differences that could
limit the efficacy of the treatment. With older delinquents, the nature of "the
adolescent" severely restricts the potential techniques available. Time-out and
extinction procedures (so successful with younger children) are generally disastrous with teenagers for reasons including their far greater physical and economic
mobility (cars, bikes, etc.), greater physical strength (removal to a time-out room
may be physically impossible for most mothers), greater peer influence and
reinforcement for alternative unwanted behaviors (boyfriends strongly reinforce
"sneaking out" after curfew), as well as the powerful and normal adolescent
developmental processes which include considerably less parental influence and
control (Coles, Alexander, & Schiavo, 1974). Change agents working with this
and other special populations of course eventually become aware of these limit-

ing conditions. However, they often have to be gleaned from between the lines of the literature.

A second omission has been in the lack of identification of different therapist skill classes. In fact, little attention has been focused on therapists as a major component of the service delivery enterprise. It appears as though we have assumed that the processes of intervention are comparable to the processes of laboratory science, wherein all people can use the same published techniques and generate the same phenomena. Yet even in science there are numerous failures to replicate, and too many findings that seem to be solely a function of experimenter bias, specific populations, geographic area, and other more ephemeral processes. Certainly in clinical settings we have all seen wide variations in therapist skill and impact. In the research literature, however, rarely are such variations in therapist skill formally reviewed as a significant source of treatment variance in family therapy outcomes. Instead, authors proceed as though the clear communication of technology produces sufficient therapist homogeneity and quality to ensure successful treatment. As programs increase in complexity, and as more agencies and therapists adopt behavioral orientations to changing problems in the family system, this assumption becomes increasingly less realistic.

In light of these issues the chapter first briefly summarizes the major underlying philosophies, techniques, and empirical support for one particular treatment model developed for families of outpatient delinquents. With this summary as background, the chapter then attempts to go beyond the usual oversimplified description of technique, and examine troublesome issues relevant to the current state of the art, including (a) the necessity for multiple levels of analysis, portraying a perspective which goes beyond the more common "response topography" approach described in the literature; (b) some commonly overlooked aspects of treatment, including variation due to the range of therapists' technical skills, the appropriate "fit" of technique to problems, and some in vivo considerations of therapy sessions such as therapist sensitivity to interactional cues; and (c) therapists as instruments of change, considering their relationship skills as critical determinants of treatment outcome.

FORMAL ASPECTS OF THE INTERVENTION PROGRAM: DESCRIPTION AND RESULTS

The program has adopted and followed a *matching-to-sample* philosophy (Parsons & Alexander, 1973) to determine both the direction and specific techniques of theory development, research, and practice. In developing intervention programs, matching-to-sample refers to using empirical research on "normal" or "adaptive" samples as a basis for determining the goals of intervention with deviant samples. Thus, in developing a change program for delinquent (status) offenders, the first step was a study comparing samples of offenders' and nonoffenders' families (Alexander, 1973). It was found that these two groups differed both in topography and distribution of several family interaction variables. Coupled with the findings of other family researchers (Ferreira & Winter, 1968; Mischler & Waxler, 1968) these findings determined the targets of intervention. Specifically, these targets were designed to help families become more efficient problem-solvers (Malouf & Alexander, 1974) by approximating their communication patterns to those of normal or adaptive families. These adaptive communication patterns were characterized by (a) high rates of reciprocated supportive communication; (b) low rates of reciprocated defensive communications; (c) greater frequency and duration of interruptions for feedback and clarification; (d) more egalitarian distribution of speech as indicated by less intrafamily talk time variance; and (e) less silence.

This matching-to-sample philosophy has several major implications which largely determined the type of intervention program that was developed. First, various aspects of family communication "styles," not a number of specific complaints or target behaviors, became the focus of intervention. This focus represented the systems theory *assumption* that family "problems" *resulted from* (rather that *caused*) the empirically demonstrated interaction differences between normal and delinquent families. Second, this matching-to-sample philosophy ensured built-in empirical feedback by posing research hypotheses. If, as intended, deviant interactional styles could be modified to approximate those of adaptive families, then presumably the problems assumed to be the result of those interactions should cease. This assumption could be empirically evaluated by correlational inferences about the properties of communication related to indices of outcome.

Finally, because the program used overt and directly measured interactions of "real" adaptive families as criteria, the treatment program was not led toward unrealistic or atypical (i.e., statistically abnormal) goal attainments. That is, many treatment models posit elusive internalized forms of "ideal mental health" such as ego strength, unconditional positive regard, or existential awareness as criterion attainment. These goals are probably unrealistic for most people, and have not easily lent themselves to empirical scrutiny. In contrast, the empirical matching-to-sample philosophy forces the investigator to acknowledge the salient observable differences between populations, and constrain himself to defining appropriate change only to those elements which differentiate the two. Per the matching-to-sample philosophy, treatment techniques were therefore chosen to impact family interaction properties directly. A central assumption was that deviant communication styles reflected families who spoke to one another in a nonproductive fashion, affording little opportunity for clear communication between members, for productive problem-solving by members, or for equal input from all members. The utility of the procedure is of course constrained by the facility with which the practitioner can manipulate or change the problematic clinical differences he has identified.

To alter the maladaptive systems characteristics, systems–behavioral therapists were trained to discriminate and modify structured components of maladaptive communication, including defensive, ambiguous, confusing, contradictory, and otherwise qualitatively undesirable verbal and nonverbal behavior (Alexander, 1973; Parsons & Alexander, 1973). In practice, therapists modeled, verbally prompted, and reinforced communications which were clear, brief, and internally consistent. Therapists encouraged accurate listening and attentive behavior, constructive feedback, as well as family members' constructive interruptions for clarity. These discrete components of productive communication were included in more global relationship structuring techniques such as behavioral contracts (Stuart, 1967). In these methods, families were urged to differentiate rules from requests, and practice mutual negotiation and behavior exchange procedures. The component properties of these techniques were designed to impact some of the qualitative interaction shortcomings of delinquent families (such as defensiveness), whereas the relationship structuring components were designed to restructure the interpersonal quantitative and distributional inequities (such as talk time). These structured interventions represent another emphasis of the program. Although the methods reflect the exchange of tangible or social reinforcers, this initial exchange has some secondary and more important properties. The topography of these techniques obscures a more important element, that of *social control*. For in addition to exchange of desirable stimuli, family members are able to initiate contact, negotiate, and protect their interests. These aspects of the intervention therefore create pervasive ''problem-solving'' attitudes which promote and maintain more discreet and long-lasting behavioral changes (Klein, Alexander, & Parsons in press).

While this training constituted the central emphasis, therapists were also familiarized with contingency procedures as potential tools to educate families in effective behavior management, with the ''reciprocity norm'' maintaining the understanding that teenagers might also find such techniques powerful in producing desired changes. Other adjunct techniques, such as bibliotherapy and token reinforcement paradigms, were used extensively in early phases of the program, but became used less and less when it became apparent they were inappropriate and relatively inefficient with the population seen in the program (Alexander & Parsons, 1973).

Because the empirical support for the treatment model has been described in great detail elsewhere (Alexander & Parsons, 1973; Klein et al., in press; Parsons & Alexander, 1973), only a brief review is presented here. As described by Klein et al. (in press), evaluation of program impact involved measurement of three different points in time, using methodological controls for potential design confounds of maturation and professional attention, and utilizing several classes of dependent measures.

The direct evaluation of program impact involved a comparison of families randomly assigned into the program or one of two comparison groups: (a) a client-centered family group program, characteristic of many juvenile court programs that emphasize awareness and communication of feelings and attitudes, and (b) a no-treatment control group. As described by Parsons and Alexander (1973), pretest sensitization was evaluated and had no impact on family process measures. On the other hand, the program significantly impacted the four measured indices of family interaction, in contrast to the comparison groups, which showed no change and did not differ from each other. Specifically, at termination, the intervention group families were less silent, had more equal talk time, and had greater duration and frequency of positive interruptions for clarification and feedback. The data thus showed that immediately after treatment deviant families more closely approximated the interaction characteristics of normal families.

The next level of evaluation involved a 6- to 18-month follow-up, using the nonreactive measure of recidivism to contrast groups. These data were taken to compare the impact of program intervention on the target problem, delinquency. In addition to the comparison groups described herein an additional treatment group (a church-sponsored "eclectic–dynamic" or insight-oriented family counseling program) was included, plus a larger group of post hoc sampled yoked controls. The behavioral–systems program was also replicated with a new sample of therapists. As can be seen in Table 1, the original program and replication significantly reduced recidivism to 26 and 27%, respectively, from the 47 to 73% ranges of the comparison conditions (Alexander & Parsons, 1973).

Table 1
Rates of Recidivism and Sibling Court Contact for Treatment and Comparison Groups

Group	N	Percent recidivism after 6–18 months[a]	Percent sibling contact after 2½–3½ years[b]
No formal treatment			
No treatment controls	6	50	67
Posthoc yoked controls	46	48	
Alternative treatments			
Client centered	19	47	59
Eclectic–dynamic	11	73	63
Behavioral–systems family program			
Original program	46	26	20
1972 replication	48	27	

[a] Data from Alexander and Parsons (1973). χ^2 differences significant at $p \leq .025$.
[b] Data from Klein and co-workers (in press). χ^2 differences significant at $p \leq .001$.

Finally, 2½ to 3½ years following program termination, several of the groups were contrasted for the rate of subsequent *sibling* involvement. This investigation tested the assertion that the systems–behavioral program, in changing interaction *styles* rather than merely modifying specific target behaviors or problem sequences, should better prepare families to resolve future developmental crises in younger siblings. As can be seen from inspection of Table 1, these predictions were again supported. The systems–behavioral program reflected a significantly lower (20%) rate of subsequent sibling contact, in contrast to a 59 to 67 % rate in the comparison groups (Klein et al., in press).

To this point, we have attempted to describe the more formal elements of the systems–behavioral program, as well as the data which attest to its utility. We have documented the more tangible components of the development, research, and evaluation strategies, and intervention foci with this section. As is the case in reviewing most published accounts of treatment models, these elements of the program do not convey many attendant assumptions and components of the model *in practice*. Subsequent portions of this chapter will attempt to highlight some of these salient characteristics, in the hope that they might illuminate some heretofore undescribed but critical aspects of the model.

BETWEEN THE LINES: LESS FORMAL CONSIDERATIONS OF THE SYSTEMS–BEHAVIORAL MODEL

Family therapists trained in the systems–behavioral model are given a specific set for the appraisal of discrete behaviors; in particular they are trained to evaluate family members and their behavior in a relational framework. This framework affords the opportunity for therapists to lend some order to disparate classes of topographically dissimilar behaviors, forces attention to the mutual interdependence of behaviors, and lends some predictability to observed family phenomena. First, and perhaps most critically, the therapist carrying this relational set evaluates the impact of a target behavior on all elements of the "system," which usually includes the family and significant others such as best friends. A specific behavior of course has "SORKC" characteristics, that is, idiosyncratic consequences, properties, and meaning for a given individual. What the therapist must also recognize, however, is the notion that the same behavior also serves as a stimulus antecedent, consequence, or contingency for other family members. Systems formulations (Alexander, 1973) dictating the interdependence of elements within a family force the therapist to this conceptualization, and give him a larger appreciation for the impact and widespread dependency of a given behavior.

Beyond these analyses of the many properties of an individual behavior, therapists must also be able to conceptualize family members' behavior at three levels of abstraction. Systems–behavioral therapists attend to the individual impact of behavior, attend to how behaviors characterize dyadic relationships (it takes two to fight), and to how behaviors serve larger family functions (adolescents seek distance as a vehicle for independence, and must fight with their parents to attain it). For example, an adolescent may be able to leave the house after an argument with his mother, full of righteous indignation but nevertheless able to spend the evening with his girlfriend. In turn, mother's burst into tears may finally serve to draw father out from behind the paper, setting an excuse for the two of them to talk to each other, and let father harangue about the way kids ought to be raised. In this instance, discrete arguing behaviors have effects for everyone. The consequences to junior serve as a stimulus for mother, which in turn serve to set a contingency stage for mother to talk to father. Father has the opportunity for repeated assertions of "I told you so." and to remove himself from his typical henpecked position. At a first individual level, arguing gets junior what he ultimately wants, time with his girlfriend. At a second relational level, a conflict requiring two participants characterizes the means for mother and son ultimately to meet their interests. At a third functional level, the behavior characterizes a developmental stage of families: an adolescent manifests his independence, and mother and father are forced to deal with their relationship as a marital dyad. Note further that the mutualities defined by these levels of analysis force the therapist to different interpretations of meaning, in many ways divorced from the topography of behaviors. Son's flight from the house in apparent rage and mother's bursting into tears are probably very real aversive consequences for them; nonetheless, they are less important as consequences than as overall maintenance functions for the family system, and as corollaries to "payoffs." This distinction is crucial, since it suggests dramatically different intervention strategies. To reduce the aversive consequences associated with arguing by time-out, shaping, or assertion training would be ultimately to deprive family members of some desirable outcomes. Rather, it may be more appropriate for the therapist to structure alternative ways for family members to meet these ends.

Note further that this formulation is consistent with a fundamental tenet of learning theory, that behavior is maintained by its consequences. However, the formulation is only possible when one begins to assign higher order logical meaning to stimuli, divorced from the more immediate consequences of anger or crying. The logical properties of this assessment require the inclusion of the impact on other family members to complete the assertions.

It appears that all too often clinical psychology promulgates assessment paradigms which bear less than appropriate relationship to treatment. When considering families, neither discrete analysis of behaviors alone nor presumed internalized traits seem appropriate. The systems–behavioral model asserts that appropriate inferences regarding family behavior require several levels of analysis, and that the selection of appropriate intervention requires the therapist to evaluate individuals, dyads, and the family as a whole. This notion of "hierarchizing" the impact of behavior is crucial in evaluating families, and it affords therapists a means to avoid judgments about "what's appropriate" for a given family. Consistent with the matching-to-sample philosophy, a systems–behavioral therapist can evaluate how the family is operating at present. Presumably, the family members, by maintenance of deviant behavior, have arrived at consequences that are meaningful for them. From this inferential starting point the therapist's task is somewhat easier, since he has merely to decide what "deviant" behaviors can be replaced with more efficient ones, while maintaining the original payoffs of independence, parental contact, and so forth. Distinctions about which behaviors serve purposes most efficiently are less difficult to distinguish than what people "really ought to want" from those behaviors. The reader may note some obvious parallels with the Premack principle: but it should be equally obvious that these consistencies can only be derived from higher order systems abstractions.

In summary, systems–behavioral therapists are trained in systems model conceptualizations of behavior. This assessment abstraction forces attention to the multiple behavioral variables that affect all family members, and describes appropriate points and purposes for behavioral interventions. While these conceptualizations could undoubtedly be conducted in different semantics, the paradigm does seem consistent with the actual behavior of families, and a parsimonious means to explain them.

TECHNICAL CAVEATS

In most respects, the behavior change technology of systems–behavioral therapy consists of conventional behavior modification techniques. However, the plethora of available techniques is formidable, and their effective use requires a broad spectrum of skill attainment. A simple classification scheme shows that there are a variety of behavioral techniques available. A first set of behavioral techniques impacts a maladaptive behavior by altering its relationship to some set of externalized reinforcers. These reinforcers may be tangible (money, tokens) or of a "social" nature (such as smiling, praise). A second set of techniques modifies relationships between a behavior and some internalized state, such as systematic desensitization and anxiety. Finally, some strategies mediate behavior change through cognitive technology, such as thought-stopping or the "rational" therapies (Alexander & Barton, 1976).

It would be cavalier for a therapist to disregard this assortment of change strategies, particularly in light of the repeated demonstrations of their efficacy. Further, as argued in the preceding section, ultimately systems–behavior therapists need to be able to give families alternative behavioral means of achieving their ends. The broader a therapist's technical armamentarium, the more likely these alternatives will be both available to the therapist and the family.

It is particularly crucial that a given technique meet the functional requirements of family members. All too often, a technique is applied which does not serve the payoff needs of all family members. For example, the behavioral contract is a ubiquitous method for change with families and marital couples. In the example cited in the preceding section, if mother and son were to contract around topical content with each other and reduce arguing, mother would be deprived of the coercive paradigm to initiate contact with father. Deprived of this payoff, it is likely that she will not follow through on the contract, and will undermine its success. If mother and son continue to argue, all three family members can continue to be paid off; if just mother and son enter negotiation, then neither mother nor father can maintain their level of contact.

This anecdote is detailed again because it represents a relatively common phenomenon. Therapists many times attempt behavior change techniques prior to appropriate and complete assessment. When one or another party refuses to honor the agreement, naive family therapists assume either (a) that the technique does not work, or (b) that the family is "really sick" and there is no hope for change. Both interpretations are incorrect.

In this example, if the therapist structured some joint "negotiation" or "contract" time for mother and father, for which father could be paid off with a less coercive interaction paradigm, then perhaps subsequent mother–son negotiations might preserve the payoff status quo. With these assurances, it seems more likely that a well-proven method may be successful.

This argues for the "problem fitting" components of effective intervention with families. In far too many instances, therapists assume that a ritualized explanation of contracting procedures represents criterion therapy attainment. Therapists elaborate the procedural guidelines around one or two "problem" behaviors, and assume that a contingency strategy to impact these behaviors will be sufficient. It is as though accomplishment of a technical maneuver which has been used successfully on prior occasions is the appropriate demonstration of therapy. It should appear obvious that within families, it is important to provide "something for everyone" in behavioral interventions. This crucial assessment–treatment confounding is highlighted because it is so consistently overlooked. Techniques developed for use with individuals or dyads require a broader focus when used with families.

Therapists trained in systems–behavioral intervention are also urged to attend to within-session sources of data. While this may be stating the obvious, it appears that many therapists are so intent on evaluating verbal accounts of overt behaviors that they do not attend to the interaction process in which they are reported.

First, therapists are afforded the opportunity to observe what families actually do. Therapists can monitor the stimulus impact of family members on each other: does junior always argue with mother, no matter what the topic of discussion?, Therapists can appraise the stylistic repertoires of each family member:

Can father consistently break up the argument, and soothe mother's feelings? Finally, family members' representations of the "problems" may provide convergent or discriminant information as to their validity. Does everyone agree that sneaking out after curfew is a problem, or does dad smilingly report, "Yeah, I challenged my old man too"? Attention to aspects of family interaction can provide therapists with information about what may or may not be the problem, as well as which family member will serve as resources or obstacles in solving them.

Second, therapists are urged to attend to the realization that they are involved in a relationship with the family. In this light, therapists should further attend to what interaction skill repertoire they are modeling. Therapists who are interrupting for clarification, being verbally brief but clear, providing feedback, and involving all family members in interaction will facilitate change by in vivo demonstrations and structuring of the appropriate interaction process.

However, therapists are also sensitized to how family members may be impacting them. It is assumed that family members will display many of the same stylistic relational qualities to therapists that they do to each other. In a matching-to-sample sense, therapists must use themselves as instruments to identify the feelings that family members elicit in them. Many male graduate students in fact feel seduced by 16-year-old daughters, and many female graduate students may feel angry and frustrated when challenged by authoritarian fathers. Therapists are sensitized to the interpersonal "pull" to blame an acting-out adolescent, or to become angry toward punitive and uninvolved parents. Consistent with the notion that these characteristics are what bring families into therapy in the first place, therapists must not be manipulated by them. For the therapist to respond to these interpersonal characteristics would be prohibitively constricting. Systems–behavioral therapists rather must respond atypically to these engaging interactions, and create different ways to deal with them. They must be alert to opportunities to supplement and facilitate interventions they designate as appropriate for families by appropriately modeling them. "Practice what you preach" shows clinical utility beyond the ethical import of this canard.

It is certainly the case that to some extent, a therapist's mastery of appropriate concepts and technical expertise will determine treatment outcome. These are undoubtedly crucial elements of the change process, no matter what the therapeutic persuasion. Therapy models which focus solely on relationship qualities fail to have any demonstrable impact on family therapy outcome (Alexander & Parsons, 1973). However, some proponents of structured behavioral models are beginning to recognize that behavior change occurs in clients which cannot be explained solely by technology. In one instance, Stuart and Lott (1974) have argued that technical features of specific reciprocal contract procedures depend more on individual therapists than on client populations.

These assertions point toward what may be the critical role of therapists' relationship skills in determining successful family therapy outcome. Some preliminary investigations into the qualities of system–behavioral therapists have shown that relationship skills predict a substantial (60%) proportion on variance in family therapy outcome (Alexander, Barton, Schiavo, & Parsons, in press; Alexander & Barton, 1976). Since the training emphasized the more structured components of intervention (i.e., brevity, clarity, and relationship structuring), it was surprising to find that therapists' relationship skills bore a stronger statistical relationship to the success of the treatment model.

With the interactional emphasis in the systems–behavioral interaction model, these findings make a great deal of sense, and are being integrated into the training of new therapists. Consistent with the matching-to-sample philosophy, therapists are evaluated on and provide feedback about those relationship skills which seem associated with successful family change. Therapists are urged to relabel topographically undesirable behaviors for their functional utility, and in a nonblaming fashion. Humor and personal reactions are discussed as means to put families at ease, or appropriately reduce or intensify the affective mood of a treatment session. In one case, a family reporting how mother beat her son with a broomstick due to his obnoxious teasing was posed the question : "Are there other ways for you two to initiate contact?" This question was very nonblaming, and served to cast both mother and son as reasonable. Mother was not cast as a heartless villain, and son's seemingly malevolent intent was re-couched as a need for contact. In this instance, a subsequent problem-solving focus was made possible by the therapist's adroit response.

This anecdote is cited to illustrate that relationship skills of this sort may be qualitatively necessary corollaries of technique. With one skillful question, the therapist was able to put aside the ponderous effect associated with the telling of this tale, create a more positive "set" for his clients by labeling the situation differently, show his willingness to be productive, and move toward a more appropriate technical means for mother and son to communicate. Obvious limitations preclude an exhaustive list of such examples, but it seems clear that therapist relationship skills are an optimal, if not crucial, means for therapists to implement change.

CONCLUSION

This chapter has attempted to document in summary fashion research performed with the systems–behavioral family intervention model, chronicle its development, and convey some flavor for its practice. In particular, the chapter has attempted to illuminate some of the "between the lines" characteristics of the model which typically go unreported in conventional accounts.

As indicated in the introduction, the state of the art in behavioral approaches to change requires careful and critical scrutiny. While on the one hand the techniques and philosophies of behavior modification are gaining widespread acceptance, its adherents are also facing more complex and troublesome issues. Some of these include growing numbers of consumers who openly express distrust, legal–ethical concerns, and more failures and disenchantment as poorly trained people try in oversimplified and naive ways to apply behavioral principles in contexts in which they are inappropriate, or at least not appropriately contextually grounded. It is partially in response to these concerns that we have discussed implicit aspects of our treatment program. At a conceptual level, continued development of the program has been defined by feedback from the empirical data.

At a pragmatic level, continued development of the program has been defined by the experiences of practicing therapists, questions raised by responsible trainees, and most importantly by the families themselves. For it is the face-to-face confrontation with family clients which has dictated attention to the special classes of problems presented to well-intentioned therapists armed only with conventional treatment pardigms.

Hopefully, advocates of other models will begin to elaborate these between-the-lines issues as well. By careful observation of *all* that what we do, further research can promote the advancement of our methods and the well-being of our clients.

REFERENCES

Alexander, J. F. Defensive and supportive communications in normal and deviant families. *Journal of Consulting and Clinical Psychology,* 1973, *40,* 223–231.

Alexander, J. F., Barton, C. *Therapist behavior and family treatment outcome.* Annual Meeting, Society of Psychotherapy Research, San Diego, 1976.

Alexander, J. F., Barton, C., Schiavo, R. S., & Parsons, B. V. Behavioral intervention with families: Therapist characteristics and outcome. *Journal of Consulting and Clinical Psychology,* 1976, *44,* 656–664.

Alexander, J. F., & Parsons, B. V. Short-term behavioral intervention with delinquent families: Impact on family process and recidivism. *Journal of Abnormal Psychology,* 1973, *51,* 219–233.

Barton, C., & Alexander, J. F. *Therapist skills in systems*–behavior family intervention: How the hell do you get them to do it? Annual Meeting, American Orthopsychiatric Association, Atlanta, 1976.

Coles, J. L., Alexander, J. F., & Schiavo, R. S. *A developmental model of family systems: A social-psychological approach.* Annual Convention, National Council of Family Relations, St. Louis, 1974.

Ferreira, A. J., & Winter, W. D. Decision-making in normal and abnormal two-child families. *Family Proceedings,* 1968, *7,* 17–36.

Kiesler, D. J., Experimental designs in psychotherapy research. In A. E. Bergin & S. L. Garfield (Eds.), *Handbook of psychotherapy and behavior change: An empirical analysis.* New York: Wiley, 1971.

Klein, N., Alexander, J. F., & Parsons, B. V. Impact of family systems intervention on recidivism and sibling delinquency: A study of primary prevention. *Journal of Consulting and Clinical Psychology,* in press.

Malouf, R. E., & Alexander, J. F. Family crisis intervention: A model and technique of training. In R. E. Hardy & J. C. Cull (Eds.), *Therapeutic needs of the family.* Springfield, Illinois: Thomas, 1974.

Mischler, E., & Waxler, N. *Interaction in families.* New York: Wiley, 1968.

Parsons, B. V., & Alexander, J. F. Short-term family intervention: A therapy outcome study. *Journal of Consulting and Clinical Psychology,* 1973, *41,* 195–201.

Stuart, R. B. Behavioral contracting within the families of delinquents. *Journal of Behavior Therapy and Experimental Psychology,* 1967, *2,* 1–11.

Stuart, R. B., & Lott, L. A. Behavioral contracting with delinquents: A cautionary note. In C. M. Franks & G. I. Wilson (Eds.), *Annual review of behavior therapy and practice: 1974.* New York: Brunner/Mazel, 1974.

Robert D. O'Connor

Chapter 9
Treatment of Race and Sex Discriminatory Behavior Patterns

Race and sex inequities have existed in America for a long time. Sociologists and political scientists have often noted major discrepancies between white and nonwhite people, and between men and women in terms of social status, the availability of opportunities and prerogatives, and the perceived worth of individuals within these groups. Racism was labeled a major "social problem" in the late 1950s when nonwhite people, primarily blacks, began to demand their constitutionally guaranteed rights in sufficient numbers. More recently the issue of sexism has come to the forefront as an increasingly vivid social problem in its own right, due in a large part to similar demands voiced by members of the "women's movement."

Although racism and sexism are in many ways unique and distinct from each other, the similarities in *process* are numerous, as are the basic forms of discriminatory behavior which ensue. The space provided here does not allow for a detailed comparison, but the utilitarian case for a unified intervention approach to both issues is well supported in the data which follow.

The terms "racism" and "sexism" do not appear in any of the standardized taxonomies of psychopathology. Clinical training programs and active practitioners very carefully avoid such broad, complex problem areas for a variety of reasons, most of which appear to be more or less reasonable on the surface. It is often stated that these are areas of social concern, not individual disorders, and that psychologists are equipped to deal only with specific, personal problems. Entire volumes could be added here to the models and rationalizations elicited by

[1]The term "nonwhite" refers to members of all groups not perceived as being white. Since the core ingredient in racism is color, other more euphemistic terms are avoided and census distinctions are ignored in the present model.

129

the implied question "Why don't clinicians attack more socially critical and generally relevant problems?"

Among the primary reasons for the limited scope of clinical practice are foggy conceptualizations of social behavior, the persistence of irrelevant medical model influences on the content and style of clinical practice, and perhaps most centrally the security and personal comfort clinicians derive from conducting a private practice limited to one-to-one treatment of standard psychiatric ills. The social impact of clinical psychology, therefore, tends to be felt only by the relative few whose personal distress falls within this narrow range of problems.

Of course, there are many clinicians who are either philosophically oriented toward the more pervasive "problems of living" (e.g., Albee, 1968; Rappaport & O'Connor, 1973) experienced by most people, or conceptually and technically trained to reduce seemingly obscure "isms" and systems problems down to a workable set of behavior change strategies. The latter group is principally composed of behavior modifiers; the former might best be termed social system interventionists.

Unfortunately, the behaviorist's technical and analytic skills are not always focused on broadly relevant topics (O'Connor, Notes 1 & 2); the social interventionist psychologist does not always have sufficiently scientific tools in his or her bag of change strategies. The present chapter represents a data-based example of how the two approaches may be successfully combined.

In this particular instance, the subject matter happens to be racism and sexism or, more specifically, race and sex discrimination, and the context in which these phenomena are approached is that of employment. The approach and specific procedures used, however, can be generalized to virtually any social concern which involves problematic human interaction patterns. As an example of this diversity, many of the same social learning principles and behavior change procedures have recently been used to help revise the entire personnel management and career development system of a major government agency (O'Connor, 1976a).

While it would be not only presumptuous but scientifically premature to state the case for social learning theory solutions to major "social problems" more strongly here, it should be noted that greater numbers of people are looking toward the human behavior experts for answers to a wider variety of problematic questions today than ever before. If consultants and clinicians simply choose to entertain a wider variety of questions, many of the answers would be forthcoming, albeit with some risk. On the other hand, one might ask either "Who else?" or "Why not?"

In order to maximize the clinical utility of the present discussion, central emphasis will be placed on a model and a set of procedures for eliminating race and sex discrimination in group training sessions. The concepts and procedures which underlie the model were developed within context of a larger, more complex set of experimental equal employment studies undertaken by the author in 1973. These studies are still in progress with additional aspects of racism and sexism currently under investigation.

In any context, racism and sexism relate to virtually every aspect of the lives of people, in very specific ways. In addition to the extensive psychological damage to the self-concepts and aspirations of nonwhites and women produced by race and sex discrimination, the expectations and contingencies associated with white, male status produce a vast number of distressing if not incapacitating situations for members of this group as well. Race and sex discrimination are not simply unpleasantries incidentally correlated with other pathologies. Quite the contrary, race and sex discrimination may be the most common basic cause of psychological problems in society today. And since this has always been the case in America, it is not likely that the problem will disappear without serious, direct, and skillful intervention.

OVERVIEW

A brief literature review is ordinarily presented at this point, so as to establish the basic foundation upon which the model to follow was built. In this case, there is no specific literature to review. Results of the experimental group training programs mentioned earlier, from which the present model was derived, are soon to be published elsewhere, but the basic outcomes are briefly described here as well (O'Connor, Note 3). These outcome studies appear to be the only available instances of empirical studies which attempt to modify race and sex discriminatory behavior directly.

Historically, racism and sexism have been legal, political, moral, and philosophical issues in America. Questions involving constitutional rights, citizenship, equal access, and the like, have comprised the essence of these issues for many years. Legal sanctions, social settings, and political structures have been modified so as to comprise a more equitable system over the years, at least in theory.

On paper, one might reasonably argue that the major institutions in America have progressed toward the noble goals of equal opportunity and nondiscrimination. However, behavioral level of analysis indicates that increases in access, the integration of various institutions, and development of of legal sanctions have probably served to increase the frequency of observably discriminatory behavior. On a day-to-day measurable basis, and more than ever before, nonwhites and women are faced with the unmistakable presence of racism and sexism, despite minor changes in form and style.

As access to employment has grown, for instance, so have the clear-cut, behavioral barriers to advancement. As nonwhites and women have begun to expect equal status and valuation on the job, the discrepancies between equal employment theory and practice have become more obvious. And finally, as more and more nonwhites and women experience the myths of equality, job related and otherwise, the specific behavior patterns which negate their theoretically equal status and access become more and more apparent.

Here the utility and applicability of behavioral analyses become most apparent. When it comes to livelihood and other daily existence problems, people are interested in equal treatment, not platitudes and attitudes. When the issue is job performance appraisal, people want the focus squarely on measurable competencies rather than stereotypes and restrictive role assumptions. In summary, and especially but not exclusively in the employment arena, the increasing numbers of nonwhites and women gaining access to the workforce and other institutions, and their subsequent awareness of the basic sources of discriminatory limitation have begun to mold the issue of equality into its most workable form. *The issue today is behavior.* The changes incumbent upon employers and employees are behavior changes. As with morality, it is often said that one cannot legislate equality. One can, however, legislate and sanction specific behaviors. Present legislation sanctions equal employment opportunity in some very specific but unsophisticated ways. In the everyday world of work, these guidelines are being further specified into discrete, observable behavior change terms. Quite by accident, employment systems may have provided the forum for an analysis of interpersonal racism and sexism which may be generalized to any other social situation and perhaps to any other dysfunctional human interaction pattern as well.

BEHAVIOR CHANGE MODEL

The global phenomena of racism and sexism differ substantially in terms of style, impact, and their various dynamics, but a behavioral analysis of the resulting discriminatory interaction patterns indicates common change strategies in specific situations. At this level of analysis, the only striking difference occurs when the psychological consequences associated with race versus sex discriminatory acts are compared.

Racism generates interpersonal events which are almost always punishing to the nonwhite person. Sexism results in numerous reinforcers for women, along with the negatives. This simple but critical distinction necessitates a somewhat sophisticated selection of changeworthy behavior patterns in the case of sex discrimination, as well as a more detailed emphasis on the ultimately negative balance of effects which accrue. At the same time, race discrimination is overwhelmingly the more negative and one-sided pattern, whereas sex discrimination produces more ambivalent consequences for both men and women and is often viewed as a less damaging state of affairs. When analyzed within a specific context, such as employment, however, these distinctions are quickly overshadowed by the commonalities revealed.

The attitudes, beliefs, traditions, and rationales which relegate nonwhites and women to lesser status and discriminatory treatment on the job differ substantially, but the form, frequency, and processes are virtually identical. Effective intervention at this level can therefore be accomplished through a single set of procedures.

Leaving aside the *ism* level of discussion, an analysis of rac*ist* or sex*ist* behavior allows for the objective and measurable definition of treatment targets. Whether or not one *is* a racist or sexist in the sense of personality traits and whether or not one is afflicted with a disorder labeled racism or sexism become irrelevant questions.

Race discrimination occurs whenever a person of one color consistently interacts *differently* with persons of another color; sex discrimination occurs whenever a person of one sex consistently interacts differently with persons of another sex. When, in a particular context, this has detrimental effects, the discrimination is considered changeworthy. When these events are detrimental to the careers of a group of people, the criterion of job relevance is also met. Behavior patterns which fit this basic definition are race or sex discriminatory, and if they occur in job relevant contexts and inhibit specific opportunity and advancement, they become the focus of this chapter.

In group treatment of dysfunctional social behavior as in marital therapy, the ideal change setting includes both or all parties which contribute to the troublesome behavior pattern. Special attention, education, or training is sometimes indicated for one or the other side of an interaction pattern, but the most direct and meaningful modifications are most likely to occur when all or both parties participate in a change strategy wherein the goals require particular inputs and responses on both sides.

Dysfunctional behavior is generally defined as behavior that is particularly bothersome or incapacitating. In reference to social behavior, this can include undesirable behavior on the part of either person. When dysfunctional patterns are firmly established as in race and sex discrimination, both sides of the interaction inevitably require alteration.

At the outset of group treatment, race and sex discrimination are defined. Legal constraints and equal employment policies are such that one need not belabor the question of changeworthiness. People are aware that race and sex discrimination are unacceptable in the work setting. The first critical step is to establish the definition of race and sex discrimination in observable, measurable terms, so that participants can identify and objectively agree upon instances of it.

Modeling and role-playing sessions depicting interaction patterns which qualify as instances of job-related race and sex discrimination are carefully and systematically directed by the group facilitator. The specific interactions selected for these sessions include a range or events which do in fact occur in the particular job setting at hand, and the range includes subtle and nonsubtle instances. Participants gradually become more skillful at correctly identifying discriminatory patterns in others. The modeling and role-playing sessions provide a nonthreatening medium for sharpening participants' abilities to recognize discrimination.

In discussion format, lists of discriminatory events which have occured to participants, directly or indirectly, are then derived. At the final stage of the group session, each participant chooses behaviors from these lists according to three criteria: Selected behavior patterns must be deemed *important* by those on the receiving end, they must be patterns in which the individual is *personally involved,* and the alternative or antidiscriminatory behavior pattern must be *doable,* within the repertoire of the individual. Some examples of common patterns which are both race and sex discriminatory are as follows:

- Women and nonwhites are excluded from decision-making relevant to their jobs, because they are assumed to be too emotional or too irrational for such activities.
- The performances of nonwhites and women are differentially evaluated and rewarded (compared to white males), producing long-run "blacklash" and inappropriate expectancies in the case of overevaluation, and overt repression in the case of underevaluation.
- The efficiency of women and nonwhites is hampered by sex-typed and race-typed socializing and other sex/race-typed distractions from job duties.
- Fear of EEO lawsuits and/or personal embarrassment leads to the exclusion of nonwhites and women from additional areas of advancement-related activity. Managers and supervisors simply avoid general contact with "potentially dangerous" employees. This often includes all nonwhites and women.
- Particular women or nonwhites who voice even mild disagreement are often labeled "troublemaker" or "militant" and are sometimes actively avoided by supervisory/management personnel. Their viewpoints and opinions are subsequently invalidated in any case.
- Nonwhites and women are often transferred or rotated "for their own good" purely on the basis of interpersonal tastes and disputes, whereas white males' difficulties are more directly addressed and usually resolved in the present context.

Participants voluntarily and privately select some number of behaviors which they intend to alter. These behavior change contracts include changes in both the initial stage of a pattern and in the response to such changes on the part of others. The essence of these interpersonal contracts is that they are self-maintaining due to the supportive responses which are contracted for at the same time changes in the initiation of interactions are agreed upon.

Before participants can realistically select change targets for themselves and before they will be inclined to do so, the facilitator must outline a behavior change model which gives participants the necessary tools. People will not readily alter their established behavior patterns unless they believe that they *can*. A clear and simplified model of social interaction, including the basic principles of behavior change, is presented prior to the selection of antidiscriminatory contracts.

Drawing on the general principles of social learning theory and behavior modification (e.g., Bandura, 1969, 1977), a behavioral model of social interaction emphasizes the portion of the process which is most directly responsible for the continuation of any particular interaction pattern, the reinforcement versus punishment characteristics of each party's input. Simply put, the most basic premise states that any consistent interaction pattern is to some degree being maintained because the response of the second party is in some way reinforcing to the first party, the one who initiates the interaction. Of course, the process is much more complicated, but this emphasis, when applied to race and sex discrimination, is a critical step toward the development of voluntary two-sided behavior change commitments.

At first glace it often appears that this model places undue "responsibility" on the shoulders of the "victims" of discrimination. The fact of the matter is that, value-laden terms aside, the premise holds true in almost every instance. In the modal case, the second party is either nonwhite or female and tends to maintain discriminatory patterns by not punishing racist or sexist remarks or actions, and indeed supporting such behavior by smiling, shrugging, or otherwise indicating that the first person's behavior is acceptable. However, this does not imply that nonwhites and women are in the best position to alter these interaction patterns, since they are by and large the relatively powerless persons as compared to white males.

Although it is patently obvious that the person who initiates a discriminatory interaction could alter the pattern by simply not initiating it, that kind of emphasis, by itself, nearly always fails to produce anything more than moralistic verbal commitments on one side and disbelief and ridicule on the other. Again, with no reference to qualitative adjectives, the behavioral analysis outlines maintenance factors wherever they happen to lie, addressing only those patterns which *do* occur and with considerable predictability. Given the tremendous frequency of firmly established, ongoing discrimination patterns, it seems reasonable to focus on these behaviors after they occur, at least initially, and then to work out those patterns toward the development of preventive measures.

Having established the behavior-maintaining role of the second party, the next step is to determine the incompatible positive alternative (IPA) for each discriminatory behavior listed. The alternative "thing to do" in a given situation, which is the antithesis of the discriminatory event in the sense that one cannot do both at the same time, smiling versus frowning for instance, is generated for each item on the list of changeworthy discriminatory events. These alternatives must also be positive, rather than substitute discriminatory events, that is, they must not meet the definition of discrimination. The IPA list becomes the menu of specific, observable discrimination reduction actions upon which change contracts are then based. This is a centrally important exercise because it results in discrete and meaningful actions which discriminators can take if they so choose. In traditional procedures, participants may come to understand "the problem" and indeed feel some inclination to correct their discriminatory inclinations, but are left with no specific direction (O'Connor, 1976b). The usual outcome of such programs is a brief period of guilt, followed by general avoidance of the entire issue, including nonwhites and women.

In the present approach, participants learn precisely what it is they would have to do if they wished to alter their own race- and sex-related behavior in a way that would meet the legitimate expectations of nonwhites and women. Again, in traditional programs where antidiscriminatory behaviors are not specified and their definition legitimized (agreed upon by all), white male participants usually conclude that nothing in particular would satisfy "those people," and use this conclusion to rationalize inaction.

The other parties to these contracts, by and large but not exclusively nonwhites and female recipients of discriminatory behavior, agree to support (reinforce) the changed (IPA) behavior of their white male co-workers, if and when it occurs. Here too, this sounds more simple than it really is. Nonwhites and women are usually and justifiably skeptical about the newly intended behaviors drawn into contracts and adopt a wait-and-see attitude. Stress is again put on the controlling role of secondary responses in social interaction patterns, and the fact that the newly adopted, probably anxious (IPA) behavior patterns will almost certainly cease to occur if they are not consistently and obviously reinforced.

The central, interpersonal behavior "treatment" portion of these group sessions concludes with the private drafting of written, individual change contracts which are maintained by each participant. In a follow-up "consultation" session, each participant is asked to confide his or her successes and failures and obtain further assistance from the facilitator if necessary. Successes are rewarded (verbally) and built upon by the facilitator in the form of increasingly more significant contracts and other antidiscriminatory actions. Successful participants generally model antidiscrimination, producing like behavior among their peers. Officewide educational sessions are often held in which discriminatory events are sought out and sanctioned.

RESULTS

The data below represent a summary of the major findings from a series of pilot studies (O'Connor, Note 3) which were conducted with the support of a major federal agency during 1974 and 1975.

- A major reduction in both racial and sexual discrimination occurred across a variety of work settings. Nearly 90% of the ongoing discriminatory events identified by nonwhite and female group participants ($n = 32$, total for two groups) were completely eliminated.

- The racial/sexual attitudes of most participants became significantly more positive following successful discrimination reduction efforts.
- Virtually all participants, white and nonwhite, male and female, indicated an increased awareness of their potential for and personal role in racism and sexism.
- In follow-up interviews, the vast majority (85%) demonstrated a commitment to continue their antidiscriminatory activites indefinitely.
- Most participants expanded their efforts to additional changes (beyond those agreed upon at the conclusion of training), and enlisted a number of nonparticipants into the effort. Beyond the specific, personal goals determined during training, there were additional reductions in discriminatory behaviors (approximately 50 additional behavior changes). Other than the 32 pilot participants, well over 100 additional employees were directly influenced (agreed to alter their behavior) through the generalized efforts of pilot participants.
- Behavior analysis and management tools acquired in the pilot training sessions have been utilized by participants (particularly managers) in a variety of personnel problem-solving situations. This gratuitous side benefit helped resolve numerous psychological (interpersonal behavior and personal difficulties) problems encountered by managers in dozens of instances. These participants report a more general (beyond racism/sexism) ability to deal with others due to the analytic and intervention skills acquired in pilot training courses.
- The average course evaluation indicated by participants (white and nonwhite, male and female) was "very useful," and in follow-up interviews these evaluations *averaged* very close to the upper limit "extremely valuable" (7 on a 1–7 scale of evaluation options). The approach, therefore, has not only proven to be quite successful from an objective outcome standpoint, but remarkably acceptable and useful to this particular audience, management, professional, and support personnel.
- Given the intensive and relatively sophisticated outcome—measurement procedures built into the project, the findings argue quite clearly for expanded training along these lines. Previously unresolved questions as to whether or not discriminatory race- and sex-typed behavior and correlated attitudes can be changed significantly have been answered.

ADDITIONAL LEVELS OF ANALYSIS

Two notes of caution should be very clearly borne in mind when interpreting or utilizing the approach presented here. First, the role of cognitive conditioning processes is not to be ignored in a behavioral training program focused on race and sex discrimination. A brief but detailed presentation of the nature of the cognitive processes of prejudice, expectancy formulation, perceptual distortion, stereotyping, and attitude formulation should be conducted prior to the behavioral level analysis. If for no other reason, people tend to enter the session with these kinds of processes in mind and it is difficult to gain immediate attention to discriminatory behavior itself without first establishing the relationship between these processes and discriminatory behavior, and behavior in general.

Space does not permit a lengthy discussion here, but suffice it to say that while these cognitions certainly play important roles in the development of discriminatory behavior patterns, they are neither as amenable to direct change as are overt behaviors nor as powerful a set of behavior-controlling factors as behavioral consequences, and they are simply not very interesting from the nonacademic standpoint of equal employment. No one really cares about racist and sexist attitudes except insofar as they mediate discriminatory behavior, the topic of specific interest to all.

While people, all people, are indeed conditioned to think and believe in racist and sexist ways through the media, textbooks, and the modeling and direct teaching of our parents and peers, people's behavior is largely a function of external events, such as its social and other consequences.

Fortunately, attitudes and other cognitive events tend to change with behavior change and as a direct *function of behavior change*. Even if people were primarily interested in racist and sexist cognitions, which they are not, the most effective way to alter these events would be first to alter discriminatory behavior and then produce consistently egalitarian behavior patterns with regard to race and sex.

The second major word of caution to bear in mind has to do with the third factor that tends to produce and maintain race and sex discrimination, social and organizational *systems*. Especially in the context of employment, it would be at best very difficult, and surely inefficient, to focus only on the day-to-day discriminatory behavior patterns of individuals. Interpersonal behavior change is a critically important, sorely overlooked, necessary, but not sufficient (in itself) solution to the problem of employment discrimination.

Here as in other contexts, changing the behavior of individuals does not necessarily change systems, and vice versa. The elements shown in Figure 1 should help to clarify the need for systemic change *stimultaneous* with behavioral change. Figure 1 depicts the most commonly used terms for the major dimensions of racism and sexism.

This chapter has focused on the behavioral level of analysis. The systemic level is indicated at the upper, broader portions of the V-shaped diagram in Figure 1. In an employment context, the interpersonal approach outlined here should be the prime behavioral level focus of an intervention program. The

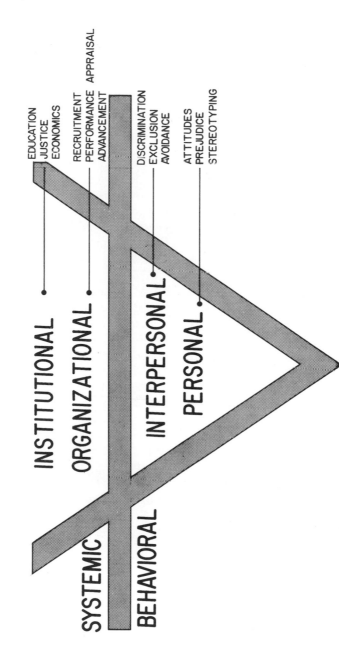

Fig. 1. Dimensions of racism and sexism.

organizational element of the systemic level, namely those policies, practices, procedures, and structures which are in themselves liable to be race and sex discriminatiory, should be the second major focal point. Without restructuring these systemic elements of an organization, it is highly unlikely that egalitarian interpersonal behavior patterns will persist. Conversely, without behavior change, egalitarian systems and structures are readily sabotaged.

CONCLUSION

This chapter represents not only an objective, empirically validated approach to one of America's most nagging and embarrassing problems, but the procedures herein are also more generally applicable to interpersonal behavior problem-solving and to personnel and career management.

In addition, it is hoped that this example of effective application of social learning principles to a "problem of living" which impacts upon us all might reinforce the relevancy search of social scientists who have the tools, and help broaden the horizons of those practitioners who aspire to become more helpful to more people.

As with any set of procedures in the early developmental stages, the specific discrimination reduction training methods described will undoubtedly undergo revision. As of this writing, in fact, a videotape-mediated sophistication of the approach has been developed by the author and his staff. These further efforts to produce sound, rational, objective, and cost-effective solutions to the equal employment dilemma should add considerable strength to the group procedures discussed in this chapter. At present, illegal discrimination pervades and seriously threatens every office, factory, agency, and organization, public and private, in Amercia. Potent procedures derived from social learning theory offer most of the tools for meaningful change. Employers need only to approach the issue from the same serious and careful posture displayed in other critical management tasks.

REFERENCE NOTES

1. O'Connor, R. D. *Behavior technology and social change*. A Symposium tri-sponsored by divisions 12, 25, and 27, presented at the annual convention of the American Psychological Association, Hawaii, 1972.
2. O'Connor, R. D. *Humanistic behaviorism*. Address presented at Veteran's Administration Hospital, Leavenworth, 1975.
3. O'Connor, R. D. *Reducing race and sex discrimination through interpersonal applications of social learning principles*. Unpublished manuscript, Center for Studies of Social Behavior, Oklahoma City, Oklahoma, 1976.

REFERENCES

Albee, G. W. Conceptual models and manpower requirements in psychology. *American Psychologist*, 1968, *23*, 317–320.

Bandura, A. *Principles of behavior modification*. New York: Holt, 1969.

Bandura, A. *Social Learning theory*, Englewood Cliffs, Prentice-Hall, 1977.

O'Connor, R. D. *Development of a behavior-specific career management system*. Project report, U.S. General Accounting Office, Washington, D.C., 1976 (a).

O'Connor, R. D. *Current status of race relations training programs*. A U.S. General Accounting Office report on race relations in the military, 1976. (b)

Rappaport, J., & O'Connor, R. D. The psychological center in a psychology department. *Professional Psychology*, 1973, *4*, 92–98.

Some of the data summarized in this chapter are based on research and training programs funded by the U.S. General Accounting Office and the Office of the Comptroller General of the United States. The author gratefully acknowledges the integrity and support of numerous officials of the G.A.O. Thanks are also due to Mr. C. Mack Hall and a number of other social scientists whose various inputs have been invaluable.

Further information and copies of the videotaped training materials discussed may be obtained by writing Dr. O'Connor at the Center for Studies of Social Behavior, 3535 N.W. 58th Street, Oklahoma City, Oklahoma 73112.

PART III

Treatment of Alcoholism and Drug Addiction

John J. Steffen
and Peter E. Nathan

Chapter 10
Treatment of Alcoholism

Behavior therapists have recently come to acknowledge the limited value of conditioning therapies alone in treating complex disorders such as alcohol abuse, largely because single symptom-directed treatments ignore the complexity of human behavior and alcoholism. For this reason and for the following, the group treatment of alcohol abusers represents a potentially useful medium for the instigation of behavior change in the alcoholic. First, the group can serve as a microcosm of society. In it, the alcohol abuser can also reenact past interpersonal difficulties related to drinking; he/she can also discover, then rehearse, new, more adaptive modes of interpersonal response. Second, group treatment, because of its intensely social nature, facilitates vicarious learning. The alcoholic can acquire adaptive responses to troublesome social situations by observing fellow group members' attempts to change. Third, group treatment may permit the saving of time and money for both patient and therapist, since it makes maximally efficient use of scarce therapist time. All of these points are discussed at greater length later in this chapter.

At this early point, the reader should also be cautioned against premature enthusiasm for behavioral group therapy for alcoholics. There is no comprehensive network of theoretical or empirical constructs to direct the practice of behavioral group therapy as there are for other group therapy approaches (e.g., Yalom, 1975). This want of a framework, in turn, is partly responsible for the paucity of research on behavioral group therapy—as contrasted with behavior therapy applied in groups, for which there is a substantial literature. As a result, no claim can be made on the basis of data for the superior efficacy of behavioral group procedures over others as applied to alcoholism. This cautionary note will hopefully be tempered in the future as behavior therapists begin to investigate the utility of behavioral group methods for treating alcohol abusers.

ETIOLOGIC CONSIDERATIONS

Although fully articulated behavioral theories of alcoholism etiology have not yet evolved, social learning theory (Bandura, 1969; Mischel, 1973) provides important initial direction for a behavioral explanation of chronic alcohol abuse.

The social learning perspective presumes that the alcoholic individual's family served and serves as a prime focus for development of his/her maladaptive drinking practices. It is from the family—later from the peer group as well—that society's rules governing alcohol consumption are acquired. Via the same mode of behavior transmission, in turn, the person who is to become an alcohol abuser learns that alcohol consumption can serve as an effective response to stressful or otherwise aversive experiences. According to this view, excessive alcohol consumption eventually becomes such an individual's major coping response to stress. This fact, coupled with increasing tolerance and physiologic addiction to alcohol, leads the alcoholic into chronic, destructive physical and psychological dependence on alcohol. Further consequences of repeated excessive alcohol consumption, including alcohol withdrawal symptoms, vocational instability, alcohol-related physical disease, and marital and familial disequilibrium, then may themselves come to serve as stressful stimuli which maintain the cycle of alcoholism.

In other words, social learning theory posits that excessive drinking is a learned phenomenon maintained by stress reduction, peer influence, and physical dependence. In addition, the consequences of drinking themselves add further stress in the form of employment, marital, and familial disturbance. Although the relationships among these determinants of alcoholism are quite complex and hence beyond the scope of this chapter, they suggest the range of factors that must be considered in the design of behavioral treatment programs for alcoholism.

ASSESSMENT AND GOAL SELECTION

This section of the chapter outlines two areas of special concern for the behavior therapist who would treat alcoholics. The first concerns the dual problems of alcoholic typology and the behavioral assessment of alcohol abuse. In this regard, we will make the point that the complexity of alcoholism and the problems associated with its reliable assessment make application of uniform therapy procedures unwise and inappropriate. The second concerns the question of suitable goals for treatment (including abstinence and controlled social drinking). The importance of this latter question has been intensified by recent controversy surrounding publication and promotion of a Rand Corporation report on a survey of alcoholism treatment to the National Institute on Alcohol Abuse and Alcoholism (Armor, Polich, & Stambul, 1976).

The etiologic complexity parallels the nosological complexity of the behavioral and emotional manifestations of alcoholism. Said another way, there is no one type of alcoholic in part because no one develops the disorder in exactly the same way, from exactly the same determinants. As a consequence, the 18-year-old college student arrested for driving while intoxicated, the 32-year-old housewife who drinks every morning, and the 46-year-old marketing vice-president who cannot work after lunch because of the three double martinis he has consumed should not be given identical treatment regimes. Although all of these individuals share a tendency to drink to exccss, we cannot assume that their abusive drinking had the same course of development, follows the same daily pattern, or is maintained by similar antecedents and consequences. While some do argue that alcoholics share similar psychological dependency needs and metabolic dysfunctions, both of which require uniform modes of treatment, these assumptions of uniformity appear to be myth, not fact (Kiesler, 1966).

Given the complex etiological and typological gaps which differentiate alcoholics, a careful, thorough behavioral analysis must always precede its treatment. Such a behavioral assessment should begin with the person's behavioral and emotional assets, as well as his or her deficits. Of special interest, with alcoholics, is the extent to which they suffer from deficits in interpersonal behavior related to their alcoholism. On completion of such a behavioral analysis, for example, it might be found that the 18-year-old is unable to refuse the offer of "just one more" from his chums despite the fact that he must drive home alone, that the 32-year-old woman drinks in the mornings because she is bored and feels she is wasting away her life at home, and that the vice-president drinks because alcohol gives him the feelings of power and competence he needs to function as he must in his high-pressure business environment.

These examples, albeit simple, suggest in barest outline the range of controlling conditions that are associated with the development of alcoholism. Though it would be naive to believe that the problem of drinking of any of the three persons cited is as simple and unidetermined as our shorthand behaviorial analysis of each suggests, it is probably just as naive to believe that one must search for purely "psychological" explanations for such purposes. In truth, of course, the former and the latter determinants of alcoholism go hand in hand, and each is as amenable to behavioral change —or as intractable—as the other. The reader who wishes to learn more about the specifics of this matter should consult one or more of several sources on multifaceted assessment in general behavior therapy (e.g., Lazarus, 1976) and in alcoholism (Nathan & Briddell, 1976). In any event, completion of a thorough behavior analysis prior to starting group treatment is, in our view, a most desirable goal.

Until recently, the only feasible goal for the treatment of alcohol abuse was life-long avoidance of alcoholic beverages—total abstinence. This restrictive view of alcohol treatment was predicated upon several assumptions, the foremost being that all alcohol abusers suffer from an inherited predisposition to alcohol abuse. This predisposition was presumed to render such individuals so vulnerable to the pharmacologic effects of alcohol that even a single drink of alcohol invariably led to drunkenness, and physical dependence.

Anecdotal reports as well as controlled laboratory research now suggest that this ''one drink, one drunk'' hypothesis may be invalid in the laboratory. Much of this work is summarized and discussed by Nathan and Bridell (1976). Further, other research groups (Pertschuk, & Stinnett, 1976; Popham & Schmidt, 1976; Sobell & Sobell, 1976) have presented data which indicate that some alcohol abusers can select, and adhere to, controlled drinking as a treatment goal without apparent effects upon familial, social, and employment activities. - NO

However, consideration of such a treatment goal must be made with great caution. Perhaps the foremost consideration in selecting controlled drinking as a treatment goal has to do with the patient's expectations about his or her ability to control alcohol consumption. If the patient strongly believes that under no circumstances would he or she be able to limit alcohol consumption, then such a goal is clearly unwise. At the same time, one must also gauge the potential impact of abstinence versus controlled drinking upon the patient's social and professional life. For example, if the patient would be unable to maintain his or her employment as an announced or admitted controlled drinker, treatment aiming at other than abstinence would clearly be inappropriate. By the same token, insistence on adherence to an abstinence treatment model in the face of repeated failure to achieve abstinence would appear to be at least as inappropriate.

This brief excursion into questions of etiology, nosology, and goal selection vis-à-vis alcoholism was designed to alert the reader to the key problems that plague the clinician and researcher in the field today.

DESCRIPTION OF THE TREATMENT MODEL

Before proceeding to explicate our behavioral model of alcoholism treatment, we must briefly explore several additional issues of relevance to our topic. These include the following: the nature of group behavior therapy; the group as a microcosm of groups in society; and the facilitation of vicarious learning in groups.

In the opening section of this chapter, a distinction was made between behavior therapy applied in groups and group behavior therapy. This distinction, on the surface, may appear to be trifling; in fact, close examination of the actual processes of change employed by the two group approaches reveals important differences in methods and goals. ''Behavior therapy applied in groups'' refers to the administration of behavior therapy techniques (e.g., systematic desensitization, assertive training, social skills, or self-control training) by a therapist in the presence of more than one patient. Although the efficacious application of these techniques does not require the presence of more than one patient, economy in therapist time sometimes requires that more than one patient be treated simultaneously. In such a case, interaction among group members is minimal, if it occurs at all; the processes of change rest primarily on the interchange between therapist and patient: the therapist instigates change in the patient.

This dimension of interaction—between patient and therapist and among group members—lies at the heart of the distinction between behavior therapy applied in groups and group behavior therapy. The latter approach encourages interaction among group members. It assumes that each member enters the group with a unique set of skills and life experiences that can be shared with other group members to the potential benefit of all. The patient is led to expect that he or she can and should provide fellow members with corrective interpersonal feedback even though he or she came into the group to learn his or her own adaptive methods of overcoming drinking problems. At the same time, this expectation does not include the assumption that a group member is invariably accurate in providing feedback or useful in sharing coping strategies. It is the therapist's responsibility to monitor the feedback group members give one another and to correct misperceptions and inaccuracies when they arise.

In sum, the major difference between group behavior therapy and behavior therapy applied in groups derives from the amount and kind of interaction taking place among group members. However, because this distinction is not always clear in practice and because each mode of treatment possesses important strengths, the group treatment model we propose here is an amalgam of the two. In particular, we envisage a behavior therapist whose role alternates between application of individual behavior therapy techniques and facilitation of constructive group interaction.

One beneficial consequence of increased involvement of group members in each other's treatment is the enhanced power relationships that develop within the group help to facilitate behavior change. To this end therapist and patients come to serve as important sources of social reinforcement for each other as patients progress toward their individual treatment goals. Further, the use of behavior rehearsal, a major component of this hybrid treatment model, is facilitated, and will probably generalize further, as more exemplars are available and become valued. The group, then, can become a microcosm of the patient's social environment but, unlike his/her actual environment, one that can foster the development of appropriate rather than inappropriate drinking behaviors.

Finally, the power of the group process can also function to encourage group members to participate throughout *all* phases of treatment, including the times when other members hold the focus of group attention. In fact, this observational learning can foster change in all members as they observe their valued peers actively working to achieve treatment goals.

TREATMENT PROGRAM: PRELIMINARY
CONSIDERATIONS

The group treatment model we propose includes five major components: pretreatment assessment, goal selection, technique application, behavior rehearsal, and in vivo practice. Before detailing these procedures, a few general comments on this approach to alcoholism treatment are in order.

First, it is assumed that this will be a time-limited closed group. The group is closed to ensure a sense of continuity among members and to avoid the loss of treatment time spent integrating new members into the group. Time limits are used to provide members with specific rather than open-ended times to reach individual treatment goals. Second, this intervention model is designed for outpatient rather than inpatient treatment because its in vivo component requires access to the real world. Third, although each of the five elements of treatment is integral to successful treatment outcome, decisions about the amount of time spent on each is at the discretion of the therapist. Finally, decisions on the sequence with which each component is introduced are, again, best left to the therapist—although assessment and goal selection should precede the other elements of treatment.

The importance of a thorough behavioral analysis cannot be overstated. In this regard several hours should be spent exploring the extent of the patient's drinking problem as well as his/her associated behavioral deficits and excesses; only in this way can the antecedents and consequences controlling such behavior be identified. To aid in this essential process, Marlatt (1976) has developed a comprehensive questionnaire to assess drinking behaviors. Among many other questions phrased with behavioral assessment in mind, the questionnaire requests data on patient's preferred beverages, amount, frequency, and manner of consumption, preferred drinking settings, and usual drinking companions. Besides identifying potential routes of intervention, this information provides the therapist with base rate data by which to gauge treatment outcome.

Suppose the therapist discovers that a male patient drinks only on weekends, when in the company of a specific circle of friends, at a circumscribed number of places. Suppose, too, that the norms of this group require that all participants drink large amounts of beverage alcohol, usually resulting in rapid intoxication, prolonged drunkenness, and severe hangover. A possible treatment plan: behavior rehearsal to assist the patient's acquisition of a new group of friends; assertive training to help him learn to refuse invitations to drink; social skills training to expand his circle of alcohol-free friends.

Data on maladaptive drinking must be augmented, of course, with detailed information on the cognitive, affective, and interpersonal concomitants of the patient's problem drinking (Lazarus, 1976). Questions asked of the patient should include thoughts or beliefs the patient has about his or her drinking;

self-statements (self-talk) the patient routinely uses while drinking; changes in effect that might occur prior to, during, or after drinking; any interpersonal events that often or always precede drinking; effects of the patient's drinking on significant interpersonal relationships. Although these questions are by no means exhaustive of those that might be asked, they provide the reader with a sense of possible areas for fruitful enquiry.

Once assessment is complete, patient and therapist jointly determine the goals of treatment. The first decision to be made has to do with the patient's terminal drinking behavior. Is abstinence or controlled social drinking to be the prime treatment goal? Problems associated with selection of the second of these goals were previously discussed. Additional decisions must be made on supplementary goals of treatment. These choices require enumeration of problems identified through the behavioral analysis and negotiation between patient and therapist on desired outcomes. Common supplemental goals of alcoholism treatment include correction of irrational beliefs about drinking, development of assertive and social skills, acquisition of more adaptive skills to cope with stress (e.g., relaxation), and improvement of marital and familial relationships. In actual practice, these goals must be stated in as clear and precise a fashion as possible to facilitate treatment success. "Improved social skills" is not an appropriate or helpful treatment goal; a more acceptable (but not perfect) goal might be "to meet new people and arrange further meetings with them." An immediate goal, in this context, would be to "sit next to someone new at church or work, introduce yourself, and strike up a conversation." With these levels of the same goal in mind, treatment could focus, in the group, on cued behavioral rehearsal for this planned encounter in vivo.

Goals selected during this component of treatment direct future group sessions. Above all, the group is used to provide patients with strategies to meet these goals and to develop a forum for shared interaction and support. The remaining components of treatment—technique application, behavior rehearsal, and in vivo practice—all take place with the group context, with each session generally containing some blend of the three.

Technique application requires the use of specific behavior therapy techniques originally developed for the individual treatment mode in the group setting. For example, the therapist might determine from prior assessment, that several, or all, group members would benefit from a course of systematic desensitization or self-control training during the group therapy. The current model programs the application of such procedures at any point during treatment.

This treatment component represents the "behavior therapy applied in groups" portion just mentioned. Our distinction between this approach and "group behavior therapy" does not preclude the use of such specific, therapist-centered procedures. In fact, the need frequently arises, during the group treatment of alcohol abusers, to provide treatment for emotional hypersensitivities (through systematic desensitization) or inabilities to delay gratification (through self-control training). Thus, the judicious use of these techniques is an essential component of a well-rounded group therapy program.

Enumeration of all individual procedures appropriate for the group treatment of alcohol abusers is not attempted here. Instead, the reader is urged to consult other resources (both in this book and in basic behavior therapy texts) that detail the specific behavior therapy techniques.

Behavior rehearsal is especially well suited for the group treatment of alcohol abusers because many problem drinkers resort to alcohol when they are confronted with stressful interpersonal situations. Behavior rehearsal can help alcohol abusers learn new methods to cope with interpersonal stress. Utilization of this technique in groups for alcohol abusers involves three distinct phases: problem identification, behavior rehearsal, and feedback on behavior from group members. The last two phases may be repeated for each problem until the patient acquires sufficient expertise to respond appropriately in each role-played situation. As with the other behavior therapy techniques, this component of treatment may be introduced at any point during treatment.

Problem identification requires the specification, during assessment or treatment, of those interpersonal events which precipitate or maintain episodes of maladaptive drinking. For example, the therapist may discover that a patient has difficulty expressing feelings of anger toward her insensitive husband. Her usual response, when hurt by him, is to "show him" by drinking excessively. This problem area, clearly, is a source of maladaptive behavior for which the woman might search out, then practice, alternative, interpersonally directed means of responding.

Behavioral rehearsal itself requires the deliberate recreation of the stressful interpersonal event for which the patient wishes to learn new methods of coping. The patient describes the event to the group and then selects a suitable number of group members to serve as dramatis personae. These group members are then further briefed by the patient on how their parts are to be played during the rehearsal. Then the scenario begins and the patient responds as he/she customarily would in real life.

The patient's initial performance—true to life—is then critically analyzed by the group (including the patient himself or herself). The therapist's role throughout this "feedback" phase is to facilitate and clarify the feedback. The therapist facilitates feedback both by providing personal feedback to the patient and by encouraging the observations of other group members. The approach should always be one which encourages positive, corrective feedback rather than negative, destructive criticism. It would be unsuitable simply to tell a patient he/she did something incorrectly; the patient should be told instead what was wrong (more accurately, ineffective), for what reasons, and what alternative ways of responding would be more appropriate and effective.

The cycle of rehearsal–feedback is repeated until both the patient and the other group members are satisfied that his/her performance is optimal for the situation. At this point the therapist may underscore the ways in which all group members, not just the target patient, have learned new methods of responding to similar stressful situations.

In vivo practice allows patients an opportunity to exercise adaptive methods of drinking in real-world social situations. In essence, the therapist conducts a practice drinking session with his/her patients. Each patient is informed that he/she is to participate in an exercise in appropriate behavior in a social drinking situation. To this end, the therapist structures a "party" at which each patient is to behave consonant with his or her drinking goal. Patients whose goal is abstinence will ingest only soft drinks, even while effectively and convincingly refusing invitations to consume something harder; patients who are to become controlled social drinkers are given specific instructions on how many drinks they are allowed to have and how they are to be consumed. The practice "party" is then held as any other similar social gathering would be, with only the above-mentioned social role restrictions on drinking behavior. These practice sessions, it is explained to the patients, are meant to enhance the carryover of their newly acquired skills to the "real life" gatherings that they will invariably encounter posttreatment.

This component of treatment is probably best given during its latter phases. By that point the patients will have become more accustomed to and at ease with each other. Also, the new interpersonal skills acquired earlier will be of assistance to patients at these practice sessions. It is desirable to hold more than one such party to facilitate the generalization of these practical drinking skills to the patients' natural environment. Social "props" to facilitate generalization may be employed in this context. Such props might include the party's location (at a member's home), music, members of the patient's family, food, and the like.

Inclusion of this component of the treatment model is intended, as already stated, to enhance the generalization of adaptive drinking behavior. Provision for aids to generalization has been a major flaw in prior treatment approaches to alcoholism. In this regard, it is often assumed that alcoholic patients, on being informed of the best way to act, will do so in the future. It is also assumed that the same patients, informed of proper ways of acting, will do so without practicing in their natural environments. Generalization of treatment, however, cannot be taken for granted. The truism, "Practice makes perfect," is especially appropriate in this regard!

CONCLUSION

The reader should know that although this model represents a reasoned behavioral approach to the group treatment of alcohol abusers, it has not yet been subjected to empirical study. However, this consideration should not deter careful clinical examination of this approach to treatment. The model proposed represents a multifaceted treatment regimen for an extraordinarily complex problem. In our view, it will only be through such a flexible mode of treatment that more effective means to treat alcohol abuse will be found.

REFERENCES

Armor, D. J., Polich, J. M., & Stambul, H. B. *Alcoholism and treatment*. Santa Monica, California: Rand Corporation, 1976.

Bandura, A. *Principles of behavior modification*. New York: Holt, 1969.

Kiesler, D. J. Some myths of psychotherapy research and the search for a paradigm. *Psychological Bulletin*, 1966, *65*, 110–136.

Lazarus, A. A. *Multimodal therapy*. New York: Springer, 1976.

Marlatt, G. A. The drinking profile. In E. J. Mash & L. G. Terdal (Eds.), *Behavior therapy assessment: Diagnosis, design, and evaluation*, New York: Springer, 1976.

Mischel, W. Toward a cognitive social learning reconceptualization of personality. *Psychological Review*, 1973, *80*, 252–283.

Nathan, P. E., & Bridell, D. W. Behavioral assessment and treatment of alcoholism. In B. Kissin and H. Begleiter (Eds.), *The biology of alcoholism*, Vol. 5. New York: Plenum Press, 1976.

Pomerleau, O., Pertschuk, M., & Stinnett, J. A critical examination of some current assumptions in the treatment of alcoholism. *Journal of Studies on Alcohol*, 1976, *37*, 849–867.

Popham, R. E., & Schmidt, W. Some factors affecting the likelihood of moderate drinking by treated alcoholics. *Journal of Studies on Alcohol*, 1976, *37*, 868–882.

Sobell, M. B., & Sobell, L. C. Second year treatment outcome of alcoholics treated by individualized behavior therapy: Results. *Behaviour Research and Therapy*, 1976, *14*, 195–216.

Yalom, I. *The practice of group psychotherapy* (2nd ed.). New York: Basic Books, 1975.

Frances E. Cheek

Chapter 11
Treatment of Drug Addiction

Since the mid-1960s, a number of investigators have attempted to introduce behavior therapy techniques in the treatment of drug addiction. In a comprehensive evaluative review of this work, Gotestam, Melin, and Ost (in press) note that three major approaches may be differentiated: (a) the treatment of drug-taking behavior, (b) the treatment of alternative behaviors, and (c) ward programs. The first approach includes aversion therapies, faradic, chemical, and verbal, and also extinction, classical and covert. In the second, approaches using systematic desensitization, and relaxation, correct conditioning, contingency contracting, and broad spectrum therapy are described. In the last, ward systems using contingency management and token economy are presented.

At the New Jersey Neuropsychiatric Institute, a broad spectrum behavioral approach has been developed, focusing on the treatment of alternative behaviors (Cheek, Sarett, Newell et al., 1967; Cheek, Laucius, Mahncke et al., 1971a; Cheek, Franks, Laucius et al., 1971b; Cheek, Tonarchio, Standen et al., 1973). Addicts are taught a set of behavior modification techniques which improve their social skills so that they may achieve better control over their behavior, cope with their life problems more effectively, and successfully reshape their lives in directions that they choose.

The techniques taught include relaxation, desensitization, self-image training, behavior analysis, behavior control, assertive training, and rational thinking. The program explains why each technique may be useful, shows how to carry it out, and teaches how to handle life problems by the use of particular techniques in particular kinds of situations.

DESCRIPTION OF THE TREATMENT MODEL

The training takes place in eight 1½-hour group sessions meeting twice weekly over a 4-week period. Groups may vary in size from 6 to 20 patients, though 10 or 12 appears best. The sessions include lectures, practice of techniques, role-playing, group discussions, reading of poetry, and homework assignments. All these materials are presented in a training manual which is given to the participant.

Since the sessions are highly structured and much material is presented in each session, it has been found best to have two group leaders for each group. Usually, one will be responsible for the scheduling of sessions, keeping of records, seeing that all material is covered in the time allotted, and also conducting the relaxation exercises. The other will act as the lecturer, presenting material and conducting discussions. Both will conduct private sessions which are routinely introduced at the beginning and end of the program as a check on each participant's understanding of what is going on, and also throughout the program if anyone seems to be having difficulties understanding or making use of the material.

At the Institute, the programs are run on a continuous basis so that as one series of eight sessions is completed another begins. Participants are allowed to enter the program at any meeting and then continue on with the next series. However, prior to such late entry to the program, each new participant is given an orientation, explaining the purposes of the program and the techniques already taught. Indeed, a half-hour orientation explaining the basic purpose of the program and introducing the various techniques always precedes the teaching of the program. Sometimes the muscle relaxation exercise (to be described later) is also offered as part of the orientation.

Then, in the *first* session of the program, relaxation training is formally introduced. The group leader (lecturer) begins by explaining why this kind of training is useful to the patient. It is pointed out that a study at the Institute has shown (Cheek et al., 1967) that addicts characteristically experience a high general level of tension as opposed to other groups of patients and to normals. The patients are told that regular practice of relaxation exercises will enable them to reduce this high general level of tension and thereby improve their personal effectiveness. It is also noted that the relaxation has been found, in this program, to have a secondary beneficial effect of eliminating destructive attitudinal sets, often characteristic of the addict, which combine hostility, resentfulness, mistrust, fearfulness, guilt, and insecurity. Such attitudes color the patient's perceptions of himself and others in a negative fashion, and similarly shape his attitudes and behavior toward others. Freed of them, he becomes open to the additional ideas and techniques taught in the program and is able to develop a more realistic, objective, and positive view of himself and others and correspondingly rational and effective behaviors.

Three kinds of relaxation training are presented. In the *muscle relaxation* procedure, the patients sit back in their chairs, close their eyes, and, as the group leader reads the instructions, tighten, hold, and then loosen the muscles in their feet, legs, hands, arms, stomach, back, chest, neck, and face. They then take two deep breaths, inhaling, holding, and exhaling slowly. Finally, as the group leader counts down from 10 to 1 the addicts bring to their minds, and hold there, a calm scene (to be explained in what follows). On a count of 5, they come slowly up and out of the state of relaxation.

The calm scene has been introduced so that it may become associated with the state of relaxation, and subsequently act as a trigger for this beneficial condition if the patient suddenly finds himself in a tense situation. The calm scene is also used in the desensitization training, to be described later.

The patients are instructed that the calm scene is to be a snapshot picture, in which is included specific details of what is seen, heard, smelled, sensed on the body, as well as a deep inward feeling of relaxation. The calm scene may be a particularly relaxing situation which the addict has enjoyed in the past, such as lying on the beach or walking quietly through the woods, or it may be an ongoing situation—relaxing in the bath at night, in an armchair listening to music, and the like. It is suggested that no person close to the patient be included (as a subsequent argument would remove the effectiveness of the calm scene) and no alcohol, cigarettes, marijuana, and so on (for obvious reasons). The group leader checks that each person has a suitable calm scene.

Two additional forms of relaxation are taught —"lightness," in which the group leader suggests that a feeling of lightness and floating is being experienced in different parts of the body, and "heaviness," in which feelings of warmth and heaviness are suggested.

This session, like all those that follow, concludes with the reading of poetry from the manual, as well as poetry or prose selections brought in by participants to illustrate the material.

Homework assignments are given out at the end of each meeting. Each participant is asked to write out his calm scene, in detail, to increase its vividness for him, and also to write out a low tension scene in preparation for the desensitization procedure of the next session. Participants are also asked to practice the relaxation at least three evenings a week in the ward. It is suggested that they may wish to do this as a group with a tape-recorded relaxation provided by the group leader.

The *second* session focuses on the technique of desensitization. It begins, as do all meetings from now on, with a relaxation exercise. This has been found to provide a positive atmosphere, facilitating learning. The patients are now taught a brief relaxation they may do by themselves, without the group leader, in which they seat themselves comfortably, then progressively tighten and relax the muscles of the feet, legs, hands, arms, back, stomach, neck, face, doing this two times, then take two deep breaths and flash their calm scene, counting down silently from 10 to 1, and coming out on a count of 5. The material of the first meeting is then reviewed and the homework assignment discussed, as in all following meetings.

The group leader now explains why desensitization training, aimed at the reduction of tension in upcoming tense situations, can be useful. It is pointed out that, as a consequence of their past misadventures, addicts have many tension-arousing situations to deal with as they try to rehabilitate themselves—facing a suspicious and hostile family, trying to get a job with a bad past record, and meeting with individuals hostile to former addicts, sometimes strategic figures such as parole or police officers. These situations may act as triggers for acute anxiety. Also, as the patient approaches them he may begin to think about them in a negative way, and thus effectively sensitize himself to them (add on tension). It is pointed out that desensitization is taught, not as a copout, so that the individual does not care about his problems, but rather to help him deal with his problems more effectively, in a calm and therefore rational way. A brief playlet from the training manual is acted out by participants to illustrate this point.

As a preparation for the desensitization training, the patients are now taught to assess their level of tension at any time, on a subjective scale from 0 to 100, so that they may have a way of measuring changes in levels of tension as they use the desensitization procedure. A chart of tension levels in the manual is helpful in this regard. They are asked to assess their tension level at the moment.

In Wolpe's desensitization procedure (Wolpe & Lazarus, 1966), a hierarchy of four or five scenes of graded tension level is employed. In this program, the technique is simplified so that only a high and a low tension scene are used. The patients are asked to work with low tension scenes (60–80) until they have had some practice with the technique, when they may move on to scenes of higher tension. Scenes of lower tension might be being accused of lying, facing a hostile nurse or social worker, and so on. Higher tension scenes (80–100) might be going before a parole board, facing the hostility of an enforcement official, being thrown out of a bar, and the like. The group leader checks that each person has a suitable low tension scene.

Next the technique of desensitization used in the program is demonstrated. The group leader first puts the group into a state of deep relaxation using the muscle relaxant method plus lightness or heaviness (whichever the group prefers). Participants are then asked to bring their tense scene to their minds for 20 seconds (imagined in detail as in the case of a calm scene). Next they are asked to shift to their calm scene for 20 seconds, then back to the tense scene. This is done three or four times. On a count of 5 they come out of the relaxed state.

After the reading of poetry, the group is asked, as a homework assignment, to write a description of a snapshot scene in which the members see themselves functioning in the near future in an effective way in what would ordinarily be a problem situation (as a preparation for the positive-realistic self-image training which is based on Susskind's idealized self-image work; Susskind, 1970). After a self-relaxation and a review of previous material and homework assignments, the rationale for self-image improvement is presented. It is pointed out that the treated alcoholic or addict has before him the difficult task of building a new, non-substance-using identity, probably in the face of hostility from those close to him, and from society in general, as a result of his past misbehaviors, and in the presence of his own tension, anxiety, hostility, and insecurity. If these feelings about himself are evidenced in his nonverbal and verbal behaviors, they will inevitably lead to hostility and rejection by others.

As well as creating disturbances in his "outer theater," these feelings lead the patient to play over past, present, and future negative scenes about himself in his imagination, his "inner theater." By the self-fulfilling prophecy, negative "inner theater" leads to negative "outer theater." Instead of such negative scenes, the patient is asked to begin to visualize positive, but realistic scenes of the near future (so that they may build on small successes) in which, for instance, he warmly greets his family on return from the hospital, presents himself well at a job interview, applies for a college course, and so on.

The group leader asks each member of the group to develop a scene in which they see themselves in the near future, in a realistically possible situation, where they might have anticipated problems but instead are handling themselves effectively. The scene chosen by each participant is checked over for suitability by the group leader.

Now, the positive-realistic self-image technique is demonstrated. Participants are first put into a state of deep relaxation, using the muscle relaxation plus lightness or heaviness, then asked to bring to their minds for 20 seconds an image of themselves as they are at that moment, focusing on their inner feeling of eagerness to grow and change. Next, they are asked to shift to their positive-realistic self-image and hold that for 20 seconds. Finally, they are asked to bring this image to their minds throughout each day, in various kinds of situations, so that it may improve their nonverbal and verbal communications with others.

To further aid the patient in reshaping his self-image positively and realistically, a game called the trade-last game is now played in the group. First, the total group is broken into small groups of six or seven and each group is instructed to chat together for about 5 minutes to become acquainted. Then each participant is given two pieces of paper. On one, the patient is asked to list what he sees as his three most positive personality characteristics (warmth, interest in others, courage). On the other, he is asked to write the name of each person in his group and then what he feels is each person's most positive physical and most positive personality characteristic.

The pieces of paper are then collected and the group leader reads out what each person has said about himself and what the others have said about him.

This simple game, which initially to some participants may seem childish and meaningless, regularly has a very powerful positive effect on the group and the individuals in it. People become more relaxed and friendly with one another and begin to feel good about themselves as they hear the various compliments read out. Later, the group leader will write on the sheet on which each participant has written about himself, what others have said about him. It is regularly observed that those most reluctant to play are most eager to get back the slip of paper with the positive things others have said about them. Many of our female alcoholics and addicts, who have typically very low self-images, have reported this was the most powerful part of the program for them. Indeed, it presents a welcome and marked departure from the kind of negative feedback which is regularly given the patient in a typical encounter or sensitivity group.

The *fourth* meeting begins with a full relaxation, including the muscle relaxation, lightness or heaviness, plus the desensitization and the self-image procedures, followed by the usual brief review of previous meetings and homework assignments.

A transition is now made from inner to outer experience. First, the lecturer explains that the program has begun with a focus on inner experience in the first three meetings because change and growth must begin *inside* the head of the participant. Now that he is calmer and more positive in his view of himself, he may begin to look objectively at his interactions with others—his "outer theater"—to see how his own behavior is influenced negatively by the hostile behavior of others and to see how he, himself, may be unintentionally shaping and maintaining undesirable behavior in others around him. He will now learn to "write his own script" for the outer as well as the inner theater in which he performs.

To help the participant understand how behaviors are shaped and maintained in interaction, he is taught what kinds of rewards are being given with examples: material rewards (e.g., money, clothing, cars), social rewards (e.g., praise, attention, affection), inner rewards (e.g., self-approval, serenity), and immediate versus delayed rewards (e.g., a college degree, proficiency in a sport). Two propositions are offered: "bad behavior produces bad behavior" and "good behavior produces good behavior" which are presented, not as hard-and-fast rules, but as useful guidelines. Several playlets from the training manual are now acted out by the group to illustrate these simple propositions.

In the *fifth* meeting, after the full relaxation and review, participants are taught simple rules for modifying the behavior of others or of themselves, so that they may not be at the mercy of the undesirable behaviors of themselves or others. It is pointed out that frequently used methods of changing undesirable behaviors of others, such as nagging and criticizing, are often unsuccessful. Moreover, even if successful they tend to make the nagger a negative stimulus. Changing one's own behavior also presents problems. It is seldom sufficient simply to decide you will change a bad habit.

Lindsley's technique, "pinpoint, record, and consequate" (Note 2), the basis for this instruction, is described. First, it is pointed out that "think small" is the basic tenet of behavior modification. If one has a dreadful wife, that cannot be worked on. But one can work on the fact that she nags continuously at the dinner table. Each nag can be noted ("pinpointed") and indeed, noted on a piece of paper ("recorded") by the husband for an observation period of 1 week. Then, he may "consequate" by telling his wife he will give her 3 minutes of social conversation after dinner (if that is a meaningful reward for her) on each day that the number of dinner table nags drops by one.

In this program, the patients are taught that the first step is to select a simple, frequently recurring undesirable behavior (like nagging) and its opposite positive behavior (praise), next to decide upon a suitable reward (such as attention), then to indicate to the person whose behavior is to be modified to indicate the negative consequences (the suitable reward or withdrawal of reward).

It is also pointed out that successful behavior modification begins with the modifier himself. To become more effective in this regard, he must increase positive behavior in general toward his target, such as attention, affection, compliments. He must also reward immediately after the target behavior occurs, as that is most effective. It is recommended that he observe the situation for a while and switch to a second reward if the first is not effective.

The patients are told that in a situation involving peers (such as a married couple) it is usually more appropriate to use a "contingency contract." In this method, a husband may, for instance, agree to give up being late for meals if his wife will improve her appearance. A formal contract is written up with bonuses for successful participation and penalties for nonperformance.

"Self-contracting," in which, for instance, the person who wishes to lose weight contracts to himself to reduce his television viewing by ½ hour per day for every 100 calories he goes over his quota for the day, is also described.

The meeting ends with instruction in three social skills which have been found to be very important in shaping and maintaining good social relations: "complimenting" (and how to receive compliments), "criticizing" (and how to receive criticism), and "apologizing" (and how to receive apologies). Specific rules of how to do it and how not to do it in each case are presented, with role-playing sessions acted out by participants.

In the *sixth* meeting, the focus on "outer theater" continues with "assertive training." After the initial procedures (relaxation, etc.) the lecturer discusses with the group the kinds of situations in which underassertive and overassertive behaviors occur (where one has to stand up for one's rights, express positive and negative feelings, etc.), how underassertive and overassertive behaviors are evidenced verbally and nonverbally, what their consequences are, and suggests how these behaviors are learned and maintained. He then offers guidelines for correct assertiveness—the six C's, which are as follows:

1. *Correct* timing.
2. *Keeping* calm.
3. *Considering* the other person's point of view.
4. *Communicating* your own feelings.
5. *Clarifying* how you would like the other person to behave.
6. Stating the negative *consequences* if the negative behavior continues and the positive *consequences* if the opposite positive behavior occurs.

It is pointed out that, using these guidelines, one will not be 100% successful, but will raise one's batting average and increase one's self-respect.

In order to illustrate underassertive, overassertive, and correctly assertive behavior, participants are now asked to play out scenes, either taken from the manual or offered by members of the group. For instance, the group leader may take the part of a wife who is sitting in her robe, drinking a martini, watching television, in an untidy house with no dinner prepared, when her husband comes in 1 hour late, without having called. Various participants will play the role of the under-, over-, or correctly assertive husband with comments from the group regarding both the verbal and nonverbal aspects of their performance.

An additional technique of self-assertion, "absurd communication," is also described. In this technique, the individual uses an indirect method such as humor to assert himself. The young girl forced to come home early by her parents may come in earlier and earlier and finally not go out at all, causing her parents a new kind of consternation. The advantages and possible disadvantages of this method are considered.

The *seventh* meeting is devoted to "rational thinking" based on Albert Ellis' "rational–emotive therapy" (Ellis & Harper, 1961). The lecturer first explains Ellis' basic point that the individual can create and magnify problems by his own thinking about the events of his life. He may "catastrophize" or "terribilize" when some negative event occurs, thinking of all the negative possibilities of the situation. This puts him into such a state of tension and anxiety that he performs ineffectively in the situation.

A technique for handling repetitious, negative thoughts or "brooding" is described; it involves

1. *Relaxation*—going through the brief self-relaxation procedure.
2. *Removing* the negative thought from one's mind.
3. *Replacing* the negative thought from one's mind with the calm scene.
4. *Repeating* the procedure till one is calmed down.
5. *Redirecting* one's thoughts toward a positive outcome of the situation.

Several common errors of thinking described by Ellis are now discussed and examples are elicited from the group. These include dichotomous thinking ("you are either for us or against us"), overgeneralization ("all drug addicts are liars"), stereotyped thinking '("hippies are dirty, untidy, immoral persons"), and so on. Ellis' 11 "rational points of emphasis" are presented. Ellis tells us that these are useful in straightening out our thinking and clearing it of the irrational ideas with which our society indoctrinates us. They include such points as "it is not a dire necessity for an adult to receive love or approval from all significant others," "nearly all instances of unhappiness are due to internal thoughts rather than external events," and so on.

The homework assigned following this meeting includes an evaluation of the program. Participants are asked to indicate the meetings they have most and least enjoyed and why. Also they are asked to fill in a behavior assessment questionnaire which requires them to consider which of several listed problems, including high general level of tension, underassertiveness, low self-image, and so forth, they had before they entered the program, whether the program has been helpful for their problems, and how they plan to use the techniques taught them in the future.

In the *eighth* and final meeting of the program, the basic purpose and content of the program are reviewed and its positive and negative aspects discussed. Then the group is asked which problems they have had, how the program has or has not already been helpful, what kinds of positive things they want to see happen in the future and what problems they might expect to face in the negative things they wish to avoid, and how they might use the techniques of the program to secure the positives and avoid the negatives. This final meeting, bringing it all together and pointing toward the future, has been seen by many participants as the most useful meeting of the program, according to follow-up evaluation questionnaires.

EVALUATION

To examine the usefulness of this approach with addicts, in November 1971 an initial demonstration program was conducted at the New Jersey Neuropsychiatric Institute, in which 29 male and 14 female addicts in the inpatient phase of a methadone maintenance program participated (Cheek et al., 1973). To evaluate the effectiveness of the program, pre- and postprogram measures of anxiety level (Taylor Manifest Anxiety Scale: Taylor, 1953), susceptibility to inner versus outer control (Rotter I–E Scale: Rotter, 1966), self-acceptance (Tennessee Self-Concept Scale: Fitts, 1965), and degree of assertiveness (developed from a series of questions regarding assertiveness in behavior therapy techniques: Wolpe & Lazarus, 1966) were obtained. Reactions to and evaluations of the program were also elicited immediately following the program and 3 months later, by means of questionnaires.

Also, to provide a more objective measure of the effectiveness of the program, it was decided to compare the 6-month outcome of the group taught behavior modification techniques, with that of the group of patients immediately preceding them in the drug treatment unit who had received only the regular program.

Accordingly, 6 months after the patients had completed the behavior modification program, the social workers responsible for checking their progress in the various methadone maintenance clinics around the state were contacted by telephone or by a direct visit to the facility and asked to rate the progress of their patients on a three-point scale as follows:

1. "Successful": Those persons who had adjusted well to the requirements of the program and were making good progress on methadone.
2. "Marginal Adjustment": Those who showed only marginal adjustment but were continuing on the program. This included drinking problems; use of other drugs, such as heroin, barbiturates, and so forth; legal problems; and severe emotional problems.
3. "Failure": Those who had not met the program requirements, had been detoxified, and not reinstated in the program.

This information was obtained for 40 or 43 patients in the program. A similar procedure was carried out with a group of 20 addicts who immediately preceded the treatment group at the drug treatment unit. The outcomes of the treated and untreated groups were compared by chi-square.

Although only a carefully controlled study would provide adequate evaluation, statistically significant changes in the pre- and postprogram test data suggested that the experimental behavior modification program reduced anxiety, improved self-image, and made for more appropriate assertiveness and increased inner control on the part of the addicts with whom we worked.

Moreover, 58% of the behavior-modification-treated group as opposed to 45% of the comparison group were rated successful on follow-up, although this difference was not significant when tested by chi-square. However, it was also noted that the greater the exposure to the program (in terms of number of sessions attended), the greater was the likelihood of successful outcome.

The subjective data lent further support to these findings. The questionnaire responses suggested that the addicts understood the aims of the program and how to carry out the techniques and make use of them in relation to their problems, both before and after leaving the hospital.

Shortly after the program was first developed for drug addicts in November 1971, it was discovered that the training could also be useful to other patient groups such as alcoholics and mentally ill patients, and also that it could be carried out effectively by paraprofessionals. Thus, it was mostly by paraprofessionals, and mainly by volunteers from the community, that during the next 5½ years, 2,612 patients at the Institute, including 1,410 alcoholics, 775 drug addicts, 188 mentally ill patients, and 239 inmates, have been trained in the program.

The patient program has also been adapted for the training of both professional and paraprofessional staff working with various kinds of clients by the addition of a first session which presents an overview of behavior modification and a last session which describes how patient and staff training programs may be set up and conducted (Cheek, Tomarchio, Burtle et al., 1975).

To date, 1,683 staff members, mostly paraprofessionals working with addicts, alcoholics, mentally ill patients, and inmates, including 114 from the New Jersey Neuropsychiatric Institute, 1,169 persons from other facilities in New Jersey, and 400 from facilities in other states, have been trained in the program.

Of these 200 persons have received special Group Leader Certificates from the Department of Health, indicating that they have successfully carried out the New Jersey Neuropsychiatric Institute behavior modification training program at their own facilities.

DISCUSSION

How might one explain the apparent effectiveness and attractiveness of this behavior modification training in self-control with addicts and other groups? In the first place, although there has been a quite appropriately negative reaction to the possible abuse of the external control aspect of behavior modification, there is a growing climate of interest in the use of behavior modification techniques to promote self-control or personal growth. The present program is an early representation of what may become a new approach in treatment, involving *education* of the client in techniques to cope with his life problems on his own. However, this educational approach is seen as an addition to, not a replacement of, more traditional approaches in psychiatry.

Another reason for the success of the self-control approach may be its emphasis on calmness and rationality, as opposed to previous therapeutic approaches, such as sensitivity and encounter methods, which were based on the letting out of emotions, usually explosively.

It is of interest that both approaches offer ways of handling tension—in encounter groups by direct expression, in behavior modification by control with relaxation. Thus, both methods offer a way of handling the extreme tension characteristic of the addict. However, the training in relaxation methods offers a way of getting rid of tension which may be successfully carried over to real-life situations, where, on the other hand, explosive patterns of behavior almost invariably result in being fired from a job, tossed out by one's family, or arrested.

A restrained style is also promoted in the training program by the examination of the consequences of behavior and by the assertive training. Here, for the addict, the emphasis on "cool" offers a useful alternative to the "machismo" philosophy which is part of the cultural heritage of the lower class male and which could lead the addict into fatally aggressive encounters with, for example, police, to protect his male image.

Behavior modification is, indeed, peculiarly suited to the cultural background of addicts and the predominantly paraprofessional staff working with them, many of whom are former addicts. Because of the nonverbal orientation of the lower class to which many addicts belong, this approach appeals in terms of its practicality and directness, emphasizing immediate problem situations and how to handle them, rather than complex and subtle analysis in terms of past experiences.

Another way in which the present approach appeals to the addict derives from the fact that most of the addicts dealt with are in an age group that responds sympathetically to the notion of working within the head. Thus, some saw the relaxation as a form of "meditation," and an effort was made to encourage identification with the youth culture in the language and style of the drug addiction workbook.

CONCLUSION

What problems and limitations have thus far appeared from this approach? Many aspects of this behavior modification training in self-control techniques seem geared to alcoholics and addicts, both as clients and as staff, and our experience to date suggests that professional staff members already trained in other therapeutic theoretical systems and styles of therapy may find difficulties in making the transfer. This is a highly didactic, structured form of group experience that may be uncomfortable for those accustomed to a more free-flowing style. Also, the group leader trained to seek out feelings, particularly hostile ones, and encourage their expression, may find it hard to switch gears and concentrate on control through relaxation and rational assessment of consequences.

Finally, though addicts have responded favorably to the program, two important questions remain: Do they actually use the techniques taught them in the program after they leave the hospital? And if so, does this really contribute to successful outcome? Only a careful comparison study can clarify these matters, a study that reaches into the period of aftercare and provides data regarding the patient's behavior in critical situations. To date, the research data offer only a promising indication that this training in behavior modification techniques, in which the development of self-control is emphasized, is acceptable and useful to addicts and to the staff who work with them.

REFERENCE NOTES

1. Cheek, F. E., Burtle, V., Laucius, J., Powell, D. Franks, C. M., and Albahary, R. *A behavior modification training program for alcoholics and their wives.* Paper presented at the 1971 meeting of the Association for the Advancement of Behavior Therapy, Washington, D.C.
2. Lindsley, O. R. *Behavior modification with families.* Seminar at Temple University, Department of Behavioral Science, Philadelphia, 1968.

REFERENCES

Cheek, F. E., Franks, C. M., & Burtle, V. Towards a behavior modification training program for wives of alcoholics. *Quarterly Journal of Studies on Alcohol,* 1971, *32,* 456–461. (b)

Cheek, F. E., Laucius, J., Mahncke, M., & Beck, R. A behavior modification training program for parents of convalescent schizophrenics. *Advances in behavior therapy*. New York: Academic Press, 1971. (a)

Cheek, F. E., Sarett, M., Newell, S., & Osmond, H. A survey of the experience of tension in alcoholics and other diagnostic groups. *International Journal of Neuropsychiatry*, 1967, *11*, 477–488.

Cheek, F. E., Tomarchio, T., Burtle, V., Moss, H., and McConnell, D. A behavior modification training program for staff working with drug addicts. *International Journal of Addictions*, 1975, *10*, 1074–1101.

Cheek, E. F., Tomarchio, T., Standen, J., and Albahary, R. Methadone plus—A behavior modification training program in self-control for addicts on methadone maintenance. *International Journal of Addictions*, 1973, *8*, 969–996.

Ellis, A., & Harper, R. *A guide to rational living*. Englewood Cliffs, New Jersey: Prentice-Hall, 1961.

Fitts, W. H. *Tennessee self-concept scale manual*. Nashville, Tennessee: Counselor Recordings and Tests, 1965.

Gotesman, K. G., Melin, L., & Ost, L. G. Behavioral techniques in the treatment of drug abuse: An evaluative review. *Addictive Behavior*, in press.

Rotter, J. B. Generalized expectancies for internal versus external control of reinforcement. *Psychological Monographs: General and Applied*, 1966, *80*, 1–28.

Susskind, D. The idealized self-image (ISI): A new technique in confidence training. *Behavior Therapy*, 1970, *1*, 538–541.

Taylor, J. A. A personality scale of manifest anxiety. *Journal of Abnormal and Social Psychology*, 1953, *48*, 285–290.

Wolpe, J., & Lazarus, A. A. *Behavior therapy techniques*. Oxford: Pergamon, 1966.

PART IV

Treatment of Psychophysiologic Disorders

Carole Kirkpatrick,
Kevin McGovern,
and Joseph LoPiccolo

Chapter 12
Treatment of Sexual Dysfunction

Although sexuality comes in many cultural wrappings, no society can successfully ignore its members' sexual expression. And, just as people must be concerned with the interface between sex and life, so have they been concerned with
the problems engendered by their sex lives.[1] For instance, there is recorded as
early as 1400 B. C. a prescription of massive doses of tiger testicles for impo-
tence. While the causes and types of difficulties may vary from drinking camel
froth for sterility to a weekend at Sandstone for marital boredom, there is presumably no society devoid of sexual problems. Historically, however, Western
society has been reluctant to acknowledge this fact. Sex therapy as a specialty
was virtually unknown in the first half of this century and was practiced largely
by analysts who saw their patient's problems as only surface expressions of
childhood conflicts. For instance, a sexually assertive woman would be considered to be suffering from penis envy and an impotent male would be said to be
suffering from unconscious incestual guilt. Thus traditionally sexual concerns, if
acknowledged at all, were not directly treated.

Eventually, however, these assumptions were challenged. The first credita-
ble sex researchers to challenge the analytic point of view publicly were, of
course, Masters and Johnson. Not only did they claim that sexual problems were
indeed widespread (an estimated 50% of couples) but Masters and Johnson
advocated the "revolutionary" stance of taking the sexual problem at face value.
And, through the use of prescribed "homework" assignments, they supplied
impressive evidence of treatment success. Additional features of the Masters and

---

[1]The term "sex life" in fact is a curious one, indicating both the major role of sex in life and yet
implying that sex can exist separate from the rest of one's life.

Parts of this chapter are excerpted from an earlier paper by the same authors: A behavioral group
treatment program for sexually dysfunctional couples, *Journal of Marriage and Family Counseling*,
1976, 2, 397–404. Reprinted with permission of the publishers.

Johnson (1970) approach were the use of cotherapists of the opposite gender, a treatment ban on intercourse, and the use of sensate focusing exercises. Although some features of this original format have been modified by other researchers,[2] the basic assumption—that sexual behavior is *learned* and therefore subject to *direct* modification—remains the hallmark of social learning or behavioral approaches to sexual dysfunctions.

GROUP APPROACHES TO TREATMENT

Recent publications have established that couples with sexual dysfunctions can be successfully treated through behaviorally oriented therapy programs (Masters & Johnson, 1970; LoPiccolo & Lobitz, 1972; Kaplan, 1974; Kohlenberg, 1974). Treatment is typically carried out by male and female cotherapists, meeting with the dysfunctional couple for 15 to 20 sessions. Through these programs, clients with erectile failure, premature ejaculation, and orgasmic difficulties receive communication and skills training aimed at teaching more adaptive patterns of sexual behavior. The overall efficacy of these treatment programs for sexually dysfunctional couples has been demonstrated, and the treatment procedures have been described elsewhere (Masters & Johnson, 1970; LoPiccolo & Lobitz, 1972, McGovern, Stewart, & LoPiccolo, 1975; Snyder, LoPiccolo, & LoPiccolo, 1975).

The most frequently noted drawback to these programs, however, is that the modification of sexual behavior can be expensive (for the client) and time-consuming (for the therapist). One solution would be to treat dysfunctional clients in a group setting, thereby treating more people in a less costly format. In fact, it would appear that sexual problems are ideally suited to group treatment because (a) a limited number of problems are shared by a large number of people,[3] (b) treatment procedures remain relatively constant for any one particular problem, and (c) treatment is usually time-limited with specific behavioral goals that can be easily tracked by multiple participants.

At this point in time, though, there is very little evidence available to indicate that the behavioral techniques employed in sexual treatment programs can be applied to group settings.

Some investigators have reported success with groups designed for single individuals or persons whose partners do not wish to be involved. For instance, Romano (1973) reported on the successful group treatment of spinal injured patients. The University of California School of Medicine at San Francisco has one of the largest reported offerings of groups: preorgasmic women's groups, gay groups, men without partners groups, and bisexual groups (Mann, 1975;

[2]Kaplan (1974), for example, reports that solo therapists achieve comparable results.

[3]For example, it has been estimated that 28% of married women in this country have never had an orgasm (Kinsey, Pomeroy, Martin, & Gebhard, 1953). Likewise, many men have trouble with premature ejaculation as evidenced by Kinsey's figures that 75% of men ejaculate in less than 2 minutes (Kinsey et al., 1953).

Vandervoort & Blank, 1975; Barbach, 1974; Zilbergeld, 1975). These authors report a high degree of satisfaction with these groups including extrasexual benefits in terms of self-esteem and confidence, less rigid sex role expectations, generally improved happiness, and so on (Wallace & Barbach, 1974; Zilbergeld, 1975), but very little outcome or follow-up data regarding sexual performance are presented. With the exception of Vandervoort and Blank's (1975) brief description, there are no reports in the literature of behaviorally based group treatment programs for couples. And, although these authors call the work "promising," they suggest that finding couples who want to be in a group at the same time is too time-consuming.

THE DEVELOPMENT OF A GROUP TREATMENT PROGRAM

By 1973, the University of Oregon Psychology Clinic had been offering a behaviorally oriented treatment and research program for sexually dysfunctional couples for about 3 years. Therapy was done by male–female cotherapy teams seeing individual couples, usually for a 15-week period. Treatment included the use of homework assignments, daily record forms (on which couples described their homework sessions), and follow-up evaluations. This treatment program, like other behavioral approaches, had proven highly successful, especially for women who had never had an orgasm and men who complained of premature ejaculation. At this time it occurred to the authors that, if our program was so successful with individual couples, why not increase our efficiency by treating several couples simultaneously and thereby reduce our long waiting list? Since our program was time-limited, behaviorally focused, and employed relatively standard treatment procedures, it appeared ideally suited to modification for a group format. Thus began the development of a group treatment model.

The first question was who to include in the group—couples who share the same sexual problem or couples who are similar in other ways (such as life-style, education, age). The shared-problem approach was chosen because our treatment is predominantly a problem-centered one. Although other group programs are based on life-style rather than problem similarity (Vandervoort & Blank, 1975), our hypothesis was that a shared problem would provide a powerful common bond among couples.

The second issue to be faced was the incentive that should be offered to try a new treatment program. We anticipated that couples would be reluctant initially to talk about sex with other unknown couples. However, considering our lengthy waiting list, the one advantage a group could offer is reduced waiting time. Thus, if a couple was willing to forego individual therapists, they would receive treatment 3 to 12 months sooner.

Basic to our model of group treatment was the development of various group treatment procedures. The procedures outlined herein served many over-lapping functions, but basically were designed to (a) develop group rapport of a common bond among participants; (b) facilitate sharing, both of problems and effective solutions; (c) reduce anxiety; (d) increase communication skills within each couple; and (e) facilitate collective problem-solving.

Thus, a number of treatment techniques were adapted or designed specifically for the group treatment program. Those treatment components unique to the group treatment mode, as opposed to individual therapy, are briefly described:

1. Warm-Up Exercises.   Several activities were constructed to get participants acquainted and feel at ease with each other. Such activities were done at the beginning of the session, and included

    a. Group Milling: Members walked around ("milled") and either ver-bally or nonverbally greeted each other. After a period of this greeting activity, participants then exchanged one written piece of information about themselves to another group member (e.g., "I like drag races," "I was born in New York"). Verbal conversation between pairs en-sued.
    b. Blind trust walk: People paired off and one person led the other per-son who was blindfolded through various experiences. The therapists usually arranged the pairing off so spouses would be partners.
    c. Hopes and fears exercise: The participants wrote each of his or her hopes and fears pertaining to the group experience on index cards. The cards were collected, shuffled, and then read out loud to the group, accompanied by group discussion.

2. Relaxation Training.   Group members were taught deep muscle relaxation in the group and were given a relaxation tape to take home for further use.
3. Roundtable Procedure.   At each group meeting, the four couples would take turns giving a 5-minute overview of their weekly activities. This pro-vided an opportunity to share common cognitive, emotional, and behavioral reactions of the previous session or homework assignments.
4. Behavioral Rehearsal.   Many problems shared by all couples, or specific to one couple, were worked on by direct behavioral rehearsal. For example, if one or more couples had difficulty initiating or refusing sexual interactions, then all persons in turn would be directed to address their partner, giving several initiation and refusal responses and receiving their partner's feed-back. Also, if a couple had experienced a specific problematic situation during the week, the therapists would reconstruct a similar scene for the group and let each couple role-play their "solution." These role-play proce-dures are described in detail elsewhere (LoPiccolo & Miller, 1975).
5. Subgroups.   In order to deal with issues not shared by the whole group, the

group was occasionally subdivided into male and female halves or two couples with each therapist. The smallness and homogeneity of such subgroups fostered much personal sharing.

APPLICATION OF THE MODEL

A group of four couples was run by the authors as a preliminary test of our treatment model. The overall success of this program demonstrates that a behaviorally oriented group approach to sexual dysfunctions shows promise as an equally effective and efficient alternative to individual treatment.

Since treatment procedures for women with primary inorgasmic dysfunctions and men with premature ejaculation have already been well established (Masters & Johnson, 1970; LoPiccolo & Lobitz, 1972), four couples with these presenting problems were selected from our treatment program's waiting list. Of the eight individuals, the four females were primary inorgasmic and three of the males were considered premature ejaculators. A primary inorgasmic woman is one who has not experienced an orgasm through any mode of physical stimulation (i.e., masturbation, oral stimulation, or intercourse). Prematurely ejaculating men often reach orgasms several seconds before or after vaginal penetration.

Each couple came in for a standard screening interview conducted by the authors. The purpose of this interview was to assess the couple's current sexual functioning and to explain the group program. In this explanation, the therapists emphasized the need to learn new behavioral skills and communication patterns. The first four couples interviewed were considered acceptable for treatment and agreed to the group method. Although homogeneous with respect to their sexual problems, the couples were heterogeneous regarding demographic characteristics of age, education, number of children, and life-styles. For example, the oldest couple were in their 40s, had been married 17 years, had two children, and were religiously active; whereas the youngest couple were in their 20s, had lived together 3 years, had no children, and professed no religious beliefs.

Prior to the start of group treatment, each couple completed the standard assessment package, consisting of:

1. A general background information form assessing current sexual attitudes and behaviors.
2. The Sexual Interaction Inventory, an assessment device which gives couples specific ratings of current sexual satisfaction across a variety of dimensions (LoPiccolo & Steger, 1974).
3. The Locke–Wallace Marital Adjustment Test, used in order to provide an index of marital satisfaction as a whole.

Each couple was asked to complete the assessment package 2 weeks prior to treatment, at termination, and at a follow-up point 6 months after termination. Thus, data at three points in time are available for all couples except one who did not respond to our follow-up request.

The treatment program consisted of 15 3-hour evening group sessions. The first 13 sessions were held on a weekly basis; the last two sessions were spread over a 6-week period to maximize the fading of treatment into self-directed maintenance.

The therapists provided the couples with an informal atmosphere. The clients were encouraged to dress informally and sit on cushions placed on the floor. After the first 90 minutes of each session, there was a 15- to 20-minute coffee break. The therapists used this time to consult with the observers. With this information, the therapists decided if it was necessary to make program changes for the second part of the training session.

At the end of each group session, the therapists gave the four couples their weekly homework assignments. The couples kept detailed records of their assignments on prepared data sheets. These records were collected 6 hours prior to the next treatment session to aid the therapists in planning treatment strategies for the next session.

The primary focus of the group treatment was to change the orgasmic responses of the men and women by improving couple communications and sexual skills. Accordingly, all couples were taught principles of constructive feedback, were given sexual topics to discuss and explore during the week (e.g., fantasy, turn-ons, and erotic literature), and were assigned various practice exercises in initiating, mood setting, and nonverbal communication. In addition, each person completed individual assignments during the week. The women followed the 9-step masturbation program (see LoPiccolo & Lobitz, 1972, for further details) to increase the probability of orgasmic response, while the men were taught to control their ejaculatory latency through the use of the squeeze and pause techniques. All couples also followed a progressive series of sensate focusing exercises.

The data displayed in Table 1 demonstrate that the group therapy program was effective in changing the sexual behavior of the three premature ejaculators. The fourth male reported a 30-minute latency during the program.

As can also be seen in Table 1, dramatic increases in female orgasmic performance took place during treatment. Mean responses are given because all four women performed similarly. By the end of treatment all four females were orgasmic 100% of the time in masturbation. In addition, each woman reported experiencing an orgasm with penile insertion and concomitant manual stimulation on at least two consecutive occasions. The percentage of orgasmic response is lower for genital caressing and intercourse than masturbation. It was expected that greater stimulus generalization would occur over time with continued practice. However, the follow-up data do not demonstrate that the high frequency of orgasmic response learned through masturbation had sufficiently generalized to

Table 1
Pre, Post, and Follow-Up Mean Scores on Sexual Response Items

Sexual response	Pre	Post	Follow-up	
1. Male's ejaculatory latency	3	8	8	Male 1
(minutes of continuous	3	8	7	Male 2
intromission)	3	11	5	Male 3
	30	30	30	Male 4
2. Female orgasmic response (percentage of time orgasmic)				
a. In masturbation	0	100	92	
b. Through manual stimulation	0	81	60	
c. In intercourse	0	75	33	
3. Duration of foreplay (minutes)	7	18	10	
4. Frequency of intercourse (times per month)	5	10	5	

Note. $n = 4$ females, 4 males.

intercourse. Increases during treatment in the length of foreplay and frequency of intercourse are also evident in Table 1.

The couples' responses to the Sexual Interaction Inventory (Figure 1) and the Locke–Wallace Inventory (Table 2) demonstrated, in addition, that the group treatment was effective not only in changing the couples' general level of sexual satisfaction but also their reported marital happiness.

Although the major goals of the group treatment program were met by each of the four couples, several of the follow-up data suggest some behavioral regression following termination. Already noted was the low female orgasmic generalization. Likewise, the amount of time spent in foreplay activities and the frequency of intercourse decreased after the program terminated (Table 1). Similar trends following termination were observed in other treatment measures,

Table 2
Pre, Post, and Follow-Up Scores on Locke–Wallace Marital Adjustment Inventory

	Pre	Post	Follow-up
Mean	96.12	116.25a	109.42b
SD	11.75	15.97	9.79

Note. $n = 8$.
a Pre–post t test $= 2.77$ ($p \leq .05$, one-tailed).
b Pre–follow-up t test $= 2.45$ ($p \leq .05$, one-tailed).

Figure 1

SEXUAL INTERACTION INVENTORY
Pre, Post, and Follow-Up Mean Scores

N=4 couples

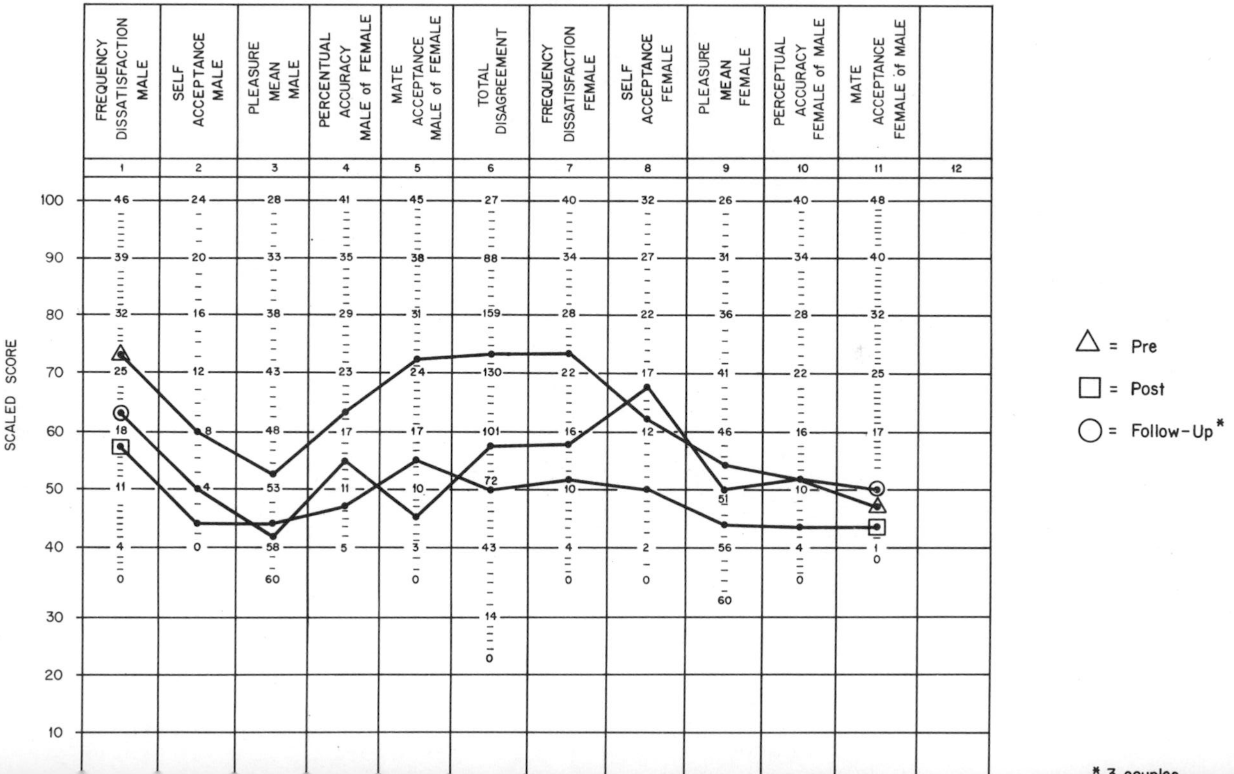

△ = Pre
□ = Post
○ = Follow-Up*

* 3 couples

178

including the Sexual Interaction Inventory (Figure 1). However, in terms of self-reported satisfaction with the quality of sex at follow-up, all couples remained at termination levels of satisfaction—either 5 or 6 on a six-point scale of sexual satisfaction.

DISCUSSION

The results of this preliminary report suggest that the group treatment program for sexually dysfunctional couples is an effective mode of treatment. Furthermore, group treatment may have some significant advantages over individual treatment. First of all, the presence of other couples seemed to act as a disinhibitor, rather than as a stimulus for anxiety. Our couples reported feeling more comfortable knowing that others had similar problems. Couples may also feel less pressure in a group setting since the therapists do not focus solely on them. In addition, the more informal structure afforded by the group may be more comparable to clients' other experiences with organizational groups, class discussions, and the like. For many of our clients, individual therapy would be a novel experience, creating anxiety regarding social norms.

The presence of other couples also seemed to have a powerful modeling effect in our group. As therapists, we were impressed with the ease of teaching alternative behaviors via role-playing and behavior rehearsal. In fact, each couple developed proficient behavior rehearsal skills. During some sessions the couples would model alternative interactions for the other couples. On other occasions, a couple would mirror or replicate the dysfunctional or constructive behaviors of another couple. Through these procedures, the couples observed, practiced, and incorporated new patterns of interaction.

The presence of other couples also seemed to produce more rapid attitude change. This change was seen most dramatically in the group division by sex. For the women especially, having the opportunity to share thoughts and feelings with three other women like themselves, produced rapid attitude change toward their own sexuality. Within 3 weeks women who had never experienced orgasm or sexual arousal were sharing fantasies, noticing genital sensations, enjoying masturbation, and were eagerly looking at nude males displayed in magazines.

In summary, the group treatment program seemed to have afforded some distinct advantages over individual treatment. The camaraderie, modeling, and opportunity for disclosure with peers made possible a therapeutic climate that was safe, supportive, and conducive to rapid attitude and behavior change.

Although our group was surprisingly free of competitiveness, romantic entanglements between different spouses, reluctance to self-disclosure in front of strangers, or strong personal dislikes, these are important issues to consider,

Fig. 1   Sexual Interaction Inventory

especially for couples with sensitive sexual problems. These common problems that often hamper group therapy were avoided through careful preplanning sessions. Prior to each therapy meeting, the therapists and observers carefully read each couple's daily record forms. After reviewing these forms, the therapists developed a treatment plan for the next therapeutic session, carefully structuring activities to maximize positive feelings and constructive problem-solving.

In addition, the authors recognized that each couple would demonstrate different rates of therapeutic progress. In order to discourage competitiveness or fear of failing, the therapists met individually with one of the couples each week for half an hour before the general group session. During these brief sessions, the therapists dealt with any issues that were impeding the couple's progress. In no case, however, did the therapist give different homework assignments to any of the couples. Each couple was expected to continue with the regular weekly assignments. However, some of the couples were encouraged to repeat a number of their past assignments.

CONCLUSION

One of the more intriguing issues raised by this study is whether group therapy can be too powerful. Is it possible that the couples' changes in attitude and behavior may have been affected more by the group process, rather than a product of a new husband and wife relationship? Is it possible that after the group disbanded, the primary source of reinforcement was withdrawn? This hypothesis is consonant with the regression effect observed at follow-up. Although maintenance was maximized through the construction of maintenance lists, lessening the directiveness of therapy, and fading out treatment over a number of weeks, the follow-up data revealed that the couples were not spending as much time in sexual activities.

Once the program was terminated, each couple lost an important source of continuous reinforcement. As one couple reported when the group did not meet one week, "This has been the highlight of our week. We didn't know what to do without the group." This loss of support and encouragement may largely account for the regression effect. The fact that attendance and camaraderie were extremely high also supports this hypothesis. If the same effect is observed in other programs utilizing a group treatment approach, alterations of the treatment procedures are suggested, and perhaps a more comprehensive maintenance program should be established.

On the other hand, some behavioral regression is to be expected as well as the fact that measures of frequency and foreplay often do not correspond to the subjective experience of sexual satisfaction. At this point there is no basis for choosing one interpretation over the other. Whether the behavioral regression at follow-up represents a natural settling from the "high" of termination or represents a deficit in the treatment maintenance procedures can only be answered by subsequent investigation.

In addition, the question of efficiency as opposed to efficacy is somewhat unresolved. Mean therapist time per session was 6 hours per therapist, as compared with an average of 3 hours per session when seeing a couple individually. However, considering the lack of previously established group treatment procedures, this allocation of resources was not excessive. A major portion of the therapists' time was spent carefully designing, discussing, and debriefing each treatment session. Additionally, it is not known what effects reducing group sessions to 2 hours would have had. Research is currently underway to reduce the amount of therapist time spent in group treatment. Hopefully, these studies will shed new light on a promising treatment approach.

REFERENCES

Barbach, I. Group treatment of preorgasmic women. *Journal of Sex and Marital Therapy*, 1974, *1*, 139–145.

Kaplan, H. *The new sex therapy*. New York: Brunner/Mazel, 1974.

Kinsey, A., Pomeroy, W., Martin, C., & Gebhard, P. *Sexual behavior in the human female*. Philadelphia: Saunders, 1953.

Kohlenberg, R. Directed masturbation and the treatment of primary orgasmic dysfunction. *Archives of Sexual Behavior*, 1974, *3*, 349–356.

Lobitz, W. C., & LoPiccolo, J. New methods in the behavioral treatment of sexual dysfunction. *Journal of Behavior Therapy and Experimental Psychiatry*, 1973, *3*, 265–271.

LoPiccolo, J., & Lobitz, W. C. The role of masturbation in the treatment of orgasmic dysfunction. *Archives of Sexual Behavior*, 1972, *2*, 163–171.

LoPiccolo, J., & Miller, V. A program for enhancing the sexual relationship for normal couples. *Counseling Psychologist*, 1975, *5*, 41–46.

LoPiccolo, J., & Steger, J. The Sexual Interaction Inventory: A new instrument for assessment of sexual dysfunction. *Archives of Sexual Behavior*, 1974, *3*, 585–595.

Mann, J. Is sex counseling here to stay? *Counseling Psychologist*, 1975, *5*, 60–64.

Masters, W., & Johnson, V. *Human sexual inadequacy*. Boston: Little, Brown, 1970.

McGovern, K., Stewart, R., & LoPiccolo, J. Secondary orgasmic dysfunction. I: Analyses and strategies for treatment. *Archives of Sexual Behavior*, 1975, *4*, 265–276.

Romano, M. Sexual counseling in groups. *Journal of Sex Research*, 1973, *9*, 69–78.

Snyder, A., LoPiccolo, L., & LoPiccolo, J. Secondary orgasmic dysfunction. II: Case study. *Archives of Sexual Behavior*, 1975, *4*, 277–84.

Vandervoort, H., & Blank, J. A sex counseling program in a university medical center. *Counseling Psychologist*, 1975, *5*, 64–66.

Wallace, D., & Barbach, L. Preorgasmic group treatment. *Journal of Sex and Marital Therapy*, 1974, *1*, 146–154.

Zilbergeld, B. Group treatment of sexual dysfunction in men without partners. *Journal of Sex and Marital Therapy*, 1975, *1*, 204–214.

Margaret A. Chesney

Chapter 13
Treatment of Dysmenorrhea

Dysmenorrhea, or pain during menstruation, is one of the most frequent complaints in medicine. Upon examining the literature, the reported incidence of dysmenorrhea in women of childbearing ages varies from 25 to 80% depending on the criteria used. The painful nature and prevalence of this problem serve to suggest that the economic, social, and, most important, the psychological costs of dysmenorrhea are considerable.

There are two major classifications of dysmenorrhea. This chapter focuses on a treatment for *primary dysmenorrhea,* menstrual pain occurring in the absence of pathological conditions in the pelvic organs. *Secondary dysmenorrhea,* on the other hand, is menstrual pain that results from organic pelvic disorders.

This chapter presents first a brief literature review regarding the etiology and treatment of primary dysmenorrhea (hereafter referred to simply as dysmenorrhea). Then the author's behavioral group treatment of dysmenorrhea is described in detail. Finally, the limitations of this treatment and future directions for dysmenorrhea study and treatment are discussed.

LITERATURE REVIEW

Dysmenorrhea is described both as short episodes of cramplike abdominal pains and prolonged dull aching pains throughout the body. Accompanying these pains may also be such symptoms as nausea, headache, irritability, and gastrointestinal disturbances. Research examining the etiology of these symptoms presents a number of contradictory explanations. However, there is general agreement that a combined psychological and physiological approach to the study of dysmenorrhea should be considered (Paulson & Wood, 1966).

Research exploring the physiological causes of dysmenorrhea has presented various findings and hypotheses involving muscular, hormonal, ischemic, and mineral corticoid explanations. Recently, several of these hypotheses have been integrated in a theory presented by Dalton (1969) which argues that, "There are two very different and, in fact, opposite types of dysmenorrhea, known as *spasmodic* and *congestive*" (p. 39).

Spasmodic dysmenorrhea, according to Dalton, is spasms of acute pain beginning on the first day of menstruation. This pain is so severe as frequently to cause vomiting and fainting. Also, the pain is limited strictly to the sections of the body controlled by the uterine or ovarian nerves, that is, the back, inner sides of the thighs, and lower abdomen.

Congestive dysmenorrhea, the opposite type, is a variation of the premenstrual syndrome. It should be noted that the term "premenstrual syndrome" or "premenstrual tension" has been applied to a wide variety of psychological symptoms which most commonly occur a few days *before* the first day of menstruation, but which may continue into the first day of the menstrual cycle (see Parlee, 1973, for a review of the literature).

Many women with premenstrual syndrome do not have congestive dysmenorrhea, but women with congestive dysmenorrhea usually experience some of the symptoms of premenstrual syndrome. The woman with congestive dysmenorrhea has advance warning of menstruation for several days. During this time, she may experience increasing heaviness and a dull, aching pain in the lower abdomen, as well as in other areas of the body including the ankles and breasts. This pain may be accompanied by nausea, lack of appetite, backache, and such psychological symptoms as lethargy, depression, and irritability.

Dalton has suggested that these two types of primary dysmenorrhea are related to imbalances between the circulating ovarian hormones, estrogen and progesterone. Women with relative elevation of their progesterone levels are likely to suffer from spasmodic dysmenorrhea. Consistent with Dalton's theory, research in this field has drawn a relationship between a relative excess of progesterone and a hypertonic cervical os (cervical opening with excessive muscular tension) (Tindall, 1971). It has been proposed that the cramplike pains of spasmodic dysmenorrhea are the result of uterine contractions attempting to force the menstruation through this hypertonic cervical os (Davis, 1964; Mann, 1963; Tindall, 1971).

Those women with a relative elevation of their estrogen levels are likely to suffer from the opposite type of dysmenorrhea, congestive dysmenorrhea. Dalton argues that this relative lack of progesterone is related to an imbalance in the corticosteroids. Thus, according to Dalton's hypothesis, premenstrual syndrome and congestive dysmenorrhea symptoms are the result of corticosteroid imbalance rather than a direct result of the reduction in progesterone. It is thought that this corticosteroid imbalance may lead to water retention resulting in the pain of congestive dysmenorrhea. A consistent expansion of Dalton's hypothesis has been put forth by Janowsky, Berens, and Davis (1973), who suggest that organic factors related to the renin–angiotensin–aldosterone system may be involved in premenstrual tension (aldosterone is a corticosteroid). Since congestive dysmenorrhea can be described as a premenstrual tension, the same etiology may be involved.

The importance of determining which of these two types of dysmenorrhea a woman may have is emphasized by Dalton. The therapy for each type, usually hormonal, is quite different; indeed, if the wrong hormone is given, the pain may be exacerbated rather than alleviated. Dalton made her differential diagnoses by clinical interview. Based on Dalton's criteria, a psychometric instrument, the Menstrual Symptom Questionnaire (MSQ), has been developed to differentiate between the two types of primary dysmenorrhea (Chesney & Tasto, 1975b). The MSQ consists of 25 items describing symptoms of dysmenorrhea. Scoring is weighted so that high MSQ scores reflect a symptom constellation characteristic of spasmodic dysmenorrhea, whereas low scores reflect a symptom constellation characteristic of congestive dysmenorrhea. Factor analysis of this questionnaire has revealed two clearly distinct factors which defined congestive and spasmodic dysmenorrhea consistent with the literature. When administered to a group of dysmenorrheic women, the ranked total scores revealed a continuous dimension within the higher scores (spasmodic) and within the lower scores (congestive), but a large hiatus existed between these polar dimensions. This pattern of scores, the reliability of the items ($r = .78$, test –retest), and the extraction of the two factors all suggest that the Menstrual Symptom Questionnaire is a psychometric capable of differentiating between the two proposed types of primary dysmenorrhea. These questionnaire results strengthen the contention that there are two types of dysmenorrhea and indirectly lend support to the hormonal imbalance theory. The Menstrual Symptom Questionnaire and instructions for its administration are available in the literature (Chesney & Tasto, 1975b).

In light of the commonly held view that hormonal imbalances play a major role in the etiology of spasmodic and congestive dysmenorrhea, hormonal therapy has become one of the most prevalent forms of treatment for this disorder. This practice is buttressed by its effectiveness, but is not universally advocated in light of the side effects (e.g., pulmonary embolism, thrombophlebitis, cerebral thrombosis, and neuroocular lesions) and nuisances (e.g., weight gain, nausea, and breast changes) which may accompany use (Tyler, 1973). Other treatments are being explored since the incidence of these side effects and nuisances is high.

Psychological treatments for dysmenorrhea have been explored because the psychological dimension has seemed particularly potent in light of the cultural taboos and the myths linked to menstruation. Consistent with this view of psychological components of dysmenorrhea, several psychological treatments have been shown to be effective, including hypnotherapy, psychodynamic therapy, and, most recently, behavior therapy (Mullen, 1968; Reich, 1972; Tasto & Chesney, 1974; Chesney & Tasto, 1975a).

In the first reported application of behavior therapy to dysmenorrhea, Mullen (1968) successfully treated a 37-year-old woman who had suffered from severe menstrual cramps (spasmodic dysmenorrhea) for 21 years. He used systematic desensitization with an anxiety hierarchy of items ranging from the end of the previous menstrual period to the day the menstrual period was to begin. Later, in a controlled study, Mullen (Note 1) used hierarchies to successfully treat five college students who had suffered from dysmenorrhea for 7 to 10 years. Students who received the systematic desensitization reported a significant reduction in symptoms whereas a control group did not.

Reich (1972) treated 12 women who had dysmenorrhea, using a group systematic desensitization focused on menstruation. These women were classified as either having high or low anxiety with the Taylor Manifest Anxiety Scale. Reich found that the low anxiety subjects benefited most from the treatment. Unfortunately, the relationship between anxiety and dysmenorrhea is not resolved by this study. It is possible that anxiety does not play a major role in dysmenorrhea and that the relaxation integral in the systematic desensitization was responsible for the treatment's effectiveness. High anxiety may have interfered with the relaxation and decreased treatment benefit for these subjects.

Using muscle relaxation training, Tasto and Chesney (1974) treated seven college students in a group for primary dysmenorrhea. Rather than utilize anxiety hierarchies, women in this program were trained in muscle relaxation and then instructed to imagine scenes associated with menstrual pain reduction. A significant reduction in symptoms was found on the Symptom Rating Scale (Mullen, Note 1) and the Menstrual Activities Scale (developed for the study).

None of these behavioral studies differentiated between spasmodic and congestive dysmenorrhea. If the discomfort of spasmodic dysmenorrhea is related to muscular contractions whereas the menstrual pain of congestive dysmenorrhea is related to water retention, then behavior therapy and muscle relaxation should be a more effective treatment for spasmodic dysmenorrhea. Chesney and Tasto (1975a) tested this hypothesis in a controlled behavioral study utilizing muscle relaxation combined with imagery associated with menstrual onset. Their study indicated that this regimen was highly effective in reducing symptoms of women having MSQ-defined spasmodic dysmenorrhea. Conversely, this approach was not effective in reducing the symptomatology of women suffering with MSQ-defined congestive dysmenorrhea.

THE DEVELOPMENT OF A GROUP TREATMENT PROGRAM

Based on the foregoing research review, the following treatment program has been developed and has been found to be effective for women with spasmodic dysmenorrhea.

Screening.   Prior to treatment, all clients are given a physical examination to verify that their dysmenorrhea is not due to a pelvic disorder. It is also advisable to have the physician discuss the method of birth control the woman may be using. This is suggested since intrauterine devices can cause dysmenorrhea; or if the woman is taking oral contraceptives, a change in prescription may alter her estrogen and progesterone levels and eliminate the dysmenorrhea.

Women diagnosed as having primary dysmenorrhea by the physician then complete the MSQ to ascertain whether their complaints reflect the spasmodic or congestive pattern. In the administration of the MSQ, it is important to stress to clients that they take care to indicate that they experience only those symptoms that they actually have, not symptoms they believe to be characteristic of dysmenorrhea but do not actually have. There is some clinical evidence that when this instruction is not stressed, scores on the MSQ may not clearly define a woman as having spasmodic or congestive dysmenorrhea.

After the women complete the MSQ, those with congestive dysmenorrhea should be advised that the treatment is not appropriate for them. Women with spasmodic dysmenorrhea begin their treatment by attending an intake interview with the therapist. The primary purpose of this interview is to determine the woman's appropriateness for group or individual therapy. With regard to history, the following information is obtained:

1. Age of first menstruation.
2. Preparation for and attitude toward menstruation.
    Age of first dysmenorrheic symptoms.
4. Explanation given for dysmenorrhea at menarche and now.
5. Brief sexual history.
6. Effect of dysmenorrhea on daily life.
7. Attempts to treat dysmenorrhea (heating pads, medication, etc.).
8. Description of other physical and psychosomatic complaints.
9. Description of any other current physical, chemical, or psychological therapies.
10. Any other concerns for which the assistance of a psychologist might be appropriate.

Since group and individual therapy are essentially identical, treating women in groups is a more efficient use of therapist time. However, there are conditions which may become apparent during the history taking which suggest exclusion of a woman from group treatment. Very high anxiety associated with menstruation or discussion of menstruation is one example of a condition for which exclusion would be advised. Another example, high secondary gain associated with dysmenorrhea, is frequently found when women describe having multiple physical and psychosomatic complaints in addition to the dysmenorrhea. It is most important to note that, inconsistent with a widely held belief, fabricated, exaggerated, or attention-seeking complaints of menstrual pain are actually very rare in the author's clinical experience.

At the end of the intake interview, women are asked to complete the Symptom Severity Scale (Chesney & Tasto, 1975a) which provides a self-report measure of the severity of dysmenorrhea symptoms during the last menstrual period. This scale is administered so that the client's status prior to treatment is available for later assessment of therapeutic effectiveness.

As implied, this treatment program can be performed with either individuals or groups of women since the procedures and exercises are the same. There is little group interaction in this treatment so that group size is usually determined by the number of recliners which can be comfortably placed in a therapy room. Owing to the sensitive nature of the treatment, the therapist in the author's groups has always been female. There are usually a total of five sessions with groups meeting either once or twice weekly. Each session is approximately 45 minutes in length.

The first session begins with the therapist and clients introducing themselves. Since it is not uncommon for even mature, highly educated women to subscribe to myths and misconceptions about menstruation and dysmenorrhea, the therapist introduces the treatment program in the context of a brief, frank, and accurate description of the menstrual cycle. Any number of anatomy texts can be consulted for this information. The author has found Vander, Sherman, and Luciano (1975), and *Our Bodies, Our Selves* by the Boston Women's Collective (1976) most helpful in this regard. An explanation of dysmenorrhea and the hormonal imbalance theory is included in this introduction. The therapist describes how it is thought that in spasmodic dysmenorrhea an excess of progesterone leads to an abnormally tight cervical os, and that the uterus responds by contracting in an attempt to force the menstruation through this tight opening. The purpose of the treatment, to relax the abdominal and uterine muscles, is then explained. It has been the author's experience that women respond very positively to learning more about their bodies and are more motivated to follow through with the program when they understand the purpose of the treatment. This introductory presentation generally takes 15 minutes.

Following the introductory presentation, the therapist trains the women in imagery formation and assessment using the Subjective Units of Imagery Scale (SUI) developed by McCullough and Powell (1972). The clients are instructed to imagine any scene that is very clear for themselves and give that scene a (SUI) rating of 10. The clients are instructed to imagine a scene that is not clear and give that scene an SUI score of 0. Then all the clients are asked to imagine several neutral scenes (walking in a park during the spring, peeling an orange) and to report on the scene's clarity with a relative SUI rating. The therapist can attempt to enhance the clarity of these neutral scenes by coaching the clients to attend to colors, textures, and elements of imagery such as the odors in the scenes. The imagery training sequence generally takes approximately 10 minutes.

The remaining half-hour of the first session is devoted to relaxation training.

The method is essentially identical to that described by Wolpe and Lazarus (1966), with the exception that the sequence of instructions for tensing and relaxing the abdomen and lower back muscles is repeated once in its entirety. Additional attention is paid to these muscles because they are involved in spasmodic dysmenorrhea.

At the close of the first session, clients are instructed to practice the relaxation daily and to record their practice on a log that is distributed. This log consists of a sheet of paper with dates listed in the left-hand column, and corresponding columns for indicating the time relaxation practice is begun and ended. This log is included because the author has found that monitoring tends to increase the possibility of practice. To facilitate this practice, relaxation instructions may be recorded on audio tapes and loaned to the clients for the first week of practice.

The second session is begun by the therapist reviewing the first session, asking for questions which have arisen, and hearing reports by the clients on their practice. Imagery is introduced into the relaxation treatment during this session. Either individual or group scenes related to the onset of menstruation are used in conjunction with the relaxation. The group scenes which are used during the second session are as follows:

1. You are at home working at some papers. You look over at the calendar and note that this week you will be starting your period. On the calendar you see all the other events scheduled for this week—you planned to attend a meeting, you promised to help one of your friends move, and you accepted an invitation to a day-long barbecue. Knowing that your period is due, you begin to wonder if you will feel comfortable and be able to do all these activities. Thinking about this, you return to your paperwork remaining calm and comfortable.
2. You are sitting at home reading. You look over at your calendar and see that you should be starting your period tomorrow. As you are sitting there you think about the schedule you have for yourself tomorrow. One thing you planned is some rigorous sport activity. You wonder if you will have any discomfort or pain when your period begins. Remaining calm and comfortable you return to your reading.

The therapist instructs the women to relax using the same instructions as in the first session. While the clients are relaxed, they are asked to imagine the first scene for approximately 3 minutes. The scene is then terminated. The clients are told to focus on deepening their relaxation and may be given some abbreviated relaxation instructions. After 2 minutes, the clients are asked to imagine the same scene a second time. After imagining this scene twice, the clients are asked to imagine a second scene twice. Between each imagined scene, the clients are told to focus on deepening their relaxation. In this manner, two different scenes are presented during the second session.

Individualized scenes have also been utilized in the group treatment program. Prior to the group session each client is given the group scenes just listed and asked to write down two similar scenes incorporating her personal activities. During the second session, rather than describing the same scene for the group of women, the therapist need only instruct the clients to imagine their scenes, identifying them by number rather than content.

Following the presentation of scenes, the therapist asks each client to give an SUI rating to their scenes to ensure that the scenes are clear. If the SUI values are consistently under 8, additional imagery training may be beneficial.

At the close of the second session, the clients are instructed to practice their relaxation with the two scenes just as in the session. They are told to do this homework once daily and record their practice on their log sheets.

The clients briefly report on their home practice of the relaxation with imagery at the opening of the third session. The third session is essentially the same as the second with the exception that two new scenes are used in conjunction with the relaxation. The group scenes which are used during the third session are as follows:

1. You awake in the morning and notice that you have begun your period. As you lie in bed, you think about all the things you planned for today. You have a full schedule including a long, quick walk with your friend. You wonder if you will have any pain or discomfort during the day. You are able to think about this discomfort, but remain calm and comfortable.
2. It is the first day of your period. You have begun an active day and are hurrying across town to a friend's house. You and your friend planned a full day of shopping for clothes. Now that you have started your period, you wonder if you will have any pain or discomfort, and if you will be able to complete your plans. As you hurry across town, you are able to continue thinking about the discomfort remaining calm and looking forward to the shopping.

Previously arranged individualized scenes can be used in conjunction with the relaxation in this session in the same manner as they were used in the second session.

At the end of the third session, the clients are instructed to practice their relaxation daily with the scenes from this and the previous session.

The clients briefly report on home practice of their relaxation with the imagery at the opening of the fourth and fifth sessions. These sessions are essentially the same as the two preceding. The same scenes used in the second and third sessions are used during these treatment sessions. Additional scenes may be written for these sessions, but have not been found to be necessary. At the close of the final session the therapist instructs the women to practice the relaxation and the scenes *at least* three times a week for several months or until their dysmenorrhea is gone. Also, the therapist suggests that the women practice relaxation during the first day of their menstrual period to aid in the reduction of dysmenorrhea.

FOLLOW-UP AND POSTMEASURE

Follow-up contacts with clients are very important to facilitate maintenance and transfer of gains following formal treatment. The first of these contacts is usually made within 2 weeks following the last session. The therapist uses this opportunity to advise clients about continued relaxation practice, and to answer any questions clients may have. One and a half months later, the therapist contacts each client a second time to tell them they will be receiving a copy of the Symptom Severity Scale in the mail for them to complete with regard to the amount of discomfort they had during their *last* menstrual period.

The Symptom Severity Scale is administered 2 months after the last treatment session. These scores can then be compared with those obtained during the intake interview to assess the effectiveness of the treatment. After performing this comparison, the therapist contacts the clients to provide feedback. If some of the women continue to experience dysmenorrhea, the therapist asks questions and makes suggestions that include the following:

1. Was her last period's discomfort as great as that of previous periods? Some women respond to the treatment gradually over several months. The therapist may suggest that the client continue regular, even daily relaxation exercises.
2. Was she practicing relaxation exercises? The therapist will almost always suggest that relaxation be practiced.
3. Did she attempt to use the relaxation during the onset of menstruation? The therapist may suggest that the client do so, since women have reported that this voluntary relaxation is beneficial.
4. Does she have an idea as to why she had dysmenorrhea? Was she doing something out of the ordinary or particularly strenuous?

The therapist may suggest that the client continue relaxation practice, and monitor her behavior and discomfort during her next menstrual period. Usually when this 2-month follow-up is not positive, advising women to practice their relaxation exercises more frequently or asking them to come in for a "booster session" is all that is needed to lead to marked improvement. If no improvement is noted after these follow-up measures, referral to a physician or gynecologist is recommended.

CONCLUSION

Although the behavioral treatment described in this chapter is effective in reducing spasmodic dysmenorrhea symptoms, it is important to note that the specific mechanisms responsible for this effectiveness are unknown. It has not yet been determined whether the effectiveness of this treatment is a function of conditioning or "voluntary relaxation" of the abdominal muscles at menstrual onset. It is possible that following treatment, the onset of menstruation is capable of eliciting a conditioned relaxation response. The author's clinical experience suggests that *both* such conditioning and "voluntary relaxation" may be operating, though not always together. Prior to incorporating in the treatment instructions for clients to practice relaxation at menstrual onset, some women were symptom-free after treatment, without any conscious effort to relax during menstruation. Other women reported reducing their dysmenorrhea directly by commencing relaxation exercises when menstruation began or when the first signs of dysmenorrhea were felt. The group treatment described herein includes this "voluntary relaxation" in light of its possible role in the treatment's effectiveness.

In addition, it has not yet been determined whether scenes, either in hierarchies or not, are important elements of this behavioral treatment. It is possible that the relaxation alone is sufficient. If future investigations reveal that the relaxation alone is effective, then serious doubt would be cast on the role of anxiety as a major contributor to dysmenorrhea.

The majority of the author's clinical experience with this treatment program has been with nonparous, college-age clients. Since there are complex hormonal changes with age and pregnancy, application of this group treatment for older or parous women needs further exploration. However, there is no reason apparent at this time that the treatment will not be equally effective with groups of these women.

Since this efficient group treatment program is not difficult to implement, nurses and paraprofessionals could be easily instructed in its administration, including the screening and follow-up procedures. The actual treatment sessions could be recorded on a set of audio tapes to be used by behavior therapists, nurses, or paraprofessionals during the sessions, or sent home with the clients to use in their home practice.

This chapter has presented a brief review of the literature which suggests that there are two separate types of primary dysmenorrhea. Research on a behavioral treatment for one of these two types, spasmodic dysmenorrhea based on this behavioral treatment was then described in detail. Finally, limitations regarding the behavioral analysis of this therapy and future directions for group treatment of this human problem were discussed.

REFERENCE NOTE

1. Mullen, F. G. *Treatment of dysmenorrhea by professional and student behavior therapists.* Paper presented at the Fifth Annual Meeting of the Association for the Advancement of Behavior Therapy, September 1971, Washington, D.C.

REFERENCES

Boston Women's Health Collective. *Our bodies, our selves* (2nd ed., rev. and exp.). New York: Simon & Schuster, 1976.

Chesney, M. A., & Tasto, D. L. The effectiveness of behavior modification with spasmodic and congestive dysmenorrhea. *Behaviour Research and Therapy,* 1975, *13,* 245–253. (a)

Chesney, M. A., & Tasto, D. L. The development of the menstrual symptom questionnaire. *Behaviour Research and Therapy,* 1975, *13,* 237–244. (b)

Dalton, K. *The menstrual cycle.* New York: Pantheon Books, 1969.

Davis, C. H. Dysmenorrhea. In B. Carter (Ed.), *Gynecology and obstetrics.* Hagerstown, Maryland: W. F. Prior Company, 1964.

Janowsky, D. S., Berens, S. C., & Davis, J. M. Correlations between mood, weight, and electrolytes during the menstrual cycle: A renin–angiotensin–aldosterone hypothesis of premenstrual tension. *Psychosomatic Medicine,* 1973, *35,* 143–154.

Mann, E. C. Primary dysmenorrhea. In J. V. Meigs & S. H. Sturgis (Eds.), *Progress in gynecology,* Vol. 4. New York: Grune & Stratton, 1963, pp. 123–146.

McCullough, J. P., & Powell, P. O. A technique for measuring the clarity of imagery in therapy clients. *Behavior Therapy,* 1972, *3,* 447–488.

Mullen, F. G. The treatment of a case of dysmenorrhea by behavior therapy techniques. *Journal of Nervous and Mental Disease,* 1968, *147,* 371–376.

Parlee, M. B. The premenstrual syndrome. *Psychological Bulletin,* 1973, *80,* 454–465.

Paulson, M. J., & Wood, K. R. Perceptions of emotional correlates of dysmenorrhea. *American Journal of Obstetrics and Gynecology,* 1966, *95,* 991–996.

Reich, S. K. *The effects of group systematic desensitization on the symptoms of primary dysmenorrhea.* Unpublished doctoral dissertation, University of New Mexico, 1972.

Tasto, D. L., & Chesney, M. A. Muscle relaxation treatment for primary dysmenorrhea. *Behavior Therapy,* 1974, *5,* 668–672.

Tindall, V. R. Dysmenorrhea. *British Medical Journal,* 1971, *1,* 329–331.

Tyler, E. T. Contraception control: The pill is best for most. In D. P. Lauler (Ed.), *Reproductive endocrinology.* New York: Medcom, 1973.

Vander, A. J., Sherman, J. H., & Luciano, D. S. *Human physiology: The mechanisms of body function* (2nd ed.). New York: McGraw-Hill, 1975.

Wolpe, J., & Lazarus, A. A. *Behavior therapy techniques: A guide to the treatment of neuroses.* Oxford: Pergamon, 1966.

PART V

Acquisition of Prosocial Skills

Barry W. McCarthy

Chapter 14
Acquisition of Coping Skills

In this chapter we discuss a model that integrates three divergent trends in the conceptualization and treatment of human problems: the use of behavioral techniques, the use of group treatment methods, and the use of short-term, crisis intervention strategies. These three approaches form the basis for a time-limited, goal-limited behavioral group model. The coping group has been developed at the American University Counseling Center to meet the needs of clients when a waiting list exists (as it almost invariably does at public mental health facilities). A prime purpose of the group is to provide service to clients who otherwise would not be served, and to do so in an effective and efficient manner. Since this behavioral group model is quite new, there is little clinical or research literature on the coping group model or on the acquisition of coping skills. We believe that this is an important area in the group treatment of human problems, and throughout this chapter we hope to raise issues that need to be given further clinical and empirical investigation. We consider acquisition of coping skills via the goal-limited, time-limited group to be one of the newest and most exciting areas in behavior therapy.

LITERATURE REVIEW

Behavioral interventions are shorter term and more goal directed than more traditional therapeutic techniques. However, behavioral techniques have not been widely utilized in crisis intervention therapies. The majority of crisis intervention services have focused on individual as opposed to group interventions. Krumboltz and Thoreson (1975) have described the effectiveness of short-term individual behavioral therapy. Likewise, time-limited, goal-limited groups in such areas as anxiety management (Suinn & Richardson, 1971), weight reduction (Wollersheim, 1970), sexual functioning (Barbach, 1975; Zilbergeld,

1975), changing depressive behavior (Lewinsohn, Weinstein, & Alper, 1970), assertion (Alberti & Emmons, 1974), and personal effectiveness (Liberman, King, DeRisi, & McCann, 1975) have proven to be effective treatment modalities. There is also literature reflecting the effectiveness of crisis intervention treatment not only in suicidal crises (Dorpat, 1973) but also in family crises (Bard, 1970) and general psychological distress, especially among adolescents and young adults (McCarthy & Berman, 1971). Generally, crisis groups are conducted from a nonbehavioral framework, and emphasize empathy, group support, and identifying available individual and community resources.

THE COPING GROUP MODEL

The group to be described is called the "coping group." The model for the group is time-limited (meets twice a week for 5 weeks), goal-limited (each client has one to three individual goals), and open-ended (members enter and leave the group throughout its existence), and behavioral strategies and techniques form the theoretical basis for the group. The coping group model was developed at a university counseling center, but could be applicable to a wide variety of settings including community mental health centers, psychological clinics, and public counseling agencies. One of the prime reasons for establishing a coping group is that by the end of a semester the counseling center finds all of its regular groups full and a rather long waiting list for individual therapy appointments. New clients coming for therapy are given a 20-minute screening interview on the day they come to the center. The person conducting the initial interview is either a staff psychologist, an intern, or an extern. If the client is determined to be experiencing an immediate and major psychological problem, he or she is given priority status on the individual waiting list and typically receives an individual therapy appointment within a week. Other clients are given four options: referral to a sliding fee clinic or private practitioner for individual therapy, returning for therapy to the center the following semester, seeing a peer counselor for support or for an individual skill-building contract if the screener sees that as an appropriate alternative, or participating in a coping group. Approximately one-third of the clients choose to join the coping group.

Before going to the first group session, the client is scheduled for an hour individual interview with the group therapist. There are two goals of this individual interview. The first is to clarify expectations and build a rapport with the client. The second is to specify one to three goals for the client to work on during the group. Clients often have ambivalent feelings about entering this type of treatment modality. The typical client's therapy expectation is that he will see someone individually who will listen to him and give him insight into his problems. The therapist attempts to refocus these expectations and develop a positive view of the time-limited, goal-limited group approach. The concept stressed is that many skills are more readily learned in a group because the person has an opportunity to observe and try out new behaviors and strategies, and to receive feedback from a therapist and peers on changes. Another expectation developed in the interview is that the client will work on the self-change program between sessions. To facilitate practicing his new skills, the client is given the option of working with a peer counselor (Wasserman, McCarthy, & Ferree, 1975) to get *in vivo* practice utilizing and refining new skills.

The client is further advised that the group will be of most value to him if he comes to each group meeting with an individual behavior or issue on which he would like to focus. He will receive most help if he can clearly request time in the group and focus his concern in a specific problem or skill area. The therapist and client proceed to establish one to three problem areas that the person will work on in the group. A goal attainment scale is constructed for each behavior (Kiresuk & Sherman, 1968) with the client retaining a copy to help him evaluate his progress. We discuss the value of vicarious learning in that the client can observe how other group members specify problems and develop strategies and techniques to deal with their behaviors. Other group members often serve as models for appropriate behaviors and attitudes. Since much of the work of the group utilizes the modality of behavior rehearsal, a short role-play is conducted to familiarize the client with this procedure. The individual session terminates by checking out with the client if he is satisfied with his individual goals, whether his expectations about the group are clear and realistic, and whether he has any questions or wants to clarify any concerns.

The individual interview serves as a further screening procedure. On some occasions, less than 10%, the therapist determines that this client would not be appropriate for a coping group, and a more appropriate referral is made.

The group itself meets twice a week for the duration of the semester; thus there are approximately 10 sessions. The group begins when there are at least three clients. We find that eight clients are the maximum for a group of this type. It is our clinical impression that the optimal group membership is six clients.

The group sessions are 90 minutes. The expectation is that each client will have the opportunity to focus on his problem area, although there is no demand that each person must participate in each session. There is a group norm that no one client can dominate a session or use more than 40 minutes of group time. Since it is an open-ended group, the group composition changes somewhat each session. For instance, there are some members who are only able to make one session a week because of time conflicts.

During the first session, a new member is allowed to be relatively inactive, briefly introducing himself and stating personal goals, and then listening to other individuals work on their problems. However, when behavior rehearsal is used the new member might be encouraged to play the role of the other person. This allows a new member a chance to interact in the group, yet with a relatively nonthreatening task.

The problems that clients will be working on during the group can be divided into three categories. The first is inappropriate emotional responses (especially anxiety-based problems), the second is inappropriate cognitions and self-defeating self-statements (especially revolving around guilt and lowered self-esteem), and third the absence or inhibition of appropriate operant skills (especially lack of assertiveness and problem-solving skills). One of the advantages of a group is that there are usually members who are good models for each of these problem areas. Thus, if one client is nonassertive, a role-play might be conducted using a more assertive client to model appropriate behavior. In the same manner, if one client has difficulty with putting himself down and falling into "guilt traps," a group member who has more positive attitudes might describe how he would think about a situation, what self-statements he would employ, and how he would then deal with the situation without feeling guilty or putting himself down. Other than the obvious advantage of having both a professional and a peer providing appropriate models and techniques, it has the additional advantage of allowing a client to be in a helping role. Being able to develop strategies to help another person and thus acknowledging that the person has strengths and coping techniques and can teach them to another is a very positive learning experience. One of the best ways to really learn a skill is to teach it to someone else, for thus both the person's skill and confidence level are greatly elevated.

These three problem areas are the main blocks to effective coping. In the group, the members are acquiring (either through working on problems themselves or through vicarious learning) the three most crucial coping skills: monitoring and controlling emotional responses, development of appropriate and self-enhancing cognitions, and learning assertive and problem-solving skills. A person who has mastery of these three coping skills should be able to deal with almost any psychological issue.

DESCRIPTION OF A TYPICAL SESSION

Let us review what might occur in a typical coping group session. There would be six members and the group therapist. First names are used in the group and will be used in this description. One member is a male (George) whose problem concerns a lack of assertion, this is his fifth session; a test-anxious female (Sue), this is her second session; a depressed and guilt-prone female (Ann), this is her eighth session; a male (Tom) who is undecided about whether to return to school, this is his sixth session; a female (Terri) who had been involved in a good deal of inappropriate drug and sex behavior, this is her sixth session and she is considering termination; and a new member who is a very shy, withdrawn female (Judy). After a brief introduction made by the new member, (the therapist will purposefully sit next to the new member to provide a sense of support), there is a 5-minute go-around to identify the individual issues that people want to work on today. Terri had done her assigned therapeutic homework successfully and she has decided that now she can cope well with her problems and will leave the group. Before a person leaves the group, she is encouraged to review her goals and before the last session write out the things that she has learned in the group. If appropriate, the client is encouraged to identify one or two remaining problems and develop some strategy that she will use to cope with these issues on her own in the future. This homework assignment was given in the previous group session and Terri reviewed it for herself and the group. Her original goals were either to eliminate completely or reduce her drug use to twice a week, to obtain birth control information, and to begin using some form of contraception. She reported that at present she was using only marijuana, between two and four times a week, and felt that this was appropriate for her. She had gone to a woman's clinic and obtained an IUD which although at first uncomfortable was now no problem. In terms of learning points, she reported that gaining more information by reading student-written drug and sex pamphlets had been particularly helpful. In the coping group, clients will often receive assignments to read relevant material between sessions. Examples of frequently assigned readings (which are loaned to clients) are *Your Perfect Right* by Alberti and Emmons (1974), "Anxiety Management Training and Deep Muscle Relaxation" (McCarthy, 1975), *Human Sexuality* by McCary (1973), and *Sexual Awareness: A Practical Approach* by McCarthy, Ryan, and Johnson (1975). Another thing which Terri identified as being helpful involved hearing from a group member as to how he had altered his drug-taking behavior by changing stimulus control cues, that is, he only used drugs with friends on nights when he did not have class the next day. Simply discussing the problems and not being judged evil or being made to feel guilty was very validating for Terri. At that point Ann, who had been close to Terri and impressed with her changes, asked in an almost pleading way how one changes guilt feelings. Terri's response was that knowing that others did not put her down made it less likely that she would feel bad about herself. A brief discussion of guilt followed with the therapist making the point that guilt is the most self-defeating of the human emotions in that when the person feels guilty, it serves to lower self-esteem and results in the person being more likely to repeat the behavior which caused the feeling of guilt in the first place. George disclosed that the self-statement he used was that since it is now done (his example was having an accident with the family car), feeling guilty about it will not change what happened. Ann acknowledged she understood the use of more appropriate and self-enhancing cognitions, but had a hard time integrating these attitudes into her life. It appeared to the therapist that although Ann was benefiting from the group, she might need more individual work focusing on cognitive restructuring

(Lazarus, 1971). Ann's homework assignment for that next week was to write down her guilty self-statements and next to them more appropriate self-statements.

In terms of remaining problems, Terri was still a primary nonorgasmic woman. She decided that on her own she would read and try out techniques revolving around self-exploration/masturbation techniques (Barbach, 1975; McCarthy et al., 1975), and if the self-help approach was not successful, then she would enter a preorgasmic women's group. When clients leave the coping group they are encouraged to engage in independent coping and self-help methods rather than immediately returning for more psychotherapy. However, they are made aware of other psychotherapeutic resources.

The group next focused on Sue's test anxiety problem since she had a test coming up in a week. She had been given a handout on anxiety control at the previous session. She felt she had a somewhat better understanding of her anxiety in test situations. She reported that she had engaged in "catastrophizing" about flunking out of school. In addition, she became aware that her hands would become increasingly tense and as she continued writing, her hands would begin to shake. The therapist described the techniques of deep muscle relaxation and coping self-thoughts. Terri commented that her coping self-thought in a test situation was "I've studied enough, if I work hard during the exam I'll get at least a C." Tom reported that in those subjects which he liked and studied for tests were no trouble because he felt confident. When pushed to specify his positive self-thought he said "I've done the work so I deserve to do well on the test." Judy reported she got anxious before tests, but during the test itself was calm because she focused only on the test, not on any extraneous nonproductive thoughts. Essentially, her self-thought was "worrying about doing badly is a waste of time." Sue was asked to choose a positive coping thought to focus on and she chose a variation of Judy's, that is, "I'm ready to take this exam and thinking about flunking out of school is a waste of time." The therapist then conducted 15 minutes of deep muscle relaxation, using guided imagery of a test situation with the addition of positive coping self-thoughts. Although the focus was on Sue's test situation most group members had experienced some test anxiety so that it was a relevant exercise for them also. In discussing the experience afterward, Ann (who had done the relaxation exercises before in an earlier group session) commented that the relaxation techniques could be utilized in a wide variety of situations and mentioned her use of them before an anxiety-provoking talk she had with a teacher. The therapist focused on the strategy of being able to monitor and control anxiety, and how this could be generalized to a wide variety of situations. Sue decided she would practice the exercises while studying, an hour before the exam, and use the hand tensing/relaxing exercises and coping self-thought during the exam itself.

George's homework assignment from the last group was to practice a variety of assertive responses. Using the typical homework feedback format, George first reported what had gone well, which was his ability to ask his parents for an additional $25 to buy some clothes. Also, he had been able to keep good eye contact with his resident advisor when talking with him. However, George reported several projects which went much less well. He was unable to be appropriately assertive with his roommate, and the interaction degenerated into a vindictive argument. Also, he was unable to obtain a date for the weekend. George was able to acknowledge his skills were getting better and that he had felt positive after the successes, but also reported being discouraged especially regarding his inability to obtain dates. Even before being asked, Ann volunteered to engage in a role-play with George to allow him a chance to practice his dating initiation skills and receive some feedback on them. George agreed to focus on nonverbal skills, especially being facially animated and maintaining a relaxed body posture. These nonverbal cues were briefly modeled by the therapist. Each group member was given a specific behavior to observe, that is, Judy focused on his eye contact, Tom on his body posture, and so on. This is one method to keep group members attentive and involved as well as providing them an opportunity to give specific feedback. The behavior rehearsal included two vignettes, one with Ann and one with Judy. George noticed that if his nonverbal behavior was more appropriate, then his confidence increased and verbal requests flowed more smoothly. The therapist drew an analogy concerning Sue's nonverbal test behavior and Ann's nonverbal behavior when she was feeling depressed. Sue agreed she tightened up during tests and that this accelerated her anxiety. Ann agreed to think about her nonverbal behavior when depressed, but she seemed less impressed by this point. Judy was asked to be aware of how her nonverbal behavior, including that day in the group, can reinforce her perception of herself (and other people's perceptions of her) as being shy and withdrawn. Judy was given a homework assignment of recording her nonverbal behavior in situations in which she acted in a passive, withdrawn manner. George was given a homework assignment to practice his initiating skills with a peer counselor from the Companion Program.

At this point, the group had only about 7 minutes left, and Tom's problems had not been attended to nor had Tom been very active in the group. This replicated a pattern of previous group sessions. When asked how he perceived the group, Tom replied that he enjoyed it, found it a valuable learning experience, and in fact more interesting and worthwhile than most of his classes. He even mentioned that he was thinking of majoring in psychology. It was evident to the therapist that Tom was using the group to avoid confronting his problems. A contract was made with Tom that he would be the first one to deal with issues in the next group, and to facilitate his preparing for the group he was asked to fill out a "steps to problem-solving" form with a focus on deciding whether to return to college next year.

The last few minutes of the group session are spent going around the group, with each member stating specific learning points from this session and to check out their "homework" for the next sessions.

DISCUSSION

Though most members enter the group with a specific crisis problem, the initial crisis is often quickly resolved or is redefined in terms of building skills or developing coping strategies. The major focus of the group is on the individual client developing his or her skills or adopting appropriate coping strategies rather than on group process or group interaction issues. However, members do learn from each other and contribute to other members' behavior change. The process of vicarious learning is actively promoted in the coping group. The therapist (or sometimes a group member) states the coping mechanism being utilized, how this can be generalized to other situations, and its possible applicability to other group members. Although the focus of the group is on individual problems, there are several mechanisms for other group members to learn: vicarious learning, pinpointing coping strategies, introduction to specific behavioral techniques, and playing the helping role for another group member.

The coping group model borrows heavily from the concepts of multimodal behavior therapy (Lazarus, 1976). The modalities of behavior, affect, cognition, and interpersonal relationships are given the most emphasis in the coping group. The message to the clients is that they are responsible for their own behavior, and that the best way to change behavior is through a series of small steps and utilization of reinforcement techniques. There is also an emphasis on being aware of and avoiding self-defeating psychological "traps" and instead to use more self-enhancing coping techniques (especially positive self-thoughts). A major emphasis is on the educational components of this group: use of homework assignments, clients keeping behavioral diaries or data cards, extensive use of bibliotherapy, and use of peer counselors to serve essentially as tutors to help the client practice and refine skills between sessions.

The group is time-limited in that it terminates when the academic semester ends. During the course of the group 15 to 22 students had been group members. At the conclusion of the group there are typically between five and seven students left. A major part of the last coping group session is spent assessing gains made and discussing problem areas which need further work. Several options are discussed with clients. They can develop self-change programs themselves (usually with the help of written resource material, especially Watson and Tharp, 1972) or seek further treatment at the counseling center. The client can be referred either to the behavioral group program, the interactional therapy group program, or to individual therapy. Often an agreement is made for the client to attempt to utilize some of the learnings from this group and to design a self-change program, and if by the next semester the issues are still problematic, then the person returns for professional services.

LIMITATIONS AND SPECIAL CONSIDERATIONS

Let us now examine some of the limiting factors in a coping group. Clearly, it will not meet the needs of a client who desires or demands a great deal of individual attention. In fact, each semester we find that we have to refer to individual therapy at least one client who attempts to dominate or who serves to inhibit the group. The client who is very highly anxious and is unable to interact in a group situation would be inappropriate because there is not enough time to reduce anxiety systematically and shape appropriate group behavior. A third type of client who does not do very well in a coping group is one who is more interested in focusing on existential or feeling-oriented issues. This is especially true of the client who has had a good deal of relationship-oriented psychotherapeutic experiences. This client tends to rebel against the task-oriented and skill-oriented approach of the coping group.

It is the author's belief that one of the crucial ingredients of the coping group model is the initial meeting with the therapist and client. In addition to serving to establish a rapport, providing a positive expectancy toward the coping group, and developing individual behavioral goals, it serves to screen out clients who would be more appropriate for other treatment modalities. Through the individual session, the client can be made aware of self-help, peer counseling, bibliotherapy resources, and other professional therapy resources which might be used subsequent to the coping group.

We believe that in a behaviorally oriented treatment facility it could be possible to use the initial coping groups as an assessment device. Adult clients would routinely be placed in a coping group (after initial interview). For many clients this intervention would in itself be enough to deal with the problem. For other clients, depending on the issues and behavioral problems which were discussed or which manifested themselves in the coping group, the therapist and the client could determine to use other treatment modalities including specific behavioral groups, an individual behavioral therapy contract either with a professional or paraprofessional, a self-control behavior change project, or perhaps more relationship-oriented individual or group therapy.

Another limitation is that the coping group is time-consuming and draining on the therapist. A single therapist is used because it is much more economical to the center, but for that 5-week period the coping group is his major clinical responsibility. There is no reason to believe that the coping group could not be conducted by coleaders in order to share the therapeutic responsibility, as well as to provide a second model for the clients. However, for cotherapy to be effective in a time-limited, goal-limited group the cotherapists need to work well together and be able to devote planning and processing time to ensure maximal effectiveness from the coleading mode.

A very important limitation in the coping group model is the lack of research on its specific components and a lack of controlled, empirical validation of its effectiveness. It is our hope that this description of the coping group model will promote research on it.

CONCLUSION

This chapter has discussed a coping group model which utilizes concepts from the areas of behavioral techniques, group treatment methods, and the use of short-term, crisis intervention strategies. The model has been successfully conducted several times, although it has not been subjected to rigorous experimental validation. However, it is a model that holds a great deal of promise in that it is economical, focuses on individual client needs and goals, is flexible, can serve as an assessment technique, and makes use of a multimodal approach to the individual and the group.

REFERENCES

Alberti, R., & Emmons, M. *Your perfect right*. San Luis Obispo, California: Impact Press, 1974.

Barbach, L. Group treatment of orgasmic women. *Journal of Sex and Marital Therapy*, 1974, *1*, 139–145.

Barbach, L. *For yourself: The fulfillment of female sexuality*. Garden City, New York: Doubleday, 1975.

Bard, M. *Training police as specialists in family crisis intervention* (Report PR70-1). Washington, D.C.: U.S. Government Printing Office, 1970.

Dorpat, T. Suicide, loss, and mourning. *Life-Threatening Behavior*, 1973, *3*, 213–244.

Kiresuk, T., & Sherman, R. Goal attainment scaling. *Community Mental Health Journal*, 1968, *4*, 443–453.

Krumboltz, J., & Thoreseh, C. *Counseling methods*. New York: Holt, 1976.

Lazarus, A. *Behavior therapy and beyond*. New York: McGraw-Hill, 1971.

Lazarus, A. *Multimodal behavior therapy*. New York: Springer, 1976.

Lewinsohn, P., Weinstein, M., & Alper, T. A behavioral approach to the group treatment of depressed persons. *Journal of Clinical Psychology*, 1970, *26*, 525–532.

Liberman, R., King, L., Derisi, W., & McCann, M. *Personal Effectiveness*. Champaign, Illinois: Research Press, 1975.

McCarthy, B. *Anxiety management training and deep muscle relaxation*. Mimeo, Washington, D.C., American University, 1975.

McCarthy, B., & Berman, A. A student-operated crisis center. *Personnel and Guidance Journal*, 1971, *7*, 523–528.

McCarthy, B., Ryan, M., & Johnson, F. *Sexual awareness: A practical approach*. San Francisco: Boyd & Fraser, 1975.

McCary, J. *Human sexuality*. Philadelphia: Van Nostrand, 1973.

Suinn, R., & Richardson, F. Anxiety management training. *Behavior Therapy,* 1971, *2*, 498–510.

Wasserman, C., McCarthy, B., & Ferree, E. Student paraprofessionals as behavior change agents. *Professional Psychology,* 1975, *6*, 217–223.

Watson, P., & Tharp, R. *Self-directed behavior: Self modification for personal adjustment.* Monterey: Brooks/Cole, 1972.

Wollersheim, J. Effectiveness of giving therapy based upon learning principles in the treatment of overweight women. *Journal of Abnormal Psychology,* 1970, *76,* 262–274.

Zilbergeld, B. Group treatment of sexual dysfunction in men without partners. *Journal of Sex and Marital Therapy,* 1975, *1,* 204–214.

Henry R. Novotny

Chapter 15
Acquisition of Social Competency Skills

The social competence training (SCT) approach is a composite, voluntary program of instruction and group treatment. Developed at a correctional facility, SCT is by no means restricted in application to a correctional, or even to an institutional, setting. SCT is easily adaptable to serve the needs of most specifiable social situations, business enterprises, training facilities of various kinds, and clinical practice.

As applied at the correctional facility, SCT consists of two parts (Novotny & Enomoto, 1976). First, it provides a training program for the inmates which includes weekly group sessions supplemented by classes, individual counseling, and tutorial sessions. Second, it provides a parallel program for the correctional staff which includes college courses, lectures, workshops, and supervised group work. SCT emphasizes the need for the staff to serve as mature models of competent, prosocial behavior.

As an educational and training program which is designed to help individuals achieve a more personally rewarding and socially productive existence, SCT focuses on a number of related target objectives. One is to teach program participants to assess accurately challenging social situations and to increase their awareness of available options and resources. Recognizing the need for sometimes cooperative and sometimes competitive social conduct, SCT employs the standard techniques of assertion training, such as modeling and behavioral rehearsal, to teach the required social competence. The program emphasizes the desirability of systematic self-management. Another objective of SCT is to promote democratic and prosocial standards of personal conduct by enforcing appropriate group norms, stressing long-range benefits of prosocial conduct, by repetitive rehearsal of desired behaviors, and by the influence of group pressure and modeling effects provided by group leaders. To facilitate effective and self-determined behavior, SCT instructs participants to rely on modes of reasoning with predictive power which make intelligent and purposeful behavior possible. The program teaches how to set personal goals, how to analyze and assess behavior functionally in terms of its predictable consequences, how to subordinate immediate impulses to longer range objectives, how to structure time and make schedules, and how to develop and apply objective criteria for outcome evaluation.

SCT is a comprehensive and conceptually integrated approach which strives for practicality and effectiveness. It utilizes the theoretical framework of social learning theory and employs techniques which derive, for the most part, from the principles of learning. SCT differs from the strictly behavioristic model because it accepts the influence of cognitive processes on behavior. The program avoids ethical and legal difficulties by being carried out on a strictly voluntary basis with a free and informed consent of the participants. SCT also avoids the use of drugs, medical interventions of any kind, and of aversive procedures.

More than 30 counselors and officers at the California Correctional Institution (CCT) at Tehachapi, and several hundred inmates, have participated in the SCT program, in addition to 25 students at the California State College at Bakersfield (CSB) and Tehachapi schooolteachers. The program has been received positively by both the correctional staff and the inmates.

BACKGROUND

In the fall of 1972, the author, then an Associate Professor of Psychology at the California State College at Bakersfield, visited the California Correctional Institution at Tehachapi to initiate a program of psychological services for the inmates. The institution had neither a psychologist nor a psychiatrist on its full-time staff at the time, and the new program was expected to supply some of the needed services as well as to provide an oportunity for CSB graduate students to do their field work and to learn about corrections. The project had the unwavering support of the then Superintendent of CCI, Jerry J. Enomoto, who has since become the Director of Corrections for the State of California.

Since the author was at that time already conducting assertion training groups at the Center for Behavior Therapy in Beverly Hills, it seemed only natural to apply the approach also at CCI. A success from the beginning, the program was progressively modified and adapted to the correctional environment. More effective techniques were developed for handling angry, hostile, and even violent behaviors, emphasis was placed on resolving normative questions, and ways were found to respond to the influence of outside ideologies which tended to polarize and to radicalize the inmate population.

While maintaining its behavioral orientation, the program was conceptually broadened and more emphasis was placed on cognitive determinants of behavior.

College courses, originally offered only to the CCI staff, were extended also to the inmates. Reading material which included reexamination of value and ethical issues supplemented the standard texts on assertion training (Alberti & Emmons, 1970; Fensterheim, 1972; Neuman, 1969; Serber, 1972) and on social learning theory (Bandura, 1969, 1971).

SOCIAL COMPETENCE TRAINING: THEORY AND APPLICATION

Following the formulation by Albert Bandura 1969, 1971), SCT uses social learning theory as its theoretical framework. The influence of environmental conditions on behavior is acknowledged, but cognitive determinants of behavior are accepted as well. According to social learning theory, behavioral and emotional responses can be learned either by direct experiences or vicariously by observation. One can also devise self-regulatory influences by a purposeful and systematic management of operative reinforcement contingencies. The highest degree of personal autonomy and independence from extrinsic influences is reached when one begins to monitor and to regulate one's behavior by self-administering reinforcements according to one's own design and purposes.

SCT in practice represents a program of "instruction in social skills and self-management" and "normative clarification." A schedule of group sessions is suplemented by lectures, workshops, tutorial sessions, and individual counseling. Videotaped examples of competent coping behaviors are shown to participants. The program adopts a number of well-defined target objectives. One, of course, is to teach effective and prosocial coping skills using assertion training techniques such as modeling and behavioral rehearsal. Group participants are taught to interpret more accurately encountered social situations and are trained to differentiate between the real, actual limitations imposed by existing, objective conditions and imagined, fictitious, and self-imposed constraints based mainly on one's ignorance, hopes, fears, and expectations. They are trained to watch for all available feedback from others, to estimate reliably their own resources and capabilities, to accept responsibility for their actions as well as emotions, and to conceptualize problem situations from their own perspectives in ways that would help them to select effective courses of action.

A second important objective of SCT is to instruct program participants in the skills and techniques of self-management. It is emphasized that a lasting change in one's behavior—such as abstaining from drugs or modifying one's eating habits to lose weight—is achieved usually only with an accompanying, judicious rearrangement of external reinforcement contingencies. One's daily routines and social life must be reexamined and, when necessary, modified. Self-oriented but democratic and prosocial standards of personal conduct are promoted by an enforcement of appropriate group norms, by emphasizing long-range benefits of prosocial behavior, by repetitive rehearsal and copious social reinforcement of effective but prosocial responses, and in general by systematic group pressure and influence of group leaders.

Yet another important objective of SCT is teaching reliance on modes of reasoning which have predictive power and which therefore make intelligent and purposeful conduct possible. The SCT approach reflects the author's conviction that epistemological considerations deserve more attention from both researchers and therapists than they are currently receiving. The way in which one conceptualizes social situations and events, the way in which one seeks and retains information, and the way in which one selects and designs one's future courses of action are obviously very powerful co-determinants of one's conduct (Novotny, 1971, 1974, 1975).

Striving to promote autonomous and effective behavior, SCT teaches how to select one's objectives, how to analyze and assess one's behavior functionally in terms of the consequences one can predict, how to make long-range goals prevail over immediate, short-lived impulses, how to make schedules and structure time, and how to select and apply objective measures to evaluate one's progress as well as the eventual outcome of one's efforts. SCT is an action-oriented program in which one asks, "What will you do about it?" rather than "How do you feel about it?" There are several reasons for this approach. First, it is much easier and more reliable to monitor changes in behavior than changes in feelings and attitudes. Second, feelings seem frequently to follow, rather than to precede, behavior. Third, some of the program participants typically grew up without adequate models of mature behavior and lack basic social skills; it is consequently very doubtful that a discussion of their feelings would ever help them overcome their deficits. If anything, the "how do you feel" aproach would encourage their dependency on the supportive empathy of other group members as well as of the group leaders.

In the final analysis, it is action rather that feelings that helps individuals reach their objectives. At least from the social viewpoint, feelings without action are functionally irrelevant. As an outcome-oriented program, SCT is then more concerned with, for example, compassionate behavior than compassionate feelings. Emphasizing the objective of helping those under stress, SCT group leaders encourage a search for an effective, helping, behavioral intervention. Group members are urged to help rather than to sympathize; to be outcome—rather than feelings-oriented.

"Self-image," "self-esteem," and "self-respect" are frequently employed terms referring to the feelings and notions which one has learned to associate with the thought of oneself, one's conduct, and one's presumed abilities, virtues, talents, and potentials. In the popular usage, one should "feel" self-respect and "have" a "good" self-image. The difficulty is that, subjectively defined, such feelings of self-worth may, or may not, be consistent with one's actual objective performance and behavior. They may be only products of personal fancy and of undeserved, sometimes well-intentioned, flattery by others. For instance, many a sympathetic counselor tries hard to "build up" his/her client's self-image.

In the SCT perspective, feelings of self-worth formed in disregard of one's actual performance are seen as basically maladaptive since they do not allow an accurate assessment of one's chances in competitive situations. If not based on verifiable performance, and associated with realistic expectations, a positive self-image is viewed as most likely resulting in unfulfilled desires, experiences of failure, frustration, and general unhappiness. SCT therefore acceepts "feelings" of self-worth as highly desirable, perhaps indispensable personal characteristics of a happy and successful individual but promotes such feelings and beliefs only in forms in which they do not conflict with reality. Feelings of self-worth, it is suggested, should be earned rather than imagined. Feelings of self-respect, for instance, should be earned in a similar manner as others' respect must be earned. The social value of an individual should be based on his performance.

SCT distinguishes between basic, enduring sentiments and short-lived, emotional reactions to often incidental stimulus situations. It is proposed that one's goals should reflect the former and that, in general, immediate impulses should be subordinated to deeper and more pervasive emotions. It is pointed out that much of impulsive behavior is counterproductive and regretted later on. SCT values spontaneous conduct but not behavior resulting from irrational phobias, leading to disastrous consequences, or consisting of antisocial behavior. In the SCT perspective, there is no "a priori reason for a schism between reason and emotions" (Strupp, 1976, p. 563). In fact, seeking a reconciliation between the two is one of the program's main objectives.

SCT also acknowledges that any lasting, profound change in one's cognition and conduct, in one's general outlook and life-style, must be accompanied by a parallel emotional change. The program finds useful the idea of a childhood "injunction" which one accepts from his/her parents, on which one bases one's "scripts" and "games," and which if dysfunctional, one must terminate by a process of "redecision" (Goulding, 1972). SCT then assumes that both immediate impulses and long-lasting sentiments can be modified by group pressure, by additional information, by a systematic reconceptualization of response and stimulus situations, by reconditioning of psychological reactions associated with emotions, and by learning effective social coping skills. One very important rule of SCT is that feelings cannot be used to explain and to justify behavior.

SCT groups usually meet between 14 and 16 times for weekly, 2-hour sessions after which certificates of completion are awarded to participants who satisfied the criteria of performance and attendance. Each group has typically two coleaders, one of each sex, who act more as task-oriented coaches and instructors than insight- and process-oriented facilitators. The group leaders must represent adequate models of mature and effective social conduct. Behavior of group members is evaluated in such terms as "effective" or "ineffective" and "productive" or "counterproductive." Group leaders try to minimize the fre-

quency of experienced failures and to maximize the frequency of encourage-
ments and acknowledgments of success.

Focus is kept on members' behavior observed in the group rather than on
behavior reported and described. It is emphasized that talking about behavior is
much easier but less productive than demonstrating it and that behavior well
learned and rehearsed is likely to be used. Behavioral homeworks are assigned
between group sessions and progress reports are kept. In general, emphasis is
placed on the more positive aspects of life and on the new achievements by the
participants. At the same time, group members are held responsible for their
conduct and their maladaptive or ineffectual responses are conceptualized as
consequences of poor self-management. Videotapes are sometimes used to show
examples of effective coping behaviors. To promote purposeful and responsible
conduct, SCT groups typically spend a substantial amount of time on techniques
of preventing confrontative situations and of mediating conflicts. Typical problem situations are analyzed and discussed, and alternative courses of action are
modeled and rehearsed.

SCT distinguishes between "angry" and "aggressive" behavior. In the
SCT terminology, angry behavior is characterized by quite specific, "angry,"
emotional responses to rather well-defined stimulus situations. Such directly
evoked angry responses can usually be either extinguished or modified in a
relatively straightforward manner. Evidence seems to indicate that, having been
conditioned, angry behavior can be unlearned rather easily.

By aggressive behavior, on the other hand, SCT refers to more complex
responses associated with more global and enduring cognitive and emotional
characteristics such as one's social views and general emotional makeup. Viewed in this perspective, aggressive behavior becomes much less a function of the
immediate stimulus situation and, therefore, more resistant to any simple and
basically noncognitive treatment. In the SCT vocabulary, aggressive behavior is
then social conduct which may be seen as substantially codetermined by conscious, and presumably well-considered, social opinions, convictions, and
philosophies.

It is usually much easier to agree upon what has been an angry response than
what has been an aggressive one. Angry behavior can be typically defined and
evaluated in terms of the stimulus characteristics and the observed quality, intensity, and adaptiveness of the response. Whether a behavior is to be seen as
aggressive, on the other hand, may well depend on the evaluator's value system
and perception of the social context within which the action took place.

Defining angry behavior in terms of immediate observables frequently
simplifies the therapeutic situation by cutting through ideological debates about
which conduct was aggressive and which was "right" and which was "wrong."
Although aggressive behavior may sometimes even be viewed as effective and
admirable, for instance when seen as a "bold pursuit of one's goals" or "self-
assertiveness," angry behavior is invariably considered undesirable and de-

bilitating; it is usually accepted by group members without opposition as suitable material for group concern and corrective action.

PROGRAM EVALUATION

The social competence training approach depends to a great extent on the well-tested procedures of assertion training and behavior therapy. These techniques have been evaluated with very positive results in such a large number of studies that it is impossible to list even a representative sample. The reader may perhaps find of special interest the work by McFall and Twentyman (1973) and some of the references listed in a bibliography by Bandura (1971). A direct evaluation of the SCT program as a whole was carried out at the California Correctional Institution and has already been reported elsewhere (Novotny & Enomoto, 1976). What follows is a summary of the reported findings.

The SCT approach was first applied as a correctional program at CCI in the fall of 1972. Initially a small and mostly self-financed project, SCT was funded at a modest level during the fiscal year 1974–1975. The reported evaluation examines the impact of the program during the latter period of relatively high activity when more than 30 CCI counselors and officers and several hundred inmates participated in the program. The outcome study consisted of two parts.

First, an attempt was made to estimate the extent to which the program helped individual inmates. The degree of treatment success was estimated from the degree to which program participants achieved their chosen treatment goals and from the level of their improvement in social skills and adjustment as observed by the correctional staff. The acquisition of previously absent social competencies such as coping with challenging situations at the institution, establishing new desirable family and peer relationships, setting of personal goals, planning for future, and handling various—to some degree perhaps contrived but generally representative—situations in the group were recorded and counted. In addition, multipart questionnaires were administered to both staff and inmates.

All outcome measures indicated that the SCT program was successful, at least within the limited range of objectives allowed by the institutional environment. Recorded data and group leaders' reports indicated that between 70% and 80% of participants achieved their treatment goals.

Inmates' improvement in social skills and their *functional* (to be differentiated from emotional) adjustment to the institutional life were also noted by the correctional staff, particularly inmates' progressive avoidance of belligerent behavior. Staff members reported an increased flexibility and effectiveness of inmate behavior as a result of SCT participation. (The number of written appeals increased as well.)

The response of the CCI staff to the SCT program was determined by administering a questionnaire to all CCI counselors who, as a group, were judged to be most likely familiar with the program and its effects on inmates. Eleven of the 15 counselors answered the questionnaire.

Eight stated they were acquainted with the program, seven took at least one of the courses the author offered at the institution, and six participated in at least one SCT group. Five found positive changes in inmates' behavior, none found negative ones, and six had no comment. Six thought that SCT was superior to other correctional programs and five did not know. All 11 believed that the SCT program should be continued and all thought that more information about it should be made available to the CCI personnel. Ten believed that training in SCT should be offered to the staff and nine were interested in coleading future SCT groups. Among the comments with regard to changes in inmates' behavior were the following:

> Inmates who have participated in the SCT program appear to handle authority and confrontation with people in a more satisfactory manner.
> Very definitely—for those who become more than superficially involved . . . post-group reinforcement needed.
> Their behavior has been much improved.
> In both attitude and behavior . . . a large percentage have had noticeable changes.
> Yes, two cases in particular I observed change from very aggressive, obnoxious to being more approachable.

Several of the counselors also offered more general comments about the program and the following sample is typical:

> SCT is much more structured which seems to help both staff and inmates.
> Superior to general group approach . . . needs further expansion/extention.
> Good tool but . . . not . . . a cure-all.
> Appears more feasible than regular group counseling.
> An effective additional tool.
> SCT is an approach that is easily understood and gives structure to group meetings that results in constructive inmate behavior.

Inmates' interest in the program was indicated by substantial waiting lists for group participation and by a very satisfactory enrollment in offered courses. Course evaluations by inmates, carried out on an anonymous basis with inmates' comments sent directly to the college, were also quite positive.

The second part of the study consisted of estimating the effect that SCT had on conflict prevention and resolution in the institution as a whole. The numbers of disciplinaries given by CCI staff to inmates were therefore compiled for comparable periods of the fiscal years 1973–1974 and 1974–1975. Only information on the most serious disiplinaries (CDC Form 115, Rules Violation Report) was available. With over 10% of all inmates at CCI involved in the SCT program during 1974–1975 (15 groups at a time), as compared to perhaps 1% (two groups at a time) in 1973–1974, the number of "beefs" given in the 1974–1975 fiscal year was expected to be significantly lower. The sharp decrease in the number of disciplinaries indicated by the data shown in Table 1 exceeded

Table 1

Number of Disciplinaries (115's) Given per Quarter

Fiscal year	Quarter			
	First	*Second*	*Third*	*Fourth*
1973–1974 (2 SCT groups at a time)	172	156	113	173
1974–1975 (15 SCT groups at a time)	77	80	61	59

all expectations. The 1973–1974 total, incidently, is comparable to the totals for several previous years.

Two notes of caution must be borne in mind. First, one must be careful in interpreting the figures given in Table 1 which might possibly indicate some other influence on the institutional life such as administrative changes. A thorough search, however, brought negative results. The second note regards the earlier part of the evaluation which could have been carried out only with respect to inmates' existence in the institution. Whether the SCT program produces lasting changes, as is hoped, and whether it really helps reduce recidivism, are questions which can only be answered in the years to come when participating inmates have been released from the penal institution.

Data obtained seem to indicate the following conclusions (quoted from Novotny & Enomoto p.53):

1. SCT teaches social competence in the broader sense of the term. It facilitates appropriate socialization and promotes satisfying, productive, and trouble-free modes of social existence.

2. SCT exerts a positive influence on the institutional climate, particularly in the area of conflict resolution.

3. SCT helps upgrade educationally both the staff and inmates.

4. SCT functions as a bridge between the institution and the local centers of higher learning, and between the institution and the surrounding community.

A FEW COMMENTS ON HANDLING OF ANGER

SCT rejects the idea that spontaneous and uninhibited expreession of anger and other emotions at all times should be considered an ethical and moral imperative as well as a sign of mental health and maturity. It would seem obvious that any civilized and productive social existence must inevitably include behavioral constraints. The real question then is either how to unlearn "surplus" emotions or how to express them in noninjurious ways. SCT prefers the former alternative but accepts the latter one if necessary.

Some therapists propose that angry individuals should channel their anger and hostility into vigorous but noninjurious physical activities by which the unwanted emotions would presumably be dissipated. SCT has no quarrel with such exercises as pillow punching, an activity which may be even healthy for other reasons, but accepts them only as temporary safety valves which postpone, rather than resolve, the difficulty.

On the other hand, there are therapists who recommend "clearing the air" and cleansing the mind by a free public discharge of the "pent-up" emotions. Their approach to handling angry responses is well represented by the following quotation:

Anger is a healthy emotion. It is your personality's first line of defense against assault and exploitation. But in order for anger to stay healthy, it must be expressed. Just as a trapped surge of electricity can burn out a motor, so anger, if not discharged in actions or words, is likely to turn into resentment (Lewis & Streitfeld, 1970, p. 149).

SCT agrees that anger is a "healthy emotion" in the sense that it is a common and sometimes even functional response experienced by everyone. It would certainly be unsound advice to advocate that anger, or for that matter any other emotion, should be indefinitely ignored and suppressed if inconvenient and discomforting. On the other hand, SCT is categorically opposed to the suggestion that "murderous rage" should be freely expressed because such an action "can often bring about an amicable end to even the most savage argument" (Lewis & Streitfeld, 1970, pp. 150–151). In most cases, the free ventilation of anger is only likely to aggravate the already strained relations and in some cases it may result in physical violence.

The author shared Lewis and Streitfeld's propositions, and a strained chuckle, with a specialized SCT group of convicts. Five of the group present killed their wives during arguments. After a pause, an inmate offered the observation that "Yes, I felt much better afterwards, but now she is dead, and I have five more years to go."

The "express your anger" theories are formulated by and for middle class, well-mannered, and generally reticent individuals. They are inappropriate for many or most people in the world who are poorly educated, nonverbal, and physically oriented. Many live by the principle of dominance and submission regulated by threats, terror, violence, and intimidation. For such individuals, the suggested sanctioning of angry conduct may represent the removal of the last civilizing restraint.

In the SCT program, individuals are taught to cope with anger-provoking situations by means of a three-step procedure. The first step consists of establishing program participants' priority of goals so that the effectiveness of their conduct may be evaluated. The group leaders also point out that, to enjoy life in a pluralistic and sometimes competitive society, one must learn purposeful and self-determined behavior, which means that one should act rather than react. One should act to reach one's objectives rather than react to others on the spur of the moment.

The second step consists of reconceptualizing the stimulus situation and the angry response. Although socially oriented, SCT seeks performer-centered perspectives because they tend to indicate feasible courses of action. For instance, many firsthand accounts of personal conflicts and differences include such statements as, "I can't help it, he makes me mad." In such cases, group leaders emphasize that placing the presumed control of one's emotions and behavior with another person is not very useful since it implies that one can do little more than hide, or attack the controller, or, alternatively, throw onself at his/her mercy. Neither response is a very promising one.

A more effective way of interpreting the anger-provoking situation, it is suggested, is to admit that one gets angry when one does not know how to respond. One must therefore take responsibility for one's feelings and learn a way of coping with the problem situation or with the difficult individual. Rather than viewing one's feelings of anger as justifications of one's position and action, one should interpret them as warning signals; one is facing circumstances which one is ill prepared to handle. Anger is then seen only as an ill-advised prompt to strident action which, as an unplanned reaction, is determined more by the provocative stimulus than by the performer's goals and purposes.

The last step consists of training group participants in the use of more effective social competency behaviors and conditioning them to stay calm in anger-provoking situations, that is, of extinguishing the physiological responses which underlie their feelings of anger. The outlined three-part procedure usually includes also considerations of social anxiety responses so that the technique really represents a social learning approach to the management of psychosocial stress in general.

CONCLUSION

Social competence training is a composite program of instruction and group treatment which is based on the principles of social learning theory. Relying at first heavily on the modeling and social influence of program leaders, SCT strives to effect lasting behavioral, emotional, and cognitive changes by the means of education, persuasion, behavioral practice, and instruction in self-management skills. The program promotes self-directed, autonomous, and pro-social conduct.

SCT uses techniques which can be employed to treat relatively many by relatively few. It admits the use of paraprofessionals since it is simple in principle and execution and, being task oriented, it permits objective evaluation of its outcome.

REFERENCES

Alberti, R. E., & Emmons, M. L. *Your perfect right: A guide to assertive behavior.* San Luis Obispo, California: Impact, 1970.

Bandura, A. *Principles of behavior modification.* New York: Holt, 1969.

Bandura, A. *Social learning theory.* Morristown, New Jersey: General Learning Press, 1971.

Fensterheim, H. Behavior therapy: assertive training in groups. In C.J. Sager & H. S. Kaplan (Eds.), *Progress in group and family therapy.* New York: Brunner/Mazel, 1972.

Goulding, R. New directions in transactional analysis: Creating an environment for redecision and change. In C. J. Sager & H. S. Kaplan (Eds.), *Progress in group and family therapy.* New York: Brunner/Mazel, 1972.

Lewis, H. R., & Streitfeld, H. S. *Growth games.* New York: Bantam Books, 1970.

McFall, R. M., & Twentyman, C. T. Four experiments on the relative contributions of rehearsal, modeling, and coaching to assertion training. *Journal of Abnormal Psychology,* 1973, *81,* 199–218.

Neuman, D. Using assertive training. In J. D. Krumboltz & C. E. Thoresen (Eds.), *Behavioral counseling: Cases and techniques.* New York: Holt, 1969.

Novotny, H. R. Reply to Seymour M. Lipset. *American Psychologist,* 1971, *26,* 202–203.

Novotny, H. R. Academic freedom and authoritarianism. In S. Hook, P. Kurtz, & M. Todorovich (Eds.), *The idea of a modern university.* San Francisco: Prometheus Books, 1974.

Novotny, H. R. Logic of social sciences: To be, to do, or to describe? In S. Hook, P. Kurtz, & M. Todorovich (Eds.), *The philosophy of the curriculum.* San Francisco: Prometheus Books, 1975.

Novotny, H. R., & Enomoto, J. J. Social competence training as a correctional alternative. *Offender Rehabilitation, 1(1) Fall 1976, 45–55.*

Serber, M. Teaching the non-verbal components of assertive training. *Journal of Behavior Therapy and Experimental Psychiatry,* 1972, *3,* 1–5.

Strupp, H. H. Clinical psychology, irrationalism, and the erosion of excellence. *American Psychologist,* 1976, *31,* 561–571.

Gerald W. Piaget

Chapter 16
Acquisition of Assertive Communication Skills

One of the most difficult problems facing professionals who wish to employ assertive training procedures as adjunctive group treatment tools involves response generalization. It is one thing to stand one's ground with a cooperative and essentially powerless group member, and quite another to hang tough with a wife or husband who really might withhold love, support, or the car keys in the face of unexpected assertive behavior. Clara Client usually finds it substantially easier to ask her mother-in-law not to criticize her housekeeping in the relative safety of a group room role-play than while under manipulative and punitive fire at home.

Basically, it is difficult for most people to generalize newly learned behavior patterns from low stress to high stress situations. Most people do not think very well under stress, and when the chips are down they tend to revert to their old habits and interpersonal roles, no matter how many times the ineffectiveness of these habits and roles have been demonstrated in practice. Not only are the old patterns intrinsically more comfortable, but they lead to short-term payoffs (anxiety reduction, stress avoidance, positive feedback, etc.) which are difficult to relinquish. Clara may know full well her life is going to hell in a handbasket as a direct result of her doormat behavior, yet still finds herself confused, ambivalent, and afraid when a real-life assertive opportunity comes along.

THE MODEL: CONCRETE ASSERTIVE RESPONSE PACKAGES

With the deck thus stacked against him, it falls to the group trainer or leader to provide his clients with a set of concrete assertive response packages (hereafter referred to by the acronym CARP) that are as easy as possible to employ in the face of internal and situational stress. Essentially, a CARP is a set of one or more basic verbal and/or nonverbal communication tools intended to convey an assertive message. Simple CARPs may consist of a single technique; more sophisticated ones weave a variety of interpersonal tools into a rather involved, broad-based pattern. In addition, CARPs have a content goal which may or may not be reached, and a process goal which almost certainly will be reached if the CARP is implemented correctly. Finally, the package is couched in a concrete procedural framework, a sort of cognitive map that the assertive trainee can hold in his mind and refer to as needed, so as not to be led astray in the face of manipulation or stress.

An example of a simple, one-process CARP is the broken record technique, discussed by Manuel Smith (1975) in his popular book, *When I Say No, I Feel Guilty*. In this procedure, the sender repeats an "I" statement or other short, honest statement until he is sure the receiver understands what he wants and complies or agrees. When used to deal with a manipulative receiver, the "I" statement is often paired with an acknowledgment of the receiver's stated position of feelings. For example, in the following dialogue, Ralph has just told his son, George, that the family car will not be available Saturday night. Keep in mind that as Ralph applies the broken record technique he speaks in a relaxed, easy manner that does not imply any particular annoyance or criticism of his son's request.

George: But Dad, I need the car this Saturday—everybody's depending on me.
Ralph: I understand that, George, but you may not use the car Saturday night.
George: How am I going to pick up my date if I can't use the damn car? Besides, you let Jimmy use it last night!
Ralph: George, I'm not going to give you the car Saturday.
George: That's just not fair!
Ralph: I understand how you feel, son, and you won't be able to have the car Saturday.

And so on. If this dialogue seems a bit stilted, it is because the broken record technique sounds more natural to most people when combined with certain other communication strategies in real situations. (However, even when used alone it is a powerful, if not particularly stylish, assertive tactic, and is easy for the nervous novice to keep in mind under fire.) In terms of the characteristics described earlier, it qualifies as a full-fledged CARP:

Communication technique(s): "I" statements.
Content goal: George not taking the car. (Note that the content goals are sometimes unobtainable—even in the case of father, son, and car. If George has thought to have duplicate keys made, he may be long gone by suppertime.)
Process goal: Ralph's intention to communicate to George that the car will be unavailable, and that that decision itself will not be changed. (Note that the process goals are usually obtainable. George would have to be very deaf, very

strange, or a very fast runner not to catch his father's intentions about the car in the face of the broken record CARP.)

Cognitive map: CARPs are based primarily on repetition, not creativity. No matter how angry or nervous George may get in the fact of his son's manipulations, he need only keep in mind, "repeat the statement, repeat the statement" in order to carry the interaction off without a flaw.

STRESS TRAINING

As noted earlier, the most difficult aspect of becoming assertive is learning to deal with significant others under stress. Significant others, in this case, are people whose opinions or actions have sufficient impact on the trainee to affect his behavior. Parents, husbands or wives, siblings, and children usually qualify as significant others. So does the headwaiter at The Beef House if he can intimidate the trainee into eating an overcooked sirloin.

Stress training can be accomplished most easily in the group setting by breaking the trainees up into triads, with one individual playing the assertor, the second playing the assertor's significant other, and the third playing the trainer. The assertor is coached in the application of a relevant CARP in response to neutral material from the significant other until he is comfortable with it. Then, at a signal from the trainer, the significant other begins to role-play increasingly stress-producing behavior while the assertor continues to practice his CARP.

It is absolutely essential that the new assertive pattern be practiced to reflex. Fledgling trainees have enough trouble dealing with manipulative behavior on a content level without having to figure out the process of effective, counter-manipulative communication on the spot as well. So, CARPs are practiced repetitively under conditions of progressively increasing stress, until the trainee can implement them easily and consistently no matter what the significant other may do to try to throw him off center.

As an example of stress training, consider the supervisor who, after repeated warnings, has decided to report a subordinate for chronic lateness. The CARP employed in this case involves three communication tactics: "I" statements, feeling expression, and acknowledgment. (In some cases, of course, these techniques overlap. Acknowledgment as used here means a short, verbal comment signaling that a message has been received. Acknowledgment does *not* imply that the receiver agrees with the message, but only that he or she has received it.) The dialogue that follows demonstrates how an assertor can be thrown off center by a skillful adversary and fail to maintain his CARP. We pick up on the dialogue after the significant other has begun to apply high stress.

Sarah: Joan, I have some bad news for you. I'm going to turn in a supervision report regarding the times you've been late this month.

Joan: You're *what??*

Sarah: I'm going to write you up for being late a lot.
Joan: You turncoat, I thought we were friends. Just because you're the damn super-
            visor on this floor you think you're Wonder Woman all of a sudden.
Sarah: Please don't feel that way, Joan—it's my job.
Joan: Your job, hah! I'll bet you enjoy playing cop.
Sarah: Of course I don't. That's a hateful thing to say.
Joan: Well then, the least you could do would be to give me one more chance.
Sarah: But this is the fifth time you've been late this month, and it's about the third
            time you've asked for another chance.
Joan: It hasn't been that often and you know it! Besides, I really mean it this time.
            Come on, be a buddy.
Sarah: Well . . . .

Notice that Sarah got trapped primarily because she *reacted* to Joan's accusations
and other manipulations. In the face of stress she was unable simple to acknowledge Joan's comments and repeat her intention. Instead, she tried to reason with
Joan, to explain her position, rationalize herself back into Joan's favor. Not only
is this sort of reactivity ultimately doomed to failure, but it actually adds fuel to
the significant other's manipulative fire. Let us see what might have happened
had Sarah been able to stick to her CARP and not fan the flames.

Sarah: Joan, I have some bad news for you. I'm going to turn in a supervision report
            regarding the times you've been late this month.
Joan: You're *what??*
Sarah: I'm going to write you up for being late a lot.
Joan: You turncoat, I thought we were friends. Just because you're the supervisor on
            this floor you think you're Wonder Woman all of a sudden.
Sarah: I'm honestly sorry you see it that way.
Joan: If you're so sorry then what are you going to do about it?
Sarah: What I said before: I'm going to write you up.
Joan: You consider me a friend and yet you're going to write me up?
Sarah: Right.
Joan: What a rotten, two-faced thing to do!
Sarah: Well, I can see your point of view on that.
Joan: This really pisses me off!
Sarah: I can understand that.
Joan: Look, the least you can do would be to give me one more chance.
Sarah: I can understand how this upsets you, and I'm not willing to give you another
            chance.
Joan: Why not, for Crissakes?
Sarah: Look, I'm just not willing to give you another chance.
Joan: That's not fair! Mabel's always late, and you've never turned her in for it.
Sarah: True, I haven't.
Joan: Come on Sarah, I'll shape up. Give me another chance, be a buddy.
Sarah: Look, Joan, I'm going to write the lateness report on you. I like you personally
            and I hope we can stay friends—and I am going to write you up.

Sarah was able to maintain her assertive position primarily by using the three communication vehicles included in the CARP set up for her: "I" statements, acknowledgment, and sharing feelings. Again, these are artificial exercises used as intermediary steps in the training of assertive communication patterns, and are not necessarily meant to be applied in real life exactly as they were used in the role-play situation. If Sarah ever does have to confront a supervisee in this manner, she will have a variety of additional communication tools available to her. Nevertheless, if and when push comes to shove and Sarah begins to panic, she will be able to fall back on these basic techniques.

At this point, some readers may be getting the impression that CARP trainers are in the business of turning out robots—individuals who react to situations as programmed, without thinking or feeling. In fact, the opposite is true. Most people who seek training in assertive communication already *are* robots who respond automatically, almost totally without choice, to stressful situations. They blush and stammer when asking the boss for a raise; they're pushed around by aggressive or overprotective parents; they spend long nights alone rather than seek companionship and risk rejection; they watch the lighted floor indicator over the door in elevators rather than venture eye contact with their fellow riders. They are pushed around daily by salesmen, receptionists, and waiters. These behaviors feel natural to nonassertive people because they have been practicing them all their lives. But they are robots, nonetheless, and unhappy ones at that.

The main purpose of training in assertive communication is to break these inhibitory reactive patterns, return the control of the trainee's behavior to himself, and take the puppet strings away from the whims of his environment. As an intermediary deconditioning aid, the trainee is taught to replace inhibitory automatic patterns with excitatory ones. It is important that he learn these constructive patterns reflexively for two reasons. First, if he does not have the new behaviors down pat and immediately available, he will "forget" them in the face of stress and return to his old maladaptive habits. Second, the facilitative communication tools serve as building blocks for the gradual formation of a richer, more spontaneous interpersonal life-style, just as the years of piano scales Van Cliburn must have practiced helped him become the creative musical genius he is today.

It has long been known that the repetitive rehearsal of stressful situations has counterconditioning properties. As the assertive trainee continues to develop and apply constructive interpersonal skills, the inhibitory patterns will begin to drop from his behavioral repertoire. At the same time, the constructive building blocks he has learned will become progressively less artificial as he incorporates them into his own personal style of expression. The ultimate product is a truly spontaneous individual, who chooses to do what he does and has the interpersonal skills to implement that freedom of choice. (Our operational definition of *spontaneity* is "instantaneous choice": volitional behavior that is relatively free of cognitive mediation, as opposed to stimulus–response reactivity.)

CARP CONSTRUCTION

To summarize, CARP training has two practical goals. An experiential situation is constructed within which the trainee's reactive patterns to stress can be elicited, observed, limited, and eventually extinguished. At the same time, the training situation facilitates the acquisition and repetitive practice of a variety of constructive, assertive communication techniques. With these goals in mind, the following basic criteria may be helpful to the prospective CARP trainer.

CARPs must be *applicable* in practice to relatively broad-spectrum interpersonal situations. The effective package is composed of simple, easily learned communication skills which can be practiced in an artificial setting and which relate to a variety of specific applications. Further, good CARPs are so concrete and well defined that they can be learned and practiced almost "by the numbers"—applied relfexively, without thought, in situations in which the trainee might otherwise forget his lines.

Skill implementation of the package should create an interpersonal situation wherein it is possible for both participants to come out ahead if the receiver is willing to relinquish his aggressive or invasive stance. But on a more basic level, CARPs help the trainee set up no-lose interactions *independent* of the amount of cooperation from the receiver.

Unfortunately, most individuals deal with life as if it were a zero-sum game. (Baseball is an example of a zero-sum game: If the Giants beat the Dodgers by two runs, the Dodgers must have lost by exactly two runs. In a zero-sum game, if there are winners there are also losers, and the composite scores add up to zero.) The assertive individual, on the other hand, sees life as a non-zero-sum game in which both or all parties involved can win. An important assertive skill involves employing a manner or style that allows the other person to leave the interaction feeling glad that it occurred, and with increased self-esteem, no matter what the actual outcome is. For example, the good communicator can assert his own view or preference without having to demand agreement or compliance from the receiver, and is willing to "agree to disagree" after having made his own preferences clear.

The CARP must *work in the real world*, must lead to positive consequences for the assertor. That is, it must be an effective behavioral alternative in the long run *no matter what response pattern the receivers may use to counter it* (short, naturally, of physical force, which is best dealt with by rapid retreat and an immediate reassessment of the situation). This is not to say that CARPs must end with the receiver doing or agreeing with what the assertor wants him to. A CARP is effective when, after having acted, it is clear to the assertor that the interaction in question turned out about as well as it reasonably could have, given the situational circumstances at hand. The assertor really has no control at all over the receiver's reaction to him anyway. There is no guarantee that the most inspired, mellow, and creative assertive move will lead to a desired outcome.

The effective CARP simply helps the assertor take his best shot in the face of stress which otherwise might limit his behavior, and increases the *probability* that he will get what he wants.

COMMUNICATION COMPONENTS OF CARPS

Through the years, psychotherapists and other communication-oriented professionals have evolved a potpourri of interpersonal tools that fit nicely into the assertive communication training rubric and may be used as CARP components. A list and brief description of some of these tools is now presented with the following disclaimer: no one technique is for everybody. Communication is a very personal business, and people tend to be ego-involved in their own communication styles. For assertive communication training to be effective and have long-lasting benefit, it is essential that CARPs be constructed with the style, values, and preference of the individual trainee in mind.

"I" Statements

Trainees are instructed to speak in the first person when sharing their own thoughts, feelings, or points of view. This seems to be of particular importance when giving feedback. People are experts on their own feelings and preferences, and the statement, "I like your hat," is a clean, straightforward mode of feeling communication. The statement, "You have a nice hat on," somehow infers that the sender considers himself a fashion expert on hats. "I don't like what you said" is clearly preferable to, "You said a stupid thing." Incidentally, it turns out to be quite difficult to call someone a name while talking in the first person ("I think that you're stupid" does not qualify as an "I" statement). For whatever reason, therapists and marriage counselors generally agree that in the long run, relationships work better when "I" statements are used consistently.

Repetitive "I" statements (broken record technique), as discussed earlier, comprise a simple, powerful technique for getting messages across to unwilling receivers. Energy and content for manipulation derive primarily from the behavior of the manipulatee as he colludes in one way or another with the manipulator. Substituting repetitive "I" statements for creativity and reasonableness helps the assertor minimize the ammunition he gives the receiver, even as it increases his chances that his message content will be heard.

Verification

This is an active listening skill wherein the receiver pays close attention to what the sender communicates, summarizes it in his own words, and then feeds it back. For example:

Scott: Last night when you yelled at me I got pretty upset. I don't like it when you take your frustrations about school or your parents out on me. Don't do that any more.

Joan: So you don't like what happened last night, and you'd like me to stop dumping upsets from other parts of my life on you.

Scott: Yeah. If you're that upset all the time maybe you ought to go see a shrink.

Joan: You're saying I may have a problem with this that I should try to solve.

This kind of active listening can be carried on at a variety of levels. For CARP purposes it is unnecessary, and usually is counterproductive, to try to interpret and reflect deep feelings. Trainees do not need to become nondirective therapists in order to use this technique; rather, they need simply to summarize the content and *expressed* surface feelings in the sender's message. The verification itself should be couched in the form of a *tentative* "You" statement, as above. "Aha! You're saying you hate me, you rat!" does not make it as a constructive verification. Among other things, verification can be a valuable alternative to collusion or counterattack in the face of manipulative sending.

Acknowledgment

As mentioned earlier, acknowledgment is a means whereby the receiver communicates to the sender that he has received the message sent. Acknowledgment is a process variable, and technically has nothing to do with the content of the sender's message. It is particularly important to stress that acknowledgment does not imply agreement, but simply signals receipt, thereby finishing the communication cycle in progress. As such, the acknowledgment technique provides the trainee with a valuable alternative response to manipulation and criticism.

Many trainees are stuck in the either–or fallacy when it comes to negative feedback: that is, they feel they must either agree or disagree. The problem with this sort of forced-choice situation is that, no matter which alternative the trainee chooses, he is being controlled by the sender. In such a situation acknowledgment is a valuable third alternative that provides a straightforward path out of the either–or bind.

Ralph: You shouldn't eat so much, you'll get sick.

Pamela: I see your point of view.

Sally: You're ugly and your mother dresses you funny.

Peter: I hear you.

Acknowledgment has various uses in effective communication. It is a short form of verification, has reinforcing properties, serves to finish communication cycles, and can be used as a powerful countermanipulation tool. Although it is beyond the scope of this chapter to give it the detailed analysis it deserves, awareness of the impact and use of acknowledgment procedures is critical to the process of both sending and receiving in assertive communication.

Fogging

In this variation on acknowledgment as discussed by Manuel Smith, the receiver tentatively agrees with the aggressive or manipulative sender's statement in order to defuse the interaction, but does not comply with the sender's directive.

Mother: Tilda, you're crazy to be buying a house by yourself. You don't know what you're doing.
Tilda: Maybe you're right, Mom—it is a pretty big risk. (While fully intending to proceed with her plans to purchase a house.)

The value of the fogging technique lies primarily in its capacity to defuse potentially explosive interactions. In addition, some particularly unassertive trainees find it virtually impossible to refrain from agreeing with their parents or other significant persons in their lives no matter how much they would like to change. For these individuals, fogging can serve as an intermediate step to more desirable countermanipulation tactics while confrontation anxiety and other reactive barriers are being dealt with. Here the ultimate tactical goal would be to acknowledge rather than to fog negative or manipulative input.

Mother: You're crazy to be buying a house on your own.
Tilda: (Fogging) You might be right, Mom.
Tilda: (Acknowledging) I see your point of view on that.

The disadvantage of fogging, of course, is that it is not a particularly honest device; trainees are encouraged to fake agreement in order to avoid being manipulated. While fighting fire with fire can be valuable in selected cases, our preference, with other things equal, is to teach trainees to acknowledge rather than to fog.

Sharing Feelings

This is a form of meta-communication where the assertor lets the other person know how he is feeling during the assertive interaction. Aside from its obvious humanistic value, sharing feelings may allow the assertor to partially rebalance a relationship he has thrown out of whack by, say, refusing to be manipulated. For example, the husband who has manipulated his wife successfully for years, and then is suddenly confronted with a centered, assertive individual whose countermanipulative strategies are too much for him is going to feel confused, angry, and insecure very quickly. His ego is going to be bruised, and bastard though he might have been, he is going to need all the empathy and reassurance he can get. In the next example, Joyce uses the rebalancing technique to increase the probability that, long term, she and her husband will have a good relationship independent of her new-found assertiveness.

Harry: You aren't going to be home Thursday night? How can you do that to me? I'm your husband!
Joyce: I'm sorry you feel I'm doing it to you. I want to go out Thursday for me.
Harry: If you loved me you'd stay home with me and the kids, where you belong!
Joyce: Look, Harry, I'm really sorry you're upset. I do love you, and I'm going to go out Thursday night.

Selective Agreement/Reinforcement

One of the skillful manipulator's most effective ploys involves mixing honest and manipulative statements in the same package. There are a wide variety of ways this can be done. For example:

Mother: Johnnie, you know we only want you to come home because we love you. If you loved us you'd spend your vacation with your family.

or:

Willie: Mom, it isn't fair that I only get $2.50 allowance; Ralph's mother gives him $5.00 a week.

or:

Rob: Hey, I know what you're doing! You're using those damn communication techniques on me again!

These manipulations are based on the implicit assumption that if the receiver agrees or accepts the true or complimentary part of the package, he or she will have to collude with the manipulation as well. If the receiver buys into that assumption, there is trouble ahead. His or her best counterstrategy is to agree with or reinforce the positive/complimentary statement and eiher ignore the manipulative component completely or respond to it by repeating an "I" statement. Responding to these examples:

Johnnie: I know you both love me, Mother, and I love you and Dad. And I do plan to go camping in the Sierras during spring vacation.
Mom: Ralph's mother is very generous to give him $5.00 per week, isn't she?
Suzanne: (to Rob) That's true.

Agreeing to Disagree

In a variation on selective agreement which effectively avoids the either–or fallacy (in this case, the either–or fallacy reads, "Either we have to agree on this issue or we have to argue about it."), the assertor explicitly labels a disagreement between himself and the other person and then lets the matter drop, unless the receiver takes it further on his own.

Harry: If you loved me you'd stay home Thursday night.
Joyce: I'm sorry you feel that way, Harry. We have a disagreement on that issue.
Harry: We do, do we? Well, what the hell do you plan to do about it?
Joyce: Well, I guess I plan to go out Thursday night.

Flushing

Many underdog manipulations derive their power from the discrepancy between the verbalized and the implied meaning of the manipulative statement. For example:

Martha: (her tone dripping of martyrdom) No, of course not. Why should I mind if you go out and play poker again? I'll just stay home here alone with the kids and the dishes and the TV set,.

If George responds to the implied meaning in Martha's statement—that she does not want him to go to the poker game and feels angry and hurt that he would rather do so than be with her—he stands the chance of getting martyred to death for the next 20 years or so. In the flushing technique, George responds very literally to what Martha says, rather than to what he knows she means.

George: (There must be *no hint* of sarcasm in his presentation) Wow, honey, you're really an understanding wife! I'm grateful that you're okay with my playing poker once a week. See you around midnight. (And he leaves.)

The flushing technique will not solve the primary problem between George and Martha: in this case, that they have a disagreement regarding how he will spend his evening. Rather, its purpose is to short-circuit the underdog manipulation and return the communication between them to a more honest level. After two or three flushing experiences such as this one, Martha probably will choose to be more direct in telling George when she wants him to stay home at night. (In the meantime, George may expect the tension level around home to be a bit higher than normal. The flushing technique is a very powerful countermanipulation tool, and should be used only as a last resort. It works by double-binding the manipulator, and is similar to fogging in that it requires a certain amount of dishonesty on the part of the asserter.)

These are just a few of the communication tools available for implementation in CARPs. Again, which particular techniques are employed should depend as much on the style and preferences of the trainee as on the particular situation in question.

SAMPLE CARP: REQUEST–CONSEQUENCES

The request–consequences CARP is one of the most common and most valuable of the more complicated CARPs employed in assertive communication seminars. Essentially, this is a two-phase package, each phase consisting of a statement–acknowledgment cycle.

Phase I: The assertor communicates a request to the receiver. He repeats his request, using variations on the broken record technique and such other tactics as the receiver's responses may call for, until his request is acknowledged clearly, or until it becomes apparent that reasonable assertive strategies will not lead to acknowledgment.

Phase II: If his request is granted, the assertor warmly acknowledges the receiver's compliance. If it is not granted, the assertor communicates the consequences of noncompliance to the receiver. Again, consequences are shared in "I" statement form, and are repeated until acknowledged, or until it becomes reasonably clear that the message has been received and will not be acknowledged.

In order to apply this CARP effectively, it is essential that the trainee knows the difference between sharing consequences and making threats. Basically, a threat is a statement of intent made by a sender in order to influence the behavior of the receiver, whereas a shared consequence is a statement of what is going to happen if a particular event either occurs or does not occur. A threat gets its power from the manner in which it is shared; a consequence has no power of its own and does not even have to be communicated in order to be a consequence: it simply is or it isn't. A threat obviously has to be communicated in some fashion or another to be threatening. If the receiver changes his behavior in the face of a threat, he has been intimidated by the sender; if he changes his behavior because he believes that it will lead to a consequence he does not wish to experience, he has made a free and rational choice based on his expectation of what may or may not happen to him.

The law of gravity provides a good example of a consequence that clearly is not a threat. The law of gravity states that if Ralph walks off the roof he will accelerate toward the ground at 32.2 ft/sec^2, and he will hit the sidewalk with a calculable impact and destructive force based primarily on the distance between the roof and the sidewalk. Now Mother Nature never threatened Ralph with the consequences of walking off a roof; she never even told him about them. He learned the law of gravity through experience and by word of mouth. However, it is a good law in that, unless Ralph is very strange, he will probably not go around walking off roofs unless he wishes to experience the consequences of that behavior.

Operationally, a law or rule is simply a probability of relationship between an event and a consequence. It is a good law or rule to the extent that the probability that the consequences will follow the event approaches 100%. Now, in the absence of firsthand experience, people tend to evaluate laws in terms of their experience with the agency that controls the law. Mother Nature has a lot of face validity because there tends to be a high correlation between her events and her consequences. The Department of Motor Vehicles, on the other hand, does not have as much face validity because people often can park overtime or speed on the freeway without getting caught. So there is a lot of speeding and overtime parking going on.

Individuals, too, have and/or make up their own personal rules—relationships between events and consequences—to help them control their lives and environment. Other people respect and give credence to these personal rules to the extent that they believe, from past experience, that the consequences will invariably follow the events in question. This has to be pretty much a one-to-one relationship: there is a rapid falloff in face validity with very slight variations in the event–consequence consistency. Which brings us back to the request–consequences CARP.

The trainee must follow three guidelines in order to use this CARP successfully. First, he *never* shares a consequence he cannot or may be unwilling to implement. Second, he *always* follows through with his stipulated consequences when the antecedent events call upon him to do so. Third, he bends over backwards to share his consequences with the receiver in an absolutely nonthreatening manner. Remember, the only real difference between making a threat and sharing a consequence is in the intention of the sender. Threats and consequences can sound pretty much alike to the receiver.

Sally: (Making a threat) Mark, I want you to know that if you date Susie again I'm going to break up with you.
Sally: (Sharing a consequence) Mark, I want you to know that if you date Susie again I'm going to break up with you.

So it is vital that the assertor let the receiver know that his intent is *not* to threaten, but rather to supply information upon which the receiver can base a free and conscious behavioral choice.

Sally: (Sharing a consequence very carefully) Mark, I've come to a decision, and I'd like to tell you about it.
Mark: Okay.
Sally: As you've gathered, I've been pretty upset about your dating Susie. Anyway, I've decided that if you continue to see her I'm going to break up with you. I don't mean to threaten you with this, it's just what I have to do for me.
Mark: Sure as hell sounds like a threat!
Sally: I'm sorry it does; I honestly don't mean it that way. I'd like you never to see Susie again more than anything, but it's even more important to me that you make your own decision about her. I just want you to have the information about what I've decided to do if you do see her again.

The assertor has communicated that while she feels very involved in the *content* goal of the interaction, she does not want to be involved in the decision *process*. She simply wants to make available what information she has at hand, and then let the receiver make his own decision. (Obviously, in the face of intense emotion and potential loss this sort of communication is very difficult to keep clean. In practice, assertive communication trainees are taught to be aware of what is going on and do the best they can.)

Summarily, in the request–consequence CARP, the assertor must only share consequences he can control, communicate the consequences in a nonthreatening manner, and be willing to implement the consequences if compliance is not forthcoming. If he can do these things, the assertor will find the request–consequences CARP a very useful and powerful interpersonal tool.

THE CASE OF BARBARA AND KARL

The following dialogue was taken, with minor changes, from tape recording of one of our assertive communication seminars. The participants are husband and wife, and the problem was a real one for them. Barbara is the trainee, and Karl is the stress producer (in our vernacular, the button-pusher). For training purposes, Karl was asked to exaggerate the intensity and duration of his upset, but otherwise to act pretty much as he would if the dialogue were to come up at home. The communication ploys Barbara used, which were mentioned earlier, have been labeled and appear in parenthesis. (Some of the techniques appearing in this dialogue have not been discussed.)

B: Karl, I have a request.

K: What now?

B: From now on I'd like you to tell me when you think you're going to be late getting home for dinner (''I'' statement).

K: Look, you're always nagging me about that. Get off my back, will you? I'll get home when I get home, and if dinner's cold, it's cold!

B: You seem to be hearing my request as nagging (verification).

K: Damn straight I do!

B: Okay, I hear that (acknowledgment). I don't mean it as nagging—I mean it as asking you to tell me when you're going to be late. No pressure meant (repetitive ''I'' statement).

K: Why do you want to know?

B: I'd like to be able to plan my day and have dinner timed properly, and so on. Among other things, I like eating with you and I prefer my dinners hot (sharing feelings).

K: Well, you ought to be able to plan your days all right without having to know exactly when I'm going to get home every night.

B: We seem to have a difference of opinion on that one (agreeing to disagree).

K: (No answer.)

B: Please hear me. It's important to me to know when you're going to be late getting home from the office (repetitive ''I'' statement, cleverly hidden in the third person).

K: (Sarcastically) I know, you keep telling me.

B: (Ignoring sarcasm) Okay. So, I'd like you to agree to let me know if at all possible when you're going to be late (repetitive ''I'' statement).

K: Sure, sure.

B: That's okay with you; you agree with that?

K: (Looking at magazine) Sure, sure.

B: (Brightly) Okay, honey, good—I really appreciate that (flushing; positive reinforcement). Now I'd like to share one more thing with you.

K: What now?

B: I'd like to let you know what's going to happen in the event that you don't keep our little agreement.

K: What do you mean, what's going to happen? Are you threatening me?

B: No, honey, really. No threat intended. I've just come to some conclusions about cooking dinner and you letting me know when you're going to be late.

K: Well, what conclusions?

B: Well, I've decided that I'm not willing to cook dinner for you, not knowing when you're going to be home. So, actually, the consequences of your coming home late without telling me will be that, for one week following, I won't cook dinner for you (sharing consequences).

K: You *are* threatening me, dammit!

B: No, I honestly don't mean to. See, I know I have nothing to do with whether or not you keep your bargain. I certainly want you to, and pretty much trust that you will. And I guess if you don't I will be upset (sharing feelings). But I know that there's no way I can make you keep it, and I'm not going to try. I'm just telling you what's what. You're my husband, and I love you (rebalancing), and the next time you don't let me know when you're going to be late I'm not going to cook for you for a week (repetitive "I" statement).

K: Jesus, that's the most arbitrary thing I've ever heard.

B: For sure (selective agreement).

K: Well, dammit, that really pisses me off.

B: I can understand that (acknowledgment).

K: Big deal. I work my ass off at the office, and suddenly you don't want to do your part unless I tell you exactly when I'm going to come home. What is it, do you think I like working late??

B: You think that because of this decision I've made, I somehow don't appreciate the work you do as much, and I'm not willing to do my own share (verification).

K: Well, it certainly feels that way.

B: I get that (acknowledgment). I guess we see it differently (agreeing to disagree).

K: You know, if you really gave a damn about me you'd be willing to give me some rope on this.

B: It must seem to you I'm being pretty hard-ass about this whole thing all of a sudden (verification).

K: Well, aren't you doing that? Not cooking dinner, for Chrissakes!

B: I just really want to know when you're going to be coming home (repetitive "I" statement).

K: I know that! Didn't I agree to tell you?

B: Yes, you did, and I really appreciate it, honey. So this whole issue probably isn't even going to come up, huh (selective agreement; flushing; rebalancing)?

K: So, If I screw up once, all of a sudden you aren't going to cook for a week.

B: I see your point (acknowledgment). Would you like one free screw-up (negotiated compromise)?

K: Thanks a lot, Bigheart!

B: Seriously, I'm willing to give you one free mistake for every time you let me know when you're going to be late. For the time being (negotiated compromise).

K: I'll take it.

B: You got it, love.

K: This is the weirdest thing I've ever heard of.

B: Really (selective agreement; positive reinforcement).

Any interpersonal problem between significant others lends itself to a variety of constructive solutions. In this dialogue, Barbara could have responded differently at several points, and still remained within the framework of the request–consequences CARP. In this case, she did get both messages across, and eventually got apparent compliance as well, using the communication techniques she learned in the seminar.

SUMMARY

Concrete assertive response packages are characterized by four critical elements.

1. A *cognitive frame* or *map* the assertor can follow almost by rote in the face of stress.
2. A *content goal,* which involves the behavior change (usually agreement or compliance) the assertor wishes from the receiver.
3. A *process goal,* which involves getting the assertor's intention communicated, heard, and acknowledged.
4. A set of simple, easily learned *communication techniques* which facilitate a constructive, assertive interpersonal process.

CARP training utilizes two complementary procedures.

1. *Repetitive practice,* which helps the trainee to learn the communication techniques on a reflex level. Once habituated, they replace old, less constructive interpersonal programming and become building blocks for eventual free, spontaneous communications.
2. *Practice in the face of graded stress,* which aids the trainee in generalizing his newly learned skills from the group room to the real world outside.

Concrete assertive response packages come in all shapes and sizes, and can be designed for and fitted to particular needs of individual trainees. Certain CARPs, however, seem to have value to almost everyone. The request– consequence package discussed in this chapter is one example of such a process.

REFERENCE

Smith, M. *When I say no, I feel guilty.* New York: Dial Press, 1975.

T. Antoinette Ryan

Chapter 17
Acquisition of Career Decision-Making Skills

Career development is a lifelong process through which the individual develops self-identity and achieves vocational maturity. In an ideal situation career development is a positive, healthy process through which the individual realizes the potential for becoming a fully functioning person, one who has achieved self-fulfillment, is capable of maintaining effective social relationships, is able to implement citizenship responsibilities, and is able to maintain economic efficiency. To help the individual achieve this ideal is a major goal of therapy.

Accomplishing this goal is primarily a matter of identifying behavioral deficits, and assisting clients to acquire behaviors which will contribute to a positive, healthy career development. One of the most essential behaviors for healthy career growth and development, and at the same time, one of the most commonly found behavioral deficits militating against the realization of a positive self-identity and vocational maturity is effective decision-making. When individuals either lack the capability to make decisions, other than deciding not to decide, or if their decision-making is faulty, they are precluded from realizing their potential for becoming fully functioning persons. Group therapy has been used effectively to help clients overcome behavioral deficits. A model for behavioral group treatment to develop clients' capabilities for effective career decision-making derives from a set of basic assumptions.

1. The problems of adjustment to work are in some sense problems of personality (Neff, 1968).
2. Peer support is an effective means of facilitating positive change in developmental aspects of the individual.
3. Members of a therapy group learn from each other through observation, imitation, and modeling.

4. Planned use of verbal or physical rewards after a response has occurred strengthens the likelihood of the response occurring again under similar circumstances.
5. Simulation allows group members to model appropriate behaviors, while others prompt and reinforce improved behaviors.
6. A therapist who consciously and systematically cues and reinforces group behavior can more quickly and thoroughly induce behavioral change in the target response class than a therapist who uses intuitive and unplanned approaches.
7. Simulating the client's problem situation provides an opportunity for practice in coping with the problem under conditions of minimum threat and maximum reinforcement.
8. The inability to make a choice is a conflict situation, which produces anxiety and thus constrains the adequacy of self-concept and militates against self-fulfillment.

HISTORICAL OVERVIEW

The use of behavioral group therapy has gained wide recognition since this treatment modality was initiated in the early 1960s. The behavioral principles which proved to be viable for therapists working with individual clients have been equally sound when applied to group therapy.

Krasner (1962) defined psychotherapy as a lawful, predictable, directive process which would be investigated parsimoniously within the framework of reinforcement learning theory. In behavioral group treatment the therapist selectively reinforces behaviors which facilitate behavior change. Dinoff, Horner, Kuppiewski, Rickard, and Timmons (1960) used verbal prompts and reinforcement techniques to increase personal and group references made by clients in therapy groups. Williams and Blanton (1968) showed that psychotherapy clients could be reinforced for expressing statements with feeling content. Their studies showed that once a client was verbalizing freely, the potential for shaping, modifying, and directing responses into areas which would benefit the client was limited only by the degree to which the therapist was able to define appropriate responses to be reinforced. Ryan (1964) used planned cueing and reinforcement to help 18- to 20-year-old male clients improve their decision-making skills. As behavioral group therapy has evolved over the years, the trend has been toward greater sophistication on the part of the therapist in using behavioral techniques in the group setting. Whereas the therapist of the 1960s focused primarily on cueing and reinforcing techniques, the trend has been toward systematically employing a variety of behavioral techniques, including goal-setting, problem presentation, simulation, social modeling, desensitization, hypnosis, and assessment. The conceptual model presented herein for behavioral group treatment to develop clients' career decision-making capability relies primarily on functional analysis, cueing, reinforcing, contracting, simulation, and social modeling.

MODEL OF BEHAVIORAL GROUP TREATMENT TO
DEVELOP CAREER DECISION-MAKING SKILLS

This model of behavioral group treatment includes three essential elements: (a) selection and organization of clients; (b) establishment and maintenance of a structural setting; and (c) selection and utilization of behavioral techniques.

The selection of clients to comprise the treatment group is a key factor insofar as success of therapy is concerned. The group should be characterized by both heterogeneity and homogeneity. Heterogeneity in regard to sex, level of decision-making problem, marital status, and personality variables is desirable. This kind of heterogeneity, in terms of background and personality variables, facilitates the use of social roles within the group. At the same time the group should be homogeneous as far as sharing the common problem, inadequate career decision-making skills. The group should be relatively homogeneous in terms of socioeconomic background and educational achievement. If members are too disparate in those areas, it is likely that difficulties will be encountered in communicating, and this will introduce another problem, thereby compounding the primary problem of career decision-making. Stone, Parloff, and Frank (1954) suggested running a larger trial group first and then drawing members for smaller treatment groups on the basis of the individual's performance in the trial group.

Size is a critical variable in organizing the group so it will have the greatest chances for success. Groups that are too small suffer by virtue of not having the potential for providing role models within the group; small groups are adversely limited in their potential for generating alternatives to solve problems. The amount of interaction among members is limited. In groups that are too large, members can get lost. Large groups militate against optimum reinforcement. In a finite period of time, there is a limit to the number of reinforcers which can be provided. If reinforcers are distributed over too many receivers, the effectiveness of the reinforcement technique is greatly curtailed. The optimum size of the group for developing career decision-making skills is six to eight members. Goldstein, Heller, and Sechrest (1966) support this size for the treatment group.

The definition of roles is important in organizing the group. There are two roles to be filled, leader and participant. The therapist is responsible for implementing the role of the leader. The clients are participants. At the outset the behavioral expectations for these roles should be defined. The leader role is essentially that of director. This establishes the therapist in a position of authority with recognized expertise. This, in turn, contributes to his or her power as a social model and his or her effectiveness as a dispenser of rewards. The clients must know that they will be expected to participate, actively, to contribute to the accomplishment of shared goals. Each one will be expected to give help as well as receive help. It should be made clear, also, that each one will be expected to help in maintaining an environment of mutual respect and understanding. Confidentiality is assured with respect to the content of the sessions.

Finally, the organization should be a closed group, that is, new members are not accepted during the course of the treatment. The duration of the treatment group is relatively short, and much time is lost in initiating new members. Identification with the group is difficult for the person entering after the group has been formed and members have achieved the feeling of belonging to a special social organization. Members of the group tend to look on a newcomer as an outsider, and consciously or otherwise, treat the person as someone outside the group. When new personalities enter the group, an entirely different set of dynamics comes into play.

The structural setting is critical in behavioral group therapy. In behavioral therapy, the setting is seen as being directly related to the success of the treatment, since the environment is considered to be a critical element in the process. There are two dimensions of the structural setting which are important considerations for the therapist. The growth, and the time frame, must be one which will provide an optimum schedule for reinforcement. The ideal physical setting will provide a comfortable environment, with carpeted floors, adequate acoustics, controlled ventilation, comfortable seating, and complete privacy. Walls should be attractive but not distracting. The schedule for therapy sessions should provide for regular meetings once or twice a week, for 60 minutes. The meetings should be spaced to allow reflection time between sessions and to give the members time in which to try out the decision-making skills being developed in the groups. The schedule should be established at the outset and should be maintained. This gives a sense of security and stability. The capricious changing of the therapy schedule can have very negative effects. This should be avoided at all costs.

There are probably advantages to both limited and unlimited time frames. This model employs a limited time frame. The duration can vary from 3 to 6 months, but the calendar for the series of group sessions should be established at the beginning. The members should be aware of the time frame within which they will be working.

The rationale behind the use of a specified, limited time frame is that this serves to create a pressure on the clients to move toward the treatment goals, particularly as the end of therapy looms in sight. Time-limited groups tend to optimize outcomes, that is, maximum gains in career decision-making skills are realized in the least amount of time. In using time-limited groups, provision should be made for recycling members who fail to reach criterion levels of peformance by the end of the series of group sessions. Every effort should be made to try to get the members to the goal levels they set for themselves at the beginning. However, members should have the option of participating in another therapy group at a later time in the event they fail to develop the level of proficiency in career decision-making that they had hoped to achieve.

A modified time-limited structure can be used, in which members are given the option to phase out before the end of the series, if they reach criterion levels of performance and do not wish to continue. In this case the fact that a person is getting ready to terminate should be made explicit, to give full opportunity for the individual to serve as a social model for others in the group, and also to let the members have a chance to give reinforcement and feedback to the person who has developed the desired level of career decision-making skills. When a modified time-limited structure is used, it is important to be sure that the group does not get too small. An alternative to phasing out is to take recognition of the accomplishment made by a member reaching the criterion performance level, and, at the same time, giving the chance to set a higher goal which the person will hope to achieve in the time remaining. This has the advantage of using time as a pressure initially, while making it possible to reward achievement of the client's goals and still maintaining the person in the group as a social model.

The schedule of sessions should provide for three distinct phases. The first two sessions should be devoted primarily to establishing the ground rules, refining assessment techniques, establishing and accepting expectations, and setting up an environment of trust and belongingness. The final session should be both termination and transition. The initial session and the final one are unique in purpose and content. In the final session the clients must be prepared to bridge the gap between the treatment group, in which there is continuing reinforcement from within the group, to the outside world, in which the individual for the most part will have to find reinforcement within the person. Ideally, the therapist should begin to prepare the members for the termination session several weeks in advance. The problem of inadequate career decision-making skills is, in effect, an anxiety problem. The inability to make decisions arouses anxiety. The focus of treatment in these cases is on reduction of anxiety by helping the client to acquire behaviors, the lack of which was creating the anxiety in the first place. It becomes very important to avoid any possible anxiety which might be aroused by virtue of being separated from the group. This kind of separation anxiety is a concomitant of group treatment, and it requires skillful handling on the part of the therapist to alleviate the problem. A goal for the therapist using behavioral group treatment must be to move the client from the position of group member who is sensitized to the support and reinforcement of the group to the status of an individual who is able to make decisions independently and to deal with problems of career development from an internal frame of reference.

The bulk of the time falling between the initial and terminal session makes up the third part of the treatment calendar. It is during these interim sessions that the therapist employs behavioral techniques to the fullest extent possible. There are many behavioral techniques and it will be up to the therapist to select and use those which seem most appropriate in any given situation. Regardless of techniques that are used, it is a good idea to start each session with a brief review of the ground rules, a report by the members of where they are in relation to the ultimate goals they have set for themselves, and reports of what each one accomplished since the last meeting in relation to the expectations which the individuals had for themselves. During these reports by the clients the therapist has an opportunity for selectively cueing and reinforcing the group members. Each meeting should close with a summary of the session and a commitment on the part of the members as to what they will do in the way of career decision-making before the next session.

A positive psychological climate is an especially important part of the structural setting. Opening each session with a brief review of the ground rules helps to maintain the kind of psychological climate that is essential for effective behavioral group treatment. The rules will have been established at the opening session and consensus on accepting the rules will have been achieved. At each subsequent session the therapist should call on one or more of the group members for a restatement of the rules: (a) maintaining strict confidentiality concerning everything that takes place within the group; (b) maintaining a commitment to contribute to the group and to help one another; (c) maintaining mutual respect and appreciation for others; and (d) extending common courtesies, such as listening while others are speaking and being considerate of others. This would include such things as getting to sessions on time.

SELECTING AND UTILIZING BEHAVIORAL TECHNIQUES

The particular behavioral techniques which are to be used with any treatment group and the sequence and configuration of techniques will depend on the situation. It is the responsibility of the therapist to be skilled in using the various techniques, and to be able to analyze the situation as a basis for determining which techniques to use and how to use them.

A *functional analysis* of behavior is an assessment of behavior in the situational context to determine the cues which elicit certain responses and what happens after the responses have occurred either to strengthen and reinforce them or to weaken them. To change behavior it is necessary to either change the effects that certain behaviors have or to develop new responses to old cues. If, for example, being unable to make a career decision elicits support, interest, and concern on the part of significant others, then it is entirely possible that the individual's nondeciding reponses are, in fact, being made in order to realize these effects. This would be particularly likely in the situation in which the individual found it very satisfying to be the object of outside interest and concern. On the other hand, it may be that the cue which elicits a nondeciding response is fear. If the individual experiences a feeling of fear whenever presented with a choice, then the response in all likelihood will be to not make a choice. In order to develop a schedule of cueing and reinforcement aimed at helping the individual overcome inadequate decision-making, it would be extremely helpful if the therapist knew just what effects the nondeciding responses had and what cues elicited these responses. The technique of functional analysis could be employed to advantage in this regard. When this technique is used in group treatment, the therapist explains what functional analysis is, and contracts with each client to make such an analysis before the next session. When this is done in one of the initial sessions, the therapist is able to use cueing and reinforcement much more effectively than otherwise. The process of making the functional analysis also has benefits for the clients. Eventually it is intended that they will be able to set up and control their own internal cueing and reinforcing processes. By knowing their response–consequence and cue–response relationships, they are better able to develop and implement career decision-making skills which will support their own positive growth and development.

To reinforce is to present a verbal or physical reward after a response has occurred, which will have the effect of strengthening the likelihood of the response occurring again. In psychotherapy a client's behavior generates *reinforcing consequences* in the therapist's attentive reactions. The attention, approval, acceptance, and interest of the therapist, expressed either verbally or nonverbally, serve to reinforce, that is, to strengthen selectively the behavior of the client.

Cues or prompts are verbal or nonverbal stimuli intended to eilict responses in the content area of therapeutic concern. Reinforcement occurs when a therapist calls attention to and acknowledges something that has already been said by a client; cueing occurs when the therapist gives prompts to encourage behavior in the target response class. The therapist reinforces by acknowledging verbally client responses in the target response class with expressions such as "Good," "Fine," or "That sounds like a good idea," or nonverbal responses such as smiles or nodding the head. The therapist gives cues by prompting the clients to talk about career choices, to explore possible career options, to consider risks of various career choices, to explore possible career options, to consider risks of various career options, to clarify values in relation to career choices, and to make decisions between competing career alternatives. The therapist also selectively withholds reinforcement when members of the group engage in non-decision-making behaviors.

In group treatment, it will be found that members of the group will soon be using reinforcement and cueing with each other, since they will tend to model after the behavior of the therapist. Thus, in the group treatment process, the reinforcement and cueing techniques become extremely powerful by virtue of the fact that an individual member of the group derives the reinforcing and cueing benefits from other members of the group as well as from the therapist.

A *contract* is an agreement between two or more parties in which a specified level of performance and the consequences for attaining that level of performance are stated and agreed upon by the parties concerned. In group therapy the contract is between an individual member of the group and the other persons in the group. In this model minicontracts are used during the course of therapy, not only to help the clients strengthen their career decision-making responses, but also to teach the clients to write their own contracts with themselves or with members of their family. Clients are expected to make minicontracts each session. The last part of the session is devoted to contracting. Each client agrees to a specified level of career decision-making before the next session. For example, a client might agree to make two career decisions before the next session. In turn, the members of the group would agree to a reinforcement to be provided as a consequence to having made the two promised decisions. An essential part of contracting is goal setting. In this model the numbers of the group must set the performance level they want to achieve.

The use of *simulation* and role-playing techniques enables clients to model appropriate behaviors which others can imitate, as well as providing a means for selectively cueing and reinforcing each other for the desired behaviors. This model uses a set of simulated situations in which profiles are provided of individuals who generally are typical of the members of the group. Each profile describes an individual who is faced with a situation requiring a series of immediate and long-term decisions. As the members of the group talk through the situation in which the fictitious individual finds himself or herself, the therapist selectively provides verbal and nonverbal reinforcement for decision-making responses on the part of the group members. This use of simulation as part of the behavioral group treatment relies heavily upon role-playing and a concomitant identification with the fictitious individuals in the simulated profiles. As the clients engage in decision-making behaviors for the fictitious individuals, under conditions of reinforcement, they are little by little internalizing the decision-making process and incorporating these skills into their own behavior repertoires. As the clients are engaged in making career decisions for the fictitious persons in the simulated situations, they are in fact developing decision-making skills which they can implement in making choices related to their own career development.

In behavioral group treatment, the therapist plays a key role. The therapist is the central and most valued person in the group. Thus, the therapist's interventions have the effect of powerful social reinforcements for the group members. The therapist is viewed as a person of value, deriving from his or her recognized expertise, prestige, and authority status. The therapist serves as a *role model* for members of the group, and, as such, is in a position of being able to develop behaviors on the part of the clients by virtue of their imitating and identifying with the group leader.

It is vitally important for the therapist to overtly demonstrate career decision-making responses, as well as to reinforce the responses made by the clients.

In the course of selecting and utilizing behavioral techniques to develop career decision-making skills of clients in group treatment, it behooves the therapist to be able to *synthesize* a number of techniques into one orderly, organized whole. It is more a matter of being able to combine rational analysis, contracting, cueing, reinforcing, simulation, and social modeling, than it is to use any one technique in isolation. This model espouses as the ideal an approach in which simulation is used primarily to afford a base for clients to practice career decision-making under conditions of planned cueing and reinforcement, with the therapist serving as a social model throughout the treatment process. The use of rational analysis and contracting as integral parts of the treatment group, serves as a means to help the clients learn these techniques for continued posttreatment use and as a means of establishing a frame of reference for realistic therapy in terms of individual needs of the clients making up the group.

VALIDITY OF THE MODEL

The validity of behavioral group treatment of deficits in career decision-making skills derives from experimental studies of the model. The development of decision-making behaviors has been a viable goal of therapy since the 1950s. However, it was not until the 1960s that behavioral techniques were implemented to help clients overcome decision-making problems. Ryan (1964) used verbal reinforcement and planned cueing in individual counseling with 18- to 20-year-old male clients to help them improve decision-making behavior. In this study it was demonstrated that it was possible to either increase or decrease client's decision or deliberation responses by giving or withholding response-–contingent reinforcement. The possibility of using simulation materials to develop decision-making dates to the 1960s. Boocock (1966) at Johns Hopkins University developed a life career game which was used effectively to develp decision-making capabilities. Varenhorst (1968) used the life career game with elementary age children. In a massive study of behavioral group therapy, Ryan (1968) tested the effects of combining reinforcement techniques, social modeling, and simulation to help clients overcome career decision-making deficits. A pretest–posttest control group design was used with subjects assigned randomly to five treatment conditions. In testing major hypotheses, analysis of variance was used to determine if statistically significant differences on criterion tests obtained across treatments. Controls were implemented over initial decision-making abilities, therapist influence, and Hawthorne effect. In the simulation-–reinforcement groups, the simulation materials consisted of profiles of fictitious persons, derived from analysis of the backgrounds, personal characteristics, and problems of the clients. Each profile provided information on the fictitious person's parents, siblings, and home situation. A description of the person included likes and dislikes, abilities and achievements, important events in life, and career-related problems. Each profile provided test data. The simulation--reinforcement groups were initiated with therapist and clients deciding on expected outcomes for each member of the group. The therapist explained that the simulated materials would be the focal part of the sessions, as a means of helping members of the group overcome their problems with career decision-making. All members of the group had behavioral deficits in the area of career decision-making skills. The therapist explained that the profiles were to provide a chance for seeing "how someone like you facing a similar problem might go about solving it." Reinforcement techniques consisted of therapist verbal and nonverbal responses of encouragement and approval. An atmosphere of warmth and nonthreat was created, and the therapist purposefully attempted to serve as a social model. At the conclusion of the treatment, the results in terms of decision-making skills were compared with results from four other modalities: (a) reinforcement only; (b) simulation only; (c) active control; and (d) inactive control. Results were significant ($p < .01$) in favor of the simulation--reinforcement group therapy for developing career decision-making skills of clients having these manifest behavioral deficits.

CONCLUSION

The lack of adequate career decision-making skills constitutes a major problem for many people in this world of rapid social and economic change. The need to help clients cope with this problem is a major challenge to therapists, both in terms of the number of individuals involved and the seriousness of the problem.

A behavioral group treatment employing a systematic synthesis of planned reinforcement and cueing, simulation, and social modeling, together with functional analysis and contracting, offers a viable approach for treating this kind of behavioral deficit. In implementing this model the therapist is challenged to the utmost. This is no cookbook approach, nor is it an approach which allows the therapist a passive role. Rather, the therapist is called on to be actively engaged in a process of continuing assessment, synthesis of behavioral techniques, reassessment, and resynthesis of approach.

REFERENCES

Boocock, S. *Effects of games with simulated environments on student learning.* Unpublished doctoral dissertation, Johns Hopkins University, Baltimore, 1966.

Dinoff, M., Horner, R. F., Kuppiewski, B. S., Rickard, H. C., & Timmons, E. O. Conditioning the verbal behavior of a psychiatric population in a group therapy-like situation. *Journal of Clinical Psychology,* 1960, *16,* 371–372.

Goldstein, A. P., Heller, K., & Sechrest, L. B. *Psychotherapy and the psychology of behavior changes.* New York: Wiley, 1966.

Krasner, L. The therapist as a social reinforcement machine. In H. Strupp & L. Luborsky (Eds.), *Research in psychotherapy.* Washington, D.C.: American Psychological Association, 1962, pp. 25–40.

Neff, W. S. *Work and human behavior.* New York: Atherton Press, 1968.

Ryan, T. A. The effect of planned reinforcement counseling on client decision-making behavior. *Journal of Counseling Psychology,* 1964, *11,* 315 323.

Ryan, T. A. *Effect of an integrated instructional-counseling program to improve vocational decision-making.* Corvallis, Oregon: Oregon State University, 1968.

Stone, A. R., Parloff, M. B., & Frank, J. D. The use of "diagnostic groups" in a group therapy program. *International Journal of Group Psychotherapy,* 1954, *4,* 274.

Varenhorst, B. B. Innovative tool for group counseling: The life career game. *School Counselor,* 1968, *15,* 357–362.

Williams, R. I., & Blanton, R. L. Verbal conditioning in a psychotherapeutic situation. *Behaviour Research and Therapy,* 1968, *6,* 97–103.

PART VI

Conclusions and New Directions

David L. Sansbury

Chapter 18
Behavioral Group Techniques and Group Process Issues

In this volume, a variety of treatment techniques have been presented for both the alleviation of a range of problematic behaviors and the acquisition of a number of important life skills. All the treatments have the common element of being conducted in a group context, be it with a couple, a family, or a nonrelated aggregate of individuals. This chapter attempts to explore the full implications of the group setting for behavior therapy with particular emphasis on the actual and potential influences of group processes on the conduct and outcome of therapy. It is the thesis of this chapter that: (a) the group functioning objectives, such as high cohesiveness, altruism, and protreatment group norms, are important to patient change and should be thoughtfully attended to by the behavior therapist *and* (b) behavioral techniques can be utilized to foster the desired group functioning objectives. Thus, this chapter addresses itself to both the traditional group therapist and to the behaviorally oriented group therapist with the attitude that each can learn from the other's methods and techniques for improving their own groups for more effective patient change. It carries out this goal by presenting a synthesis of the group dynamics and the behavior therapy in groups orientations.

INTEGRATION OF GROUP DYNAMICS AND BEHAVIORAL ORIENTATIONS

In order to explicate a creative merging of the two approaches to group therapy clearly, it is necessary to present a model of group process and group development. Although Yalom (1970) has identified a list of curative factors in group therapy based on his research and that of others, he does not fully develop a model of the sequential emergence of the factors and how each may be furthered by therapist intervention. This section provides the outline of such a model.

Universality

Out of the initial coming together, sharing of problems and goals, and discovering similarities of backgrounds, conflicts, and motivations for joining the group, a sense of universality emerges. Although feelings of universality feed on themselves in that the members are able to find more and more areas of similarity, its emergence can be facilitated by a number of therapist behaviors prior to and during the first session. The selection of group members on the basis of similar educational and socioeconomic backgrounds, of similar problems, and of similar desired goal behaviors is one approach. While discussions of this approach can be easily caught up in the simple-minded, heterogeneity--homogeneity controversy without adequate resolution, there is a sophisticated view which diverts attention toward clinically isolating those specific inter-member similarities and differences leading to the most interactive, compatible, and potentially therapeutic group. In this approach the focus of attention is on the behavioral attributes of the potential member, not descriptive attributes. With an eye toward increasing the factor of universality and at the same time increasing the likelihood that appropriate models will be available in the group, both Bertcher and Maple (1974) and Rose (1972) have advocated procedures for balancing group membership on critical behavioral attributes as they relate to the group objectives.

For example, if one group member wishes to increase social assertiveness, a second member with another type of problem is chosen for his skill in interpersonal situations in addition to a shared concern with the first member over recurring depression.

A second approach to influencing the emergence of universality can occur in the first session. The questions for most new members of a therapy group are as follows: Why am I here? Do I belong here? Why are all these other people here? Are their problems similar to mine? By beginning the group with a focus on the similarity of the problems brought by the members and a focus on common goals and objectives, the therapist fosters a sense of belonging and purpose, and begins establishing therapeutic group norms. This emphasis on goals is typified in an article by Sundel and Lawrence (1972), who write

In the treatment approach to group work, goals for the solution of each member's problems are specified early in the group's history. These goals may be revised later or changed, but it is essential that the members and worker have a concrete understanding of each of their treatment goals. The evaluation of success rests on the extent to which a member's specified goal has been reached. (p. 34)

The sharing of information, the establishment of common problems, goals, and purposes, and a feeling of not being all alone in one's misery reduce the individual's personal anxiety and promote the establishment of a feeling of cohesiveness among the group members. The feelings of similarity allow the members to share in the therapeutic group processes.

Cohesiveness

Through this initial sharing one develops a sense of belongingness; each individual shares the feeling of having a place in the group. There develops a sense of oneness of purpose and the purpose helps bind the members together. This developing sense of unity and attraction of the members to the group is referred to as cohesiveness, and nearly all writers within the field of group work mention cohesiveness as a key element in the process of group therapy, and at the core of a successful group. Without the emergence of this factor, there really is no group.

It has been argued that "what goes on in the psychotherapeutic 'working-through' process is a kind of conditioned learning in which the therapist's overt and covert responses act as 'reward–punishment' cues which reinforce more mature patterns" (Marmor, 1966, p. 363). Thus, the reinforcement of selected behavior is one of the processes by which the therapist facilitates behavior change in group therapy. Yet, as Liberman (1970a) asserts, the principles of operant conditioning do not help us to select the behavioral unit to be reinforced in order to produce changes of benefit to the patient. Help with that selection comes from the literature on group therapy and group dynamics, and out of that literature comes the key concept of cohesiveness.

The possibilities for a creative synthesis in the merging field of behavioral orientation and the group process field is exemplified in the research of Liberman (1970a, b). He tested out two hypotheses: (a) "By prompting and reinforcing intermember behavior that reflects mutual recognition, interest, concern, and acceptance, the therapist can help the group members resolve their problems with intimacy and foster group cohesiveness," and (b) "A therapist who consciously and systematically prompts and reinforces group behavior noted. . .above can more quickly and thoroughly induce behavioral and personality change in the target dimensions than a therapist who uses more intuitive and unplanned approaches" (Liberman, 1970a, p. 145). His data strongly support both hypotheses.

Based on a review of studies of verbal conditioning in groups, Goldstein, Heller, and Sechrest (1966) earlier had set forth an hypothesis rather similar to Liberman's first hypothesis. Specifically, they predicted: "Therapy group cohesiveness may be increased by differential reinforcement of patient group-oriented verbalizations versus individual-oriented verbalizations" (p. 421).

The two studies most related to this hypothesis were reported by Dinoff and his colleagues (Dinoff, Herner, Kurpiewski, & Timmons, 1960a; Dinoff, Herner, Kupiewski, Ricard, & Timmons, 1960b). Their aim was to demonstrate the potential for verbally conditioning schizophrenic patients in a quasi-group therapy setting to emit therapy-relevant, personal verbalizations and group verbalizations. In the first study, after determining initial response levels over three group sessions, the 10 subjects were divided into two matched groups of 5 subjects each. Each group met separately with the investigator for six 50-minute sessions. In one group the investigator elicited and reinforced personal responses from each patient as well as reinforced any spontaneous personal remarks. In the other group, the same procedures were applied to group verbalizations. Following these meetings, the patients returned to the combined group situation and a free discussion format with the investigator not present. The subjects' verbalizations were again observed and judged for three 50-minute sessions. Four of the five subjects in the personal-focus group increased in percentage of personal responses while four of the five subjects in the group-focus group decreased in personal responses.

A second study was undertaken to measure the learning during the conditioning process itself prior to the subjects being reorganized into the larger group again. Using a similar procedure, 12 schizophrenic patients were divided into two groups, one eliciting and reinforcing personal statements and the other group statements. Following each of the three treatment sessions, the investigator left the room after instructing each group to continue its discussion for another 50 minutes. These sessions were observed and rated as before. The results indicate a highly significant increase of personal and group responses in the personal-focused and group-focused experimental groups, respectively.

Thus, there is experimental support for the position that verbal conditioning techniques may be used effectively in a group setting to alter members' verbalizations in ways that impact on and further the evolving group processes.

Krumboltz and Potter (1973) built upon and extended Liberman's concepts by further specifying the group behaviors which operationally define cohesiveness, trust and openness, and task accomplishment. They also provided an extensive list of leader behaviors as well as group exercises which could facilitate these three group processes. The specific behavioral techniques of modeling and extinction were added to the procedures of prompting and reinforcement used by Liberman.

Group Norms

One major result of increased cohesiveness is the greater value attached to the group and the development of group norms regarding permissible, desired, and unapproved behaviors. Positive attitudes develop among members of the group, each taking on greater and greater reinforcement value for the other group members. Accompanying this increased attraction, though, is the increased fear that deviant attitudes or behaviors will result in rejection, thus depriving the member of reinforcements. "The more cohesive the group, the greater the probability that members will develop uniform opinions and other behaviors with respect to matters of consequence to the group" ((Lott, 1961, p. 284). Thus, through the process of cohesiveness, the group's capacity to control behavior by providing a system of rewards and punishments is established.

There is some likelihood that one group norm which could be established early in the group's life will be a strong dependency on the leader with greatly decreased self-imitating behaviors by the members. Often therapy groups will enter into a dependency stage with the attitude that the leader is there to supply all the needs of the members and they have to but wait to be cured in turn. The behavioral group therapist needs to recognize this possibility and to systematically prompt and reward the initial attempts of the members to work directly on their problems. Throughout the course of the group, it is the major task of the therapist to harness the capacity of groups for influencing members and to direct the norms toward therapeutic goals.

The importance of directing the group's motivational and reinforcement power even in behavioral groups is clearly presented by Goldstein and Wolpe (1972):

Group pressure is a powerful motivating factor in changing attitudes and actions. The group therapist's role in actuating this potential is one of solidifying and channeling this pressure on each member in a therapeutic direction. He identifies the inappropriate and specifies the more appropriate behavior. The direction of change is kept constantly overt by references to the goals to be achieved by each member, making them clear to all present the appropriate direction for each one. The therapist does not hesitate to interrupt or correct any member's advice that tends to be irrelevant or potentially distracting or oppositional to movement toward determined goals. The therapist has the particular advantage that he is identified as the expert, that he has little difficulty in applying solidified group pressure when he so desires. (p. 146)

THERAPEUTIC CHANGE PROCESS

At this point, after the evolution of group universality and cohesiveness, and after the establishment of protreatment group norms, the stage is set for change to begin. The initial step in change is the elicitation of the issues that are troublesome to the member. This is accomplished quite openly and directly by the behaviorally oriented group therapist as evidenced in the foregoing quote, and the constant focus on the individual member's goals is a hallmark of behavioral groups. The establishment of cohesiveness and protreatment group norms helps to reduce individual member anxiety and leads to increased member-to-member interaction. Patients begin seeing each other as peers, and the group generates a feeling of altruism, "I help you and you help me." Within this supportive context, members now are willing to share and work on the problems which brought them to therapy. Some talk *about* their problems while others will readily display the problem behavior within the group. Given a here-and-now enactment of the problem behaviors along with a clear agreement on treatment goals between the patient and therapist, the process of change is underway.

The next and most crucial step in the sequence of change is that the problem behavior, thought, or feeling must be dealt with in a way that is different from the patient's previous history. The patient learns to give up old inappropriate, maladaptive, and possibly harmful ways and learns new more appropriate and adaptive behaviors. Although the state of knowledge about people-changing is still primitive and no single method or set of techniques has been shown to change all, the procedures based upon social learning theory and carried out in a group context as has been presented in this volume offer the most effective set of techniques currently available.

As members of the therapy group begin working on their problems within the group, other members observe and imitate effective behaviors and solutions. Yalom (1970) has specified "identification" as one of the 10 curative factors available in therapy groups. While this factor may emerge naturally in all therapy groups, it is not always certain that members will profit fully from this process without intervention from the therapist. It is too much to assume that group members will do just the right thing at the right time and others will attend fully and accurately to just the right stimuli. Drawing upon the existing research on modeling, the behaviorally oriented therapist will institute a more controlled and more powerful procedure. Live or filmed models are introduced who enact the desired behavior for the member who is seeking change and who has been instructed in what critical behavior to observe. Ideally, a variety of models are used or, where this is not feasible, the patient is instructed to imagine a variety of models successfully completing the desired behaviors. Following the modeling, the therapist or the model works with the patient in a process of guided participation and his successful approximations to the modeled behavior are amply rewarded verbally by the therapist and the group members.

Several recent studies substantiate the importance of providing guided participation following modeling for both increasing acquisition of desired behavior and reducing avoidance behaviors. Friedman (1971) studied the differential effects of information, modeling, and role-playing on the acquisition of assertive behavior. He assigned 101 subjects randomly to one of six treatment conditions: live modeling directed role-playing, improvised role-playing, modeling plus directed role-playing, reading assertive script, reading nonassertive script. For the male subjects, modeling plus directed role-playing was the most effective treatment whereas the women showed greatest change following the improvised role-playing.

The following two studies have focused on reducing avoidance behavior using guided participation following modeling. Bandura, Blanchard, and Ritter (1969) compared the effectiveness of participant modeling, symbolic modeling, and standard desensitization in the treatment of snake phobia. In the participant modeling condition, after demonstrating the desired behavior the model guides the observer personally through the steps involved, directly assisting if necessary. In the study, 92% of the participant modeling subjects significantly reduced their phobia. This method was more successful than the symbolic modeling condition, and both modeling groups proved superior to the standard desensitization treatment group.

In order to study the relative efficacy of two covert modeling procedures and guided participant modeling in treating avoidance behavior, Thase and Moss (1976) assigned eight subjects randomly to one of four treatment conditions: covert modeling with a similar other as model, covert modeling with themselves as model, live modeling followed by the model guiding the subject's participation, and delayed-treatment control group. The guided modeling group was significantly more effective in reducing general and specific self-reported fears and had significantly greater approach behavior than the other three groups.

A patient's successful change in behavior, whether reduced avoidance behavior or increased skill, is a model for the other group members and a motivating and supporting force for their attempts at change. One value of a balanced group is now apparent. With optimal selection, each member has a paired member who is skilled in the desired goal behavior and, thus, capable of serving as an effective peer model. Although imitative behavior is a naturally occurring group curative factor, its effectiveness can be augmented through the procedures associated with guided modeling.

There are two major effects of this modeling with reinforcement, guided participation, and verbal reinforcement in groups. First, and most obvious, is behavior change in the problem areas; that is, the patient gets better. Second, the group develops more cohesion. Based on Hullian theory, Lott (1961, p. 281) hypothesized that in a group where rewards or satisfactions have been frequent, each individual will develop a positive attitude toward every other member of the group who has been consistently present when goals have been achieved. A study by Lott and Lott (1960) tended to support this hypothesis. In nontechnical language, when people start getting better, the members like the group even more.

A second major way in which behavior change is effected through group therapy has been identified in the group process literature as interpersonal learning. The group presents the members with an opportunity to express their target or problem behaviors, feelings, and attitudes; to try out new behaviors; and to receive accurate feedback from a variety of observers in a relatively safe environment. Although aspects of this curative factor overlap the change process involving modeling and guided participation, it is presented as a distinct process because of the lack of modeling the appropriate behavior and the emphasis on discrimination learning. The therapeutic interventions which focus on feedback have been well described by Goldstein and Wolpe (1972):

> Every effort is made to encourage members to respond as honestly and openly as possible to one another. As the members become able to do so to a greater degree than customary social interchanges permit, everyone in the group is subjected to an unprecedented and valuable experience through the emotional, attitudinal, and verbally expressed action tendencies. Some furnish immediate feedback, allowing a member to form connections between his behavior and the responses of others. In the beginning, the feedback tends to be expressed in general terms—such as, "You strike me as the typical salesman type" and "You really don't like women, do you?" The therapist then works toward restatement in more concrete terms so that the recipient may more easily discriminate the particular behavior that elicits such responses. (p. 130)
>
> The goal is to make these connections as explicit as possible. Very often, being able to discriminate in this way about behavior is the first step toward change. Once a person becomes aware of the effect of his behavior, he may choose the behavior he would like to begin to change. (p. 131)

The provision of well-timed, accurate, and behavior-oriented feedback is a crucial element in discrimination learning and in the broader curative factor of interpersonal learning. To be clear in our use of the term, the definition of feedback presented by Benne, Bradford, and Lippitt (1964) would probably be acceptable to a majority of users of the term: "Feedback, as used here, signifies verbal and nonverbal responses from others to a unit of behavior provided as close in time to the behavior as possible, and capable of being perceived and utilized by the individual initiating the behavior" (p. 24).

Recently Alfred Jacobs (1974) presented a very thorough review of the use of feedback in groups and summarized the results of a series of studies by himself, Todd Schaible, and others. In general, their findings indicate that positive feedback is preferable to negative since it appears to the receiver as more accurate, having greater impact, and leading to a greater sense of group cohesiveness. Also, when it precedes negative information, it helps make the negative information more believable and gives rise to greater group cohesiveness than when the reverse order is true. When the feelings of the speaker are added to the information feedback, the information is seen as more believable. Finally, behavior-oriented feedback is seen as more valuable than other types, and the combination of positive emotional statements and identification of instances of desirable behaviors yields greater believablity, impact, and intention to change than a focus on undesirable behaviors. (pp. 44–443)

In earlier studies, Lippitt (1959) demonstrated that counseling interviews focused upon what group members thought of the member and how they wanted him to change caused significant changes in the members getting feedback. French, Sherwood, and Bradford (1966) demonstrated that a person's self-identity is influenced by the opinions that group members share with him; that the more that is communicated to the person, the more the change in self-identity; and that the more the person is dissatisfied with his present self-perception, the more likely he is to change this self-perception.

Thus feedback has been demonstrated to be an effective change agent in groups and the most effective sequence, focus, and type have been well researched. Of particular importance to this chapter is the interaction of feedback and the group process of cohesiveness. Quoting from Jacobs (1974):

If our results are generalizable to such longer and more complex attempts to change the behavior of individuals by group intervention techniques as psychotherapy and growth groups, one might speculate that setting ground rules which limited early feedback between group members to statements of positive valence, or encouraged members to deliver such statements to each other, would increase the attraction between group members as well as facilitating the acceptance of later feedback. (p. 434)

THERAPEUTIC CYCLE

Thus, it has been demonstrated that one of the direct results of both behaviorally oriented interventions discussed, one based on modeling principles and the other on discrimination learning procedures, is to increase the level of group cohesiveness. Hence the model of group development as it is evolving in this synthesis is a cyclical one. Universality helps set the stage for the beginnings of group cohesiveness which gives rise to the development of group norms. The group norms act as a motivating, rewarding, and sanctioning system which helps to induce attempts at behavior change and reinforces successes. Behavioral interventions foster the initial group processes, initiate the individual change process, and mobilize the social reinforcement value of group members for discrimination and interpersonal learning. Also and importantly, successful individually focused interventions result in increased group cohesiveness. This greater cohesiveness strengthens the group norms of altruism, support for risks and change, and openness to giving and receiving feedback. Thus, the stage is set for additional behavior change by other members and the cycle is given renewed energy.

The interaction of the group member with this cycle is clearly described by Goldstein and Wolpe (1972):

Just as group pressure motivates the initiation of new behavior, group approval of action completed serves as a powerful reinforcer of that action, further increasing the probability that the new behavior will be repeated and broadened. Once a person begins to conform to group pressure, he receives reinforcement through direct statements of approval. More importantly, he is reinforced by being accepted as having tried and by added acceptance of his pain and sharing of his joys. He comes to feel part of the group. The feeling of belonging that develops further increases the motivational and reinforcing power of the group (p. 158)

CONFLICT PHASE

Readily apparent to the therapist or theorist versed in the literature on group development is the absence of the conflict or counterdependent phase in the group model presented. It is the author's contention that behavioral groups greatly minimize the need for and, in many cases, are therapeutically effective without the occurrence of a conflict phase. In nonbehavioral therapy groups this phase results from the group leader not meeting the members' expectations regarding leadership after they had entered into a dependent status early in the group's life. Dissatisfaction and hostility arise when the leader frustrates the dependency through upsetting expectancies regarding his role. According to group development theory, this stage is seen as necessary for the development of protherapeutic group norms and independence of group members. The difference between behavioral and nonbehavioral therapy groups was anticipated by Goldstein, Heller, and Sechrest (1966) who proposed two hypotheses both firmly rooted in group dynamics and related research findings. They predicted:

(a)   In early stages of a course of group psychotherapy a leader-centered therapist orientation will be associated with less patient hostility and more patient attraction to the therapist and to the group than will a group-centered therapist orientation.
(b)   In later stages of a course of group psychotherapy a leader-centered therapist orientation will be associated with more patient hostility and less patient attraction to the therapist and to the group than will a group-centered approach. (p. 373)

Thus, the preferred therapist orientation is one in which the therapist is active, directing, structuring, encouraging, and suggesting early in the group life and, then, gradually turns over the leadership roles to the group with the result that the group is essentially self-directing in later steps. This summary is an excellent description of the typical behavioral group and helps to explain how hostility toward the leader is minimized in these groups.

In this attempted merger of behavioral and group dynamics orientations, it is important to point out the research of Robert Liberman (1970b). Liberman reviewed the group dynamics literature on the issue of dealing with authority and presented the major working hypothesis from that orientation as, "By expressing hostility and disappointment toward the therapist for not gratifying wishes for dependency, the group members would resolve their problems with authority and develop greater independence" (p. 313). In his research he sought to find out whether learning mediates the expression of hostility and disappointment toward the leader. In order to assess that, he studied two matched therapy groups for 9 months, from start to termination. In the experimental group the therapist prompted and reinforced hostility and expressions of disappointment directed toward the leader and redirected (toward the leader) potentially destructive hostility between members. The results did show a lawful relationship between therapist's prompts and reinforcements and the behavior of his group therapy patients in the dimension of hostility and disappointments expressed to the therapist. Yet, it appears as though this area of group dynamics is overrated in importance since less than 1% of all verbal acts by patients fall in this category of hostility toward leader. Further, there was no significant relationship between patients' expression of hostility toward the therapist and improvements in dominance, independence, or symptomatology.

Thus, the group dynamic-oriented therapist could facilitate the emergence of the conflict phase of group life through reinforcements and prompts, yet the evidence from this study also showed no relationship between hostility to therapist and cohesiveness. The findings do indicate that expressions of affects such as affection and hostility are manifest at an operant level for each person and can be increased or decreased by environmental stimuli. Interestingly, and to the point of the hypotheses set forth by Goldstein, Heller, and Sechrest, the data of the two studies by Liberman also show that over time the therapist's influence accounts for less of the variance in the patients' expression of cohesiveness and hostility directed toward the therapist. That is, even with a strongly behaviorally oriented therapist, "As the group matures and develops a culture of its own, the therapist who had set the tone for norms and standards becomes less important as a source of reinforcement, and the patients become more important as agents of mutual reinforcement" (Liberman, 1970b, p. 327).

CONCLUSION

To summarize, in this chapter universality, cohesiveness, altruism, and protherapeutic norm development were presented as necessary group processes to set the stage for the process of change. Also, modeling, behavior rehearsal, feedback, and social reinforcement were identified as powerful therapeutic interventions available to the group therapist. Although these procedures are derived from social learning theory, they are available and useful to any group therapist regardless of orientation. In addition, it has been the working assumptions of this chapter that: (a) the curative factors of identification, reality testing, interpersonal learning techniques mentioned, and (b) while the behaviors subsumed under the curative factors occur naturally in any therapy group, they can be brought about more effectively using these social learning techniques.

REFERENCES

Bandura, A., Blanchard, E. B., & Ritter, B. Relative efficacy of desensitization and modeling approaches for inducing behavioral, affective and attitudinal changes. *Journal of Personality and Social Psychology*, 1969, *13*, 173–199.

Benne, K. D., Bradford, L. P., & Lippitt, R. The laboratory method. In L. P. Bradford, J. R. Gibb, & K. D. Benne (Eds.), *T-group theory and laboratory method*. New York: Wiley, 1964, pp. 15–44.

Bertcher, H. J., & Maple, F. Elements and issues in group composition. In P. Glasser, R. Sarri, & R. Vinter (Eds.), *Individual change through small groups*. New York: The Free Press, 1974, pp. 186–208.

Dinoff, M., Herner, R. F., Kurpiewski, B. S., & Timmons, E. O. Conditioning verbal behavior of schizophrenics in a group therapy-like situation. *Journal of Clinical Psychology*, 1960, *16*, 367–370.

Dinoff, M., Herner, R. F., Kurpiewski, B. S., Ricard, H. C., & Timmons, E. O. Conditioning verbal behavior of a psychiatric population in a group therapy-like situation. *Journal of Clinical Psychology*, 1960, *16*, 371–372.

French, J. R. P., Jr., Sherwood, J. J., & Bradford, D. L. Change in self-identity in a management training conference. *Journal of Applied Behavioral Science*, 1966, *2*, 210–218.

Friedman, P. H. The effects of modeling and role-playing on assertive behavior. In R. Rubin, H. Fensterheim, A. Lazarus, & C. Franks (Eds.), *Advances in behavior therapy*. New York: Academic Press, 1971, pp. 149–169.

Goldstein, A., & Wolpe, J. Behavior therapy in groups. In H. I. Kaplan & B. Sadock (Eds.), *New models for group therapy*. New York: Jason Aronson, 1972, pp. 119–154.

Goldstein, A. P., Heller, K., & Sechrest, L. *Psychotherapy and the psychology of behavior change*. New York: Wiley, 1966.

Jacobs, A. The use of feedback in groups. In A. Jacobs & W. Spradlin (Eds.), *The group as agent of change*. New York: Behavioral Publ., 1974, pp. 408–448.

Krumboltz, J. D., & Potter, B. Behavioral techniques for developing trust, cohesiveness and goal accomplishment. *Educational Technology*, 1973, *13*, 26–30.

Liberman, R. A behavioral approach to group dynamics: I. Reinforcement and prompting of cohesiveness in group therapy. *Behavior Therapy*, 1970, *1*, 141–175. (a)

Liberman, R. A behavioral approach to group dynamics: II. Reinforcing and prompting hostility to the therapist in group therapy. *Behavior Therapy*, 1970, 1, 312–327. (b)

Lippitt, G. L. *Effects of information about group desire for change on members of a group*. Unpublished doctoral dissertation, American University, 1959.

Lott, B. E. Group cohesiveness: A learning phenomenon. *Journal of Social Psychology*, 1961, *55*, 275–286.

Lott, B. E., & Lott, A. J. The formation of positive attitudes toward group members. *Journal of Abnormal and Social Psychology*, 1960, *61*, 297–300.

Marmor, J. Theories of learning and psychotherapeutic process. *British Journal of Psychiatry*, 1966, *111*, 363–366.

Rose, S. *Treating children in groups*. San Francisco: Jossey-Bass, 1972.

Sundel, M., & Lawrence, H. Behavior modification in adult groups, *Social Work*, 1972, *17*, 34–43.

Thase, M. E., & Moss, M. K. The relative efficacy of covert modeling procedures and guided participant modeling on the reduction of avoidance behavior. *Journal of Behavior Therapy and Experimental Psychiatry*, 1976, *7*, 7–12.

Yalom, I. *The theory and practice of group psychotherapy*. New York: Basic Books, 1970.

Index